3 71.35
I 6/5

# An Introduction to Distance Education

*An Introduction to Distance Education* is a comprehensive look at the field today, outlining current theories, practices and goals. The book reviews the influence of past distance education theory and practice, along with current changes. It outlines the practical skills and information that are essential to effective distance education design, delivery and navigation.

This volume brings together seminal contributors who have and who are currently researching and shaping our understanding and practice of distance education. A discussion of past and present practices in higher and distance education leads to an understanding of accessible education and the appropriate use of Web 2.0 technology.

Utilizing a student-guided approach, each chapter offers the following pedagogical features to engage and support the teaching and learning process:

- **Questions for reflection, review and discussion**: Students can use these questions as triggers for further thoughts related to the topic. Instructors can use these questions for classroom and online discussion.
- **Key quotations**: Strategically placed throughout the text, these points act as a springboard for further reflection and classroom discussion.
- **Concept definitions**: Central concepts discussed in the text are defined for students at the end of each chapter.

A perfect textbook for Educational Technology Doctorate, Masters and Certificate programs, students will find *An Introduction to Distance Education* offers a solid foundation from which to explore and develop new approaches to designing and implementing online courses.

**M.F. Cleveland-Innes** is a faculty member and program director in the Center for Distance Education at Athabasca University in Alberta, Canada.

**D.R. Garrison** is the Director of the Teaching and Learning Centre and a professor in the Faculty of Education at the University of Calgary.

LT

# An Introduction to Distance Education

Understanding Teaching and
Learning in a New Era

Edited by M.F. Cleveland-Innes
and D.R. Garrison

Routledge
Taylor & Francis Group

NEW YORK AND LONDON

First published 2010
by Routledge
270 Madison Avenue, New York, NY 10016

Simultaneously published in the UK
by Routledge
2 Park Square, Milton Park, Abingdon, Oxon OX14 4RN

*Routledge is an imprint of the Taylor & Francis Group, an informa business*

© 2010 Taylor & Francis

Typeset in Caslon
by Keystroke, Tettenhall, Wolverhampton
Printed and bound in the United States of America on acid-free paper
by Walsworth Publishing Company, Marceline, MO

*Library of Congress Cataloging in Publication Data*
An introduction to distance education : understanding teaching and
learning in a new era / M. Cleveland-Innes, D.R. Garrison, editors.
    p. cm.
    Includes bibliographical references and index.
    1. Distance education. I. Cleveland-Innes, M. II. Garrison, D. R.
(D. Randy), 1945-
LC5800.I68 2010
371.35—dc22                                        2009033210

ISBN 10: 0–415–99598–1 (hbk)
ISBN 10: 0–415–99599–X (pbk)
ISBN 10: 0–203–86091–8 (ebk)

ISBN 13: 978–0–415–99598–6 (hbk)
ISBN 13: 978–0–415–99599–3 (pbk)
ISBN 13: 978–0–203–86091–5 (ebk)

This text is dedicated to the families that support the work of the devoted scholars represented here.

# Contents

    DISTANCE EDUCATION                                91
    Dr. Doug Shale

7   TEACHING AND LEARNING IN POST-INDUSTRIAL
    DISTANCE EDUCATION                               108
    Dr. Karen Swan

PART III   A UNIFIED APPROACH

8   THE FUTURE OF LEARNING TECHNOLOGIES:
    TRANSFORMATIONAL DEVELOPMENTS                    137
    Dr. Phil Ice

9   BLENDED LEARNING                                 165
    Dr. Norman D. Vaughan

10  THE FUTURE OF DISTANCE EDUCATION:
    REFORMED, SCRAPPED OR RECYCLED                   198
    Dr. Terry Evans & Dr. Brian Pauling

PART IV   SUMMARY AND CONCLUSION

11  LEADERSHIP IN A NEW ERA OF HIGHER
    DISTANCE EDUCATION                               227
    Dr. M.F. Cleveland-Innes & Dr. Albert Sangrà

12  CONCLUSION                                       248
    Dr. D.R. Garrison & Dr. M.F. Cleveland-Innes

    Contributors                                     260
    Index                                            267

# Foreword

I am delighted to be asked to contribute a Foreword to this important and timely volume of essays, providing for the reader an overview of where distance education has come from and where in all its variety it is going to. The timeliness derives principally from the observation in the book that distance education is standing at the cusp of change, as it moves from the industrial approach based on efficiencies of large scale to the new era of the digital world and ICT, where the fundamental organizational and pedagogic models are different. The volume therefore proves a very valuable overview both for those new to the field, and those well established in it.

The editors have been able to draw on some of the most able observers and analysts of developments in this field. While the chapters ask different questions and offer a range of different answers, some common themes emerge. In particular the reader will be asked again and again to examine whether the structures that have been created over the last 40 or so years, and which have in their time innovated and challenged the conventional structures of educational institutions, can now in turn adequately offer possibilities for reform and reshaping for new futures. There is a significant judgement to be made—and with a real sense of urgency—as to whether our current educational organizations which have championed distance education will be leapfrogged by those who have been born directly into the digital age. The further rise of private sector institutions, who now teach approximately one third of the world's higher education students, may base itself on its capacity to reform and retool more quickly than public sector institutions feel able to do.

What are the core characteristics of change that are driving the new revolution? The new technologies make both offers and demands in the field of pedagogy. Firstly, the so-called digital natives have an expectation of multi-media in the resources with which they engage. This proposes a significant change in making print one of the resources and not the only or even simply the dominant resource. Secondly, the resources which distance education institutions have had as the core of their mission to provide for learners can now be sourced in a variety of ways, and in particular sought by the learners themselves through the Web and all its extraordinary richness and confusion. Thus we have the perhaps banal but nonetheless pithy summary of that as representing the move from "the sage on the stage," which distance education in some ways represented too, to the guide on the side. More fairly perhaps we can see the move that took place from conventional teaching to distance education, where the production of learning resources was accompanied by a mediating and supportive teaching role, has now developed further so that this mediating role has to support the capacity of learners to make sense of the wealth of resources which they can, with guidance, find themselves. This in turn accelerates the move towards enquiry based learning, where the support of enquiry becomes the dominant mode of teaching.

Secondly, the new technologies make collaborative work for learners possible in a real sense for the first time. Distance education students, if indeed they continue to have such a denominator, can talk to each other without the barrier of geographical distance that going to study centers has represented for so many years, and which always challenged the study center experience as being universal. At the same time we know that online discussion sites can as often be empty as they are full of active learners, and that drop-out can be severe. However, we know enough of the successful cases of online learning to know that it can be done well, even if it is by no means always done well. One of the tipping points we balance on is whether educational institutions can skill themselves quickly enough in the organization and management of online learning experiences to be able to satisfy their learners, who, in an increasingly competitive world, can study elsewhere.

Two things are clear in this volume of essays: firstly, that the changes identified represent very exciting possibilities if those responsible for change and reform can conceptualize and practice them; and secondly, that the imperative is no less real than it was 40 years ago when it can be said modern distance education came of age. The demand for educational opportunity cannot now, as it could not then, be met by the bricks and mortar development of educational institutions. This volume will make the issues that the field faces clear to those who have responsibilities for developing these opportunities.

A last comment: If distance education as we recognize it does not continue as a delineated field of practice, those whose professional identity is based on that field may not continue to define themselves professionally in that way. So change is at hand not only for learners, planners and managers, but for the field of practitioners and those who support them as a whole!

Alan Tait
*The Open University, UK*
June 2009

# 1

# TEACHING AND LEARNING IN DISTANCE EDUCATION

## Enter a New Era

### DR. M.F. CLEVELAND-INNES
Associate Professor and Program Director
Athabasca University

> He that will not apply new remedies must expect new evils; for time is the great innovator.
>
> Francis Bacon (1561–1626), English philosopher

## Introduction

Within the last few decades, pervasive technology and significant social and economic development have forever changed our society. Social and economic change has made it increasingly difficult for education to operate in insular ways; attention to changing demographics, global economies and new social mores is required (Keller, 2008). The potential reach of technology seems limitless, and has already changed distance and higher education institutions in "the way we organize ourselves, our policies, our culture, what faculty do, the way we work, and those we serve" (Ikenberry, 2001: Foreword). Change in higher education to accommodate broader societal changes requires new ways of thinking about economic issues, accountability, technology and the teaching–learning process.

*Introduction to Distance Education: Understanding Teaching and Learning in a New Era* is a response to this reality. It is a comprehensive examination of the current education context, where distance education is presenting itself, and then making itself known. The modern era of

1

distance education operates in a postmodern, post-Fordist socio-economic environment. Thus, the post-industrial approach to distance education is a transforming factor in higher education; fundamentally reconceptualizing, restructuring, and significantly reshaping the teaching and learning transaction. This book provides a detailed review of the influence of industrial distance education, and the current changes occurring through the transition to post-industrial society. Most critically, it outlines what must be part of distance education design and delivery for effective education in the 21st century.

In the design and delivery of 21st-century distance education, online teaching and learning has emerged. Defined as Internet-based learning that delivers content and enables communication between instructor and students, online teaching and learning is rooted in the transaction of distance education and advanced computer and communications technology.* Absent from the developing field is a foundation of thought from the fields of distance, higher and adult education. Previous discussions on the topic of online learning pay little attention to this integration; what reference is available is superficial and separate from the premises of facilitating online learning. This text presents the conceptual and structural foundation of factors contributing to the emergence and successful implementation of online learning. It explains how we get to quality learning outcomes in the post-industrial online environment. This text provides the reader with a rationale, answering the 'why' question for the development of new teaching and learning models for a new era.

The content of the book is based upon the research and practice of multiple authors regarding educational approaches and transitions as they are shaped and influenced by new and emerging technologies and broad-based societal change. The premise is that the 21st century represents a new era of distance education identified by collaborative communities of inquiry in an online learning environment. The framework and conceptual foundation for the theory and practice of online

---

* The term 'technology' refers to person-made objects designed to extend human capabilities, in support of life activities leading to sustenance and gratification. In this discussion, the term 'technology' will refer most often to computer systems as an extension of human abilities.

education emerge from the work first introduced in the Routledge Falmer publication E-Learning in the 21st Century (Garrison & Anderson, 2003). Recent research of the editors (Cleveland-Innes & Garrison, 2009; Cleveland-Innes, Garrison, & Kinsel, 2007; Garrison & Cleveland-Innes, 2005, 2004; Garrison, Cleveland-Innes, & Fung, 2004) shapes the theory, practical guidelines, and activities described in the book.

### Review of the Book

The text divides into three main sections. Part I reviews the roots of distance education, the emergence of a new way of doing education that responded to the industrial age in society. This section covers the foundations of distance education in the industrial era, as it emerged through correspondence models, the open learning concept, and the development of new theories and practices. Technology in the industrial era enabled new ways of designing education, but also constrained innovation within the boundaries of available technologies of the time. Teaching and learning, reconceptualized in ways that shaped new roles for teachers and learners, emerged to accommodate new models for delivering education at a distance. Developments at the time fit within the dominant organizational system, allowing for new specializations, open designs and teaming for development and delivery of instruction.

Chapter 2 outlines the evolution of distance education for the reader. The story focuses on the foundational principles and practices of distance education. This is what eventually becomes known as the industrial era of distance education. After describing the industrial era of distance education, we demonstrate that we are entering a new era of distance education. This post-industrial era has emerged in the 21st century but is not yet fully understood or adequately addressed by the scholars in the field of online education.

The history of distance education makes clear a preoccupation with geographical constraints that used available technologies to neutralize distance and increase access. This contrasts with the modern or post-industrial era that reflects a focus on transactional issues and ubiquitous communications technologies (Garrison, 2000). This developmental framework shapes the structure of this book and the discussions of subsequent chapters.

Chapter 3 is written by Gary Miller. Dr. Miller argues that distance education during the industrial period developed at the intersection of three powerful forces as they presented themselves at the time: social change, technological development, and the need for educational institutions to adapt to changing social needs. Among these three forces, technology was (and is) both a cause of change—due to its impact on society—and a means by which distance education responded to those changes. Technology also affects how institutions did (and still do) organize the distance education function over time. To understand the interactions among technologies, organization, and the role of distance education better, Gary takes on a retrospective, longitudinal view.

Chapter 4, written by Margaret Haughey, takes the same long view. The chapter outlines how models of teaching and learning in distance education are extensions of theories about teaching and learning in use at the time. Set before the digital age, Dr. Haughey shows how different models of teaching and learning developed. These models both emerged from and acted back on emerging distance education. These influenced the foundational distance education model described in the chapter.

Part II addresses a changing environment. The hegemony of the industrial model set the ideals and limits for distance education and created the opportunity for the formation of new models in post-industrial times. The developments of education were and are redirected according to the philosophy and technology of the time. As the 21st century approached, information and communications technology and rapid, continuous change shifted assumptions about teaching, learning and institutional organization. Again, teaching and learning activities, reconceptualized in ways that shaped new roles for teachers and learners, emerged to accommodate new models. Education theories and practices were reshaped by postmodern, constructivist views encompassing strategies of collaborative and lifelong learning, all in support of an information and knowledge society with ubiquitous, networked environments.

In Chapter 5, Heather Kanuka and Charmaine Brooks outline the response of higher education to post-Fordist structures in society. They question the possibility that the essence of a university education can be preserved in post-Fordist times along with the requirements for flexible access, quality learning experiences, and cost-effective distance learning offerings. The chapter outlines the concept of post-Fordism, and summarizes the post-Fordist debate in higher education. The authors suggest that constructivist learning theory exists within the post-Fordist framework and describe the theory and its potential role within a post-Fordist era. They conclude with the argument that in a post-Fordist framework, distance higher education will achieve some of its goals of flexible access, quality learning experience and cost effectiveness, but not all three at once.

In Chapter 6, Doug Shale provides a developmental view of the distance education enterprise. The commitment of distance education has been to extending access to education to those who would not normally have such an opportunity. The challenge for distance education has been to bridge the spatial separation of the learner from a teacher. The separation has largely been due to the geographic locations of participating individuals. However, over time, this separation has changed to other kinds of personal circumstances on the part of the learner—life situations such as family and work responsibilities that make the requirements of face-to-face attendance difficult, if not impossible. From this point of view, the development of distance education has really been about administrative and organizational ways and means of situating an educational institution to commit itself (at least to some extent) to doing distance education, and ways and means of bridging the separation of teacher and student. Much less attention was directed to sustained two-way communication between teacher and learner. This chapter reviews how this has transpired in places across the globe.

Bridging the gap between teacher and learner in post-industrial education is the focus of Chapter 7 by Karen Swan. For Dr. Swan, what distinguishes online learning from the distance education of the previous era is not just the digital technologies from which it takes its name, but the pedagogical approaches they enable. Distance education was materials- and teacher-centered, online learning is student-centered; where distance education focused on independent study, online learning focuses on collaboration; where distance education was grounded in behaviorist and cognitive psychology, online learning is grounded in social constructivist learning theory. This chapter explores why and how online learning is embracing emerging digital technologies and social constructivist epistemologies. The chapter demonstrates that a particular confluence of emerging technologies, cultural practices and serendipity has resulted in an online teaching and learning characterized by social constructivist and inquiry-oriented approaches.

Part III looks at the most recent developments of the field, from emerging and disruptive technologies to international competition. The integration of virtual and place-based universities has led us to models of collaborative online and blended learning. The future of distance education will emerge in technology-enabled institutions with faculty development and training programs and established support for the production of virtual spaces and material.

Chapter 8 by Phil Ice is a discussion of the underlying pedagogical possibilities of technologies that increasingly tie together the physical and virtual worlds. For Dr. Ice, distance learning has had great difficulty freeing itself from the governing, linear paradigm that fails to differentiate between quantifiable training outcomes and the construction of knowledge. He sees e-learning as the rapid proliferation of new applications, communication modalities and competing visions of what the future of technological convergence will look like. Despite issues revolving around the rapid pace of transformation, contemporary and emerging technologies allow practitioners to select from an array of tools that allow for co-construction of knowledge as opposed to mere transmission of facts. This chapter is both declarative and prophetic.

In Chapter 9, Norm Vaughan reports that 80 percent of all higher education institutions and 93 percent of doctoral institutions offer hybrid or blended learning courses—the infusion of Web-based technologies into the learning and teaching process. Technologies have created new opportunities for students to interact with their peers, faculty and content in blended courses and programs. This chapter describes blended learning environments in higher education, the opportunities and challenges associated with these environments from the student, faculty and administrative perspectives, and how the Community of Inquiry (CoI) framework is used to design online blended learning courses and programs.

In Chapter 10, Terry Evans and Brian Pauling ask if distance education is to be reformed, scrapped or recycled. Drs. Evans and Pauling feel a discussion of the future of distance education needs to be about possibilities rather than predictions. In an era in which diversity, fluidity and flexibility are its main characteristics, they predict that the demand for distance education will not disappear: it is structured into our future existence. However, the fluidity around educational terms and practices means that it is also quite possible that 'distance education'—the term and its history—will be towed to the scrap yard.

Part IV completes the text with a view of teaching and learning in a networked university, as defined in the post-industrial era. Martha Cleveland-Innes and Albert Sangrà discuss the challenges and opportunities of creating a new higher education, and the leadership required to face these challenges and capitalize on the opportunities.

The book concludes with a summary chapter written by the editors. We revisit the idea that teaching and learning models in distance education are being shaped over time, and are reshaping teaching and learning in higher education in general. The limitations of post-industrial distance education are considered. Distance education theory, still in its infancy, is reviewed. We finish with questions still to be answered and consider the extent to which a new model of teaching and learning can be maintained without compromising access and required cost-effectiveness, so central to the traditions of distance education.

All chapters provide pedagogical enhancements and support for teachers and learners using the book. The supports are of several kinds. All chapters but this introduction and the conclusion offer review and reflection questions with key terms and definitions. In addition, quotes that illuminate central premises in the chapter are offered throughout each chapter.

The field of distance education, and its evolution over time, occurred because of people dedicated to the cause of improved access to education and the development of the structures and processes required to do so. These significant contributors to the field are people who were instrumental in its growth; they are the builders, creators, developers and pioneers. Understanding these people and the work they have done over time provides a more grounded view of how things have emerged and changed in distance education. Many could have been named; a select few have been included in this text. Each chapter includes a biography and photograph of one significant contributor to the field of distance education, either historically or currently, or both; either in research or practice, or both.

> *The independent study method is not, in its basic concepts, different from other teaching–learning methods.*
>
> *(Charles Wedemeyer, 1971, p. 553)*

## Conclusion

The content of the book provides discussion of the past and present context for higher and distance education, with a view to accessible education and appropriate use of technology for education. This book provides longitudinal perspectives on distance education broadly, with particular emphasis on the shape of distance teaching and learning over time. It is assumed that the evolution of distance higher education provides valuable responses to the challenges facing higher education in general. This is particularly so in reference to teaching and learning. The move from industrial distance education to post-industrial collaborative, constructivist learning in online environments gives us a window to possible changes in higher education—whether online, blended or face-to-face.

A fulsome view of distance education in all its forms, over time and space, is necessary to see both the value and the imperatives in the changes in teaching and learning that have occurred. This book is an introduction to distance, online and blended learning for students, a working reference for faculty and instructional designers, and a guide to the future for senior administrators to understand distance, online and blended learning approaches in higher education. It will have particular value to instructional technology courses and programs. Interest in technologically mediated learning is emerging in the larger field of education. Diverse approaches and innovations require that we make sense of this period of change and transition in distance education, and in education broadly.

Significant Contributor

**Professor Sarah Guri-Rosenblit** is the Director of International Academic Outreach and the Head of Graduate Studies in Education at the Open University of Israel. She earned her Ph.D. from Stanford University in 1984 in Education and Political Science. Her areas of expertise are focused on comparative research of higher education systems, distance education and e-learning. She has published books and dozens of articles in these fields. She has participated in the last decade in many international and national forums on various aspects of higher education. She was selected in 2005/6 as one of the 30 New Century Scholars in the Fulbright Program on Higher Education in the 21st Century: Global Challenge and National Response. Since 2003 she has been a member of the Scientific Committee of Europe and North America in the UNESCO Forum of Higher Education, Research and Knowledge. She is also a member in expert evaluations panels of HESC (Higher Education and Social Change) under the auspices of the European Science Foundation, and the Bellagio Conference Center of the Rockefeller Foundation. Her latest book, *Digital Technologies in Higher Education: Sweeping Expectations and Actual Effects*, was published in March 2009 by Nova Science. Her full CV and a list of publications, keynotes and conference presentations can be found at: http://www.openu.ac.il/Personal_sites/sara-guri-rosenblit.html.

### References

Cleveland-Innes, M.F. & Garrison, D.R. (2009). The role of learner in an online community of inquiry: Instructor support for first time online learners. In N. Karacapilidis (Ed.), *Solutions and innovations in web-based technologies for augmented learning: Improved platforms, tools and applications.* Hershey, PA: IGI Global.

Cleveland-Innes, M.F., Garrison, D.R., & Kinsel, E. (2007). Role adjustment for learners in an online community of inquiry: Identifying the needs of novice online learners. *International Journal of Web-based Learning and Teaching Technologies*, 2(1), 1–16.

Garrison, D.R. (2000). Theoretical challenges for distance education in the twenty-first century: A shift from structural to transactional issues. *International Review of Research in Open and Distance Learning*, 1(1). Retrieved September 29, 2008 from: http://www.irrodl.org/index.php/irrodl/article/view/2/333.

Garrison, D.R. & Anderson, T. (2003). *E-learning in the 21st century: A framework for research and practice.* London: Routledge/Falmer.

Garrison, D.R. & Cleveland-Innes, M.F. (2004). Critical factors in student satisfaction and success: Facilitating student role adjustment in online communities of inquiry. In J. Bourne & J.C. Moore (Eds.), *Elements of quality online education: Into the mainstream.* Volume 5 in the Sloan C Series, Needham, MA: The Sloan Consortium.

Garrison, D.R. & Cleveland-Innes, M.F. (2005). Facilitating cognitive presence in online learning: Interaction is not enough. *American Journal of Distance Education*, 19(3), 133–148.

Garrison, D.R., Cleveland-Innes, M.F. & Fung, T. (2004). Student role adjustment in online communities of inquiry: Model and instrument validation. *Journal of Asynchronous Learning Networks*, 8(2), 61–74. Retrieved December 2007 from: http://www.aln.org/ publications/jaln/v8n2/v8n2_garrison.asp.

Ikenberry, S. (2001). Foreword. In C. Latchem & D. Hanna (Eds.), *Leadership XE "Leadership" for 21st century learning: Global perspectives from educational perspectives.* Sterling, VA: Stylus.

Keller, G. (2008). *Higher education and the new society.* Baltimore, MA: Johns Hopkins University Press.

Wedemeyer, C.A. (1971). Independent study. In R. Deighton (Ed.), *Encyclopedia of Education IV.* New York: Macmillan.

# PART I
# THE INDUSTRIAL ERA

# 2

# FOUNDATIONS OF DISTANCE EDUCATION

## DR. D.R. GARRISON
Professor and Director
University of Calgary

## DR. M.F. CLEVELAND-INNES
Associate Professor and Program Director
Athabasca University

## Introduction

The purpose of this chapter is to map the evolution of distance education. Attention will focus on the foundational principles and practices of distance education. This is what eventually became known as the industrial era of distance education. After describing the industrial era of distance education, it will be argued that we are entering a new era of distance education—the post-industrial era. The post-industrial era has emerged in the 21st century and is not fully understood or adequately addressed by the scholars in the field.

The history of distance education has seen a preoccupation with geographical constraints along with technologies to neutralize distance and increase access. This contrasts with the modern or post-industrial era that reflects a focus on transactional issues and ubiquitous communications technologies (Garrison, 2000). This developmental shift shapes the structure of this book and discussions in subsequent chapters.

## The Evolution of Distance Education

*Industrial Era*

The beginnings of distance education date back well over 100 years to the age of correspondence education. The first half of the 20th century was a period of expansion for correspondence education. The emergence of correspondence education was a direct result of developments in communications technology: specifically the mail system and the ability to distribute course materials economically. Notwithstanding the method of delivery, it is important to recognize that correspondence education introduced 'teaching' through text. This represented a foundational change from conventional classroom teaching and learning. Certainly the success of correspondence education was due to factors such as learner access and independence in terms of time and place of study.

It was only in the latter half of the 20th century that individuals like Charles Wedemeyer (1971) began to refine our understanding of correspondence study.

Wedemeyer was a pioneer in the theoretical development of distance education and a catalyst for the age of distance and open education. He focused on the characteristic of independent study that provided access to socially disadvantaged individuals. However, Wedemeyer critically noted that much of the content was prescriptive. Unfortunately, the movement to the industrial production of course materials in the latter half of the 20th century reduced choice with regard to goals and learning activities.

Since the early 1970s, coinciding with the creation of the British Open University, distance education became very much aligned with the mass production of independent study course packages and institutional structures and efficiencies to support the 'massification' of education. It is clear that industrial distance education is focused on organizational economies of scale. This approach

> *Peters (1994, 2007) did not originally intend the industrial model to be a prescriptive theory of teaching or reflect all of distance education. The industrial model was intended as a descriptive theory and not a value judgment of the author (Peters, 2007).*

served the long-standing goal of distance education to increase access, especially for the educationally disadvantaged. The technology and scale of production was observed by Otto Peters to be consistent with the principles of industrialization. Peters (1994, 1998) wrote extensively about the organizational structure of distance education in terms of its association with the industrial production characteristics, such as division of labor, mass production and economies of scale.

Peters (1994, 2007) did not originally intend the industrial model to be a prescriptive theory of teaching or reflect all of distance education. The industrial model was intended as a descriptive theory and not a value judgment of the author (Peters, 2007). However, it has become the defining theoretical representation of the field that reflected practice. Industrialization transformed teaching in the extreme in terms of becoming depersonalized (Peters, 2007). This unique pedagogical form of industrialized learning caused "a dramatic pedagogical paradigm shift." In particular, Peters (2007, p. 61) argues that it obliged students "to become autonomous and self-regulated with regard to goals, methods, and media." Whether self-regulation can mitigate the prescriptive and isolated nature of industrial distance learning is open to debate. This point will be picked up in a subsequent section.

There were other scholars who addressed issues of interaction and dialogue. The challenge, however, was that to increase interaction necessitated reduced independence and increased cost. For this reason, Borje Holmberg (1989) offered the concept and goal of 'guided didactic conversation' that simulated interaction without the loss of independence or autonomy. While this concept included the possibility of real conversations with a tutor, most often this was simulated internal conversation that resulted from the design of the self-study materials. In essence, however, teaching remained one-way communication between the course materials and the student.

*The constraint of distance should not essentially remove two-way communication from the educational process.*

The industrial model was very good at transmitting information and instructions to the learner, but implicitly militated against sustained two-way communication as an important element in an educational experience. As a result of the industrial developments toward extreme independence, depersonalization and isolation, distance education scholars began to focus on teaching and learning issues. For example, Michael Moore (1990, 1991) introduced the concepts of structure and dialogue to address the need for interaction. This put in perspective the issues of structure (industrial design) and dialogue (interaction), thereby attempting to shift the focus to pedagogical issues over structural constraints. Distance was defined by Moore as a function of structure and dialogue. The greatest distance, according to Moore, was low structure and low dialogue.

About the same time that Moore raised the issue of real two-way dialogue, others were also arguing for emphasis on communication and collaboration. Garrison (1989) and Garrison & Shale (1990) pointed out the central role of two-way communication and dialogue in an educational experience. The point was that we must not lose sight of the fact that we are talking first about education and secondly about the structural constraint of distance. Too much focus on distance and economies of scale was shifting the focus away from communication as the essence of an educational experience. The constraint of distance should not essentially remove two-way communication from the educational process. To address this concern, two-way communication was explicit in Garrison and Shale's (1987) definition of distance education. It also included the possibility of interaction among a group of students (i.e., collaboration). Interaction and collaboration were included to recognize the growing use of audio conferencing, an emerging technology for distance education at the time.

The adoption of audio-conferencing technologies in the 1980s raised questions about the trade-off of independence and interaction (Daniel & Marquis, 1979). It became apparent that rich, collaborative educational experiences were possible and, in some situations, worth the compromise regarding time and place independence (Garrison, 1989). Today, of course, this has evolved into Internet-based audio, video and text-based conferencing. While some independence in terms of time is sacrificed for synchronous conferencing, asynchronous text-based conferencing makes possible time and place independence with sustained interaction. Clearly the emergence of new communications technology and the Internet is having a profound influence on all of education.

*Role of Media*

The first electronic technology adopted by distance education was radio in the early part of the 20th century. This was followed by television broadcasting in the second half of the 20th century. Television broadcasts were extensively used by the British Open University. They did not, of course, provide two-way communication. Dissemination of course content was reinforced and the loss of interaction that Wedemeyer decried was further eroded. However, in the late 1970s audio conferencing was beginning to get a foothold in distance education. This was described as the second generation of distance education technologies that made possible immediate communication between teacher and students (Garrison, 1985). In most cases students traveled to a local teleconference center. This loss of independence was considered by many students as more than a reasonable compromise to interact verbally and collaboratively in real-time.

While there has been an evolution of communications technology, distance education's fundamental approach and value in terms of learner autonomy has not shifted measurably. Certainly online communication and discussions have been adopted by distance education institutions. At the same time, this technology is most often an optional add-on due to the dominance of the self-instructional course package, the need for economies of scale, and continuous enrollment that makes interaction and collaboration impractical.

> *The difference between the industrial and post-industrial is that between individual responsibility (i.e., autonomy) and collaborative responsibility (i.e., community).*

Peters (2003, p. 87) quite rightly argues that "because each medium influences and changes the pedagogical structure, the question as to which carrier media to use for distance education is not only a practical . . . but also a pedagogical issue." However, he goes on to state that we should make no mistake, the "pedagogical goal here is the development of autonomously acting students who initiate, control, and evaluate their work themselves" (p. 96). As such, Peters views media as an opportunity for individualization and independent learning. He sees media as "promising possibilities for developing autonomous and self-regulating learning behavior" (p. 90). In this view, the traditional assumptions of independence are not challenged and the potential of new media and technology for two-way communication is seen only in terms of serving the assumption and goal of sustaining the autonomy of the student.

In contrast to Peters' position, Terry Evans and Daryl Nation (2003, p. 785) identify the risk of re-jigging "old industrial approaches to distance education" that are influenced by "neo-instructional industrialism." For those committed to autonomy as an ideal and the industrial model, paradigms do not shift easily. In the industrial paradigm, distance education is committed to the design of teaching that enhances autonomy and self-direction. The self-study course package remains the core of distance education, regardless of the technology of delivery or ancillary uses of media. Only the efficiency of delivering these materials has evolved in the industrial distance education paradigm.

On the other hand, there are those who see the potential of new and emerging technologies to enhance and sustain interaction and collaboration. These educators see the possibilities and opportunities to use communications technology to create sustainable communities of learners. The difference between the industrial and post-industrial is that between individual responsibility (i.e., autonomy) and collaborative responsibility (i.e., community). With the range of cost-effective communication technologies available today, the selection of communications technology is very much shaped by the educational assumptions and intended approaches. In both industrial and post-industrial educational contexts, this is greatly affected by past practice and resistance to change. There is a shift to the traditions of conventional higher education founded in discourse and the collaborative construction and confirmation of knowledge.

*Post-industrial*

In recent years, a new era of distance education appears to be emerging that has capitalized on the Internet and new communications technology. However, this is more than the adoption of new technologies. It has been accompanied with an examination and shift in pedagogical assumptions and approaches. The goal now is to provide a brief outline

*Online learning is in fact a separate branch of the educational evolutionary tree, quite different from industrial distance education.*

of the post-industrial era and its approaches to teaching and learning. A more complete discussion of this topic is provided in the second part of this book.

Evans and Nation (2003, p. 780) were two of the early distance educators who challenged the dominant paradigm that "alienated 'its students from each other and wider educational and social processes.'" In an attempt to bring distance education into the mainstream, Evans and Nation recognized the impact of the Internet on how we think about the theory and practice of distance education. They suggest that interaction through the Web is part of the 'new distance education':

> Matters such as interaction and dialogue, . . . need to be reconsidered and reformulated . . . Good distance educational design has not only recognized the importance of interaction, but also the importance of students' contexts in influencing their learning.
>
> (Evans & Nation, 2003, p. 777)

In many ways, the post-industrial era is the story of distance education adopting a set of assumptions and practices congruent with the ideal of a community of inquiry found in the mainstream of higher education. In the post-industrial era, communities of inquiry were made possible by the asynchronous nature of online learning. While students can interact when and where they chose, they can also collaboratively engage in a purposeful and cohesive group environment. The post-industrial era is very much associated with online sustainable communities of learners.

Online learning is in fact a separate branch of the educational evolutionary tree, quite different from industrial distance education. 'Online learning' is the term used here that best reflects the technology and practice of the post-industrial era. Online learning represents a range of practices based on the Internet that provides synchronous and asynchronous communication in a personal and group environment. The point is that online learning goes beyond accessing information on the Web. It is the integration of connectivity (interaction, discourse) with asynchronicity (independence) as well as the potential to combine different forms of communication (text, verbal, visual) to create unique online learning environments (Garrison & Anderson, 2003).

Online learning in an educational context is seen to be consistent with the traditional values and assumptions of higher education as they relate to both teaching and learning. In particular, our view of online learning is very much associated with supporting sustainable communities of inquiry. The Community of Inquiry framework is a purposeful educational environment that brings together the core elements of social, cognitive and teaching presence for the purposes of critical reflection and discourse (Garrison, Anderson, & Archer, 2000).

Communications technology and the Internet have been disruptive and influential to both distance and conventional higher education. They have opened the door to new thinking about approaches to teaching and learning. For this reason, constructivist and deep approaches to learning have resonated with those in the post-industrial era of distance education. Communications technology is seen as an opportunity to apply constructivist principles and deep approaches to distance education. This is the point of departure between the industrial and post-industrial eras. It has also been a catalyst for conventional higher education to examine and rethink the dominant approaches to teaching and learning.

*Blending and Convergence*

The post-industrial era of distance education is adopting many of the educational assumptions associated with interactive and collaborative learning. Moreover, the power and ubiquity of the Internet and communications technology have also been a disruptive force in conventional education. In particular, educators in higher education have begun to question their reliance on teacher-centered practices and the dominance of the lecture. Online learning may well make possible the realization of the ideals of creating and sustaining communities of inquiry. More and more we see higher education centers redesigning their courses and programs along the lines of blended learning (Garrison & Vaughan, 2008).

With the Internet's access to information, the merging of verbal and text communication, and the capability to sustain communities over time and distance, all educational institutions are pausing to rethink the role of the classroom and online learning. The landscape in higher education is changing as institutions compete for students in terms of flexible access and providing for meaningful, collaborative learning experiences. The blending of online and face-to-face approaches suggests the possibility of a merging of post-industrial distance education and conventional higher education. While mixed-mode institutions have been with us for some time, we are now seeing conventional universities more fully integrating online and classroom approaches. In Europe, we are seeing a new type of university evolving with the adoption of online learning and digitized course content (Garrison & Kanuka, 2008). With the adoption of online capabilities, conventional universities have begun to compete with distance education institutions. Garrison and Kanuka (2008, p. 16) state that an "overview of international perspectives on the changes occurring in current distance education practices, in both traditional distance and on-campus delivery, reveals there is considerable investment in convergent models of distance and campus-based institutions."

Doug Shale (2002, abstract) also notes the "growing convergence between conventional and distance learning modes, leading to the hybridization of higher education." The hybridization or blending of online and face-to-face approaches is the main force behind convergence. This is causing both distance and conventional higher education to examine their practices. At its core, blended learning is about thoughtfully taking the best of face-to-face and online learning and fusing the two uniquely to meet specific educational goals. Blended learning reflects a significant shift in instructional design. As a result of the transformational potential of blended learning, there is growing interest in approaches that blend face-to-face and online learning environments (Garrison & Vaughan, 2008).

Recent developments, such as blended approaches in higher education, raise interesting but serious questions about the evolution and possible transformation of distance

*[O]nline learning (OLL) emerged from computer conferencing and converged with the growing interest in constructivist theories of learning in traditional higher education (Garrison, in press).*

education. Will the widespread adoption of Internet and communications technology be the catalyst for distance education to abandon the industrial model? Will the dominant paradigms of distance and conventional education converge? Or will we see a diverse array of approaches and choice in distance and conventional higher education? These questions will be explored in the third part of this book.

### Conclusion

In this chapter we have provided the framework and assumptions that shape the structure of this book. We began by exploring the foundations of traditional distance education which serves as the introduction to the first part. More recent developments in distance education were also introduced which foreshadow discussions in the second and third parts of this book.

It is becoming increasingly evident that distance education is no longer limited by contextual and structural constraints. The Internet is an integral part of life globally. Most nations have moved into the Internet age and the potential for online learning communities is being realized. Are industrial distance education approaches being retained for legitimate purposes related to access or are they simply due to inertia and investment in the technology of mass production? How will the full potential of new and emerging communications technology and the Internet impact distance education? The next chapters in the first part of this book set the stage to address these questions.

### TERMS AND DEFINITIONS

**Collaborative learning:** An instructional strategy that involves joint intellectual activity among learners. Learners work together to discern meaning or come to understanding. They solve problems and create products in dependent exchange with each other.

**Correspondence study:** The original form of distance learning involving print-based material, the separation of teacher and learner and the exchange of content through the postal service.

**Industrial era:** Time period from the late 18th to early 19th century when significant changes in agriculture, manufacturing, mining and transportation changed the social and economic conditions, first in Britain and then in many places around the world.

**Interaction:** Strictly speaking, refers to mutual or reciprocal action or influence. In the practice of distance education, interaction refers to the engagement of learners with content, learning material, instructor(s) and other students. Of particular note is the change in interaction opportunities from print-based to online distance education environments. Online environments increase opportunities for interactional engagement of all kinds.

**Pedagogy:** Describes the art, science and sometimes profession of teaching.

## QUESTIONS FOR REVIEW AND REFLECTION

1. What are the pedagogical goals of Otto Peters?
2. What do Evans and Nation (2003) mean by re-jigging "old industrial approaches to distance education" influenced by "neo-instructional industrialism"?
3. Has distance education reached an evolutionary dead-end?
4. Will the potential to develop communities of learners independent of time and space transform distance education?
5. Or will conventional higher education institutions adopt the values and practices of distance education that essentially attenuate the direct influence of a teacher?

**Significant Contributor**

**Desmond Keegan** received his BA (Hons) from University College Dublin in Classical European Civilization. He received his MA from University College Dublin in Medieval European Civilization, studying under the late Professor Dr. Ludwig Bieler. He received a Post-Graduate Diploma in Education from the University of Adelaide. His Ph.D. thesis was published by Croom Helm as *Foundations of Distance Education* in 1986. The second edition was published by Routledge in 1990 and the

third followed in 1996. It was translated into Italian as *Principi di
Istruzione a Distanza* (La Nuova Italia) in 1994, into Chinese as *Yuan
Juli Jiao Yu Jichu* (Central China TV University), and was chosen as a
set text for the Open University of the United Kingdom's MA in Open
and Distance Education in 1997. Dr. Keegan was enormously influential in helping practitioners and researchers interpret and understand
the emerging field of distance education theory and practice. While he
contributed greatly to defining the field of distance education, his
greatest contribution was perhaps making accessible the ideas of other
pioneering researchers. In particular, he was instrumental in bringing
the revolutionary ideas of Otto Peters to the English-speaking world
of distance education. He also contributed to understanding the evolutionary changes that were occurring in distance education at the end of
the 20th century.

## References

Daniel, J.S. & Marquis, C. (1979). Interaction and independence: Getting the
    mixture right. *Teaching at a Distance*, 14, 29–43.
Evans, T. & Nation, D. (2003). Globalization and the reinvention of distance
    education. In M.G. Moore & W.G. Anderson (Eds.), *Handbook of
    distance education*. Mahwah, NJ: Lawrence Erlbaum.
Garrison, D.R. (1985). Three generations of technological innovation in
    distance education. *Distance Education*, 6(2), 235–241.
Garrison, D.R. (1989). *Understanding distance education: A framework for the
    future*. London: Routledge.
Garrison, D.R. (2000). Theoretical challenges for distance education in the
    21st century: A shift from structural to transactional issues. *International
    Review of Research in Open and Distance Learning*, 1(1), 1–17.
Garrison, D.R. (in press). Implications of online learning for the conceptual
    development and practice of distance education. *Journal of Distance
    Education*.
Garrison, D.R. & Anderson, T. (2003). *E-learning in the 21st century: A
    framework for research and practice*. London: Routledge/Falmer.
Garrison, D.R., Anderson, T., & Archer, W. (2000). Critical inquiry in a text-
    based environment: Computer conferencing in higher education. *The
    Internet and Higher Education*, 2(2–3), 87–105.
Garrison, D.R. & Kanuka, H. (2008). Changing distance education and
    changing organizational issues. In W.J. Bramble & S. Panda (Eds.),
    *Economics of distance and online learning: Theory, practice and research*.
    London: Routledge.

Garrison, D.R. & Shale, D. (1987). Mapping the boundaries of distance education: Problems in defining the field. *The American Journal of Distance Education*, 1(1), 7–13.

Garrison, D.R. & Shale, D. (Eds.) (1990). *Education at a distance: From issues to practice.* Melbourne, FL: Krieger.

Garrison, D.R. & Vaughan, N. (2008). *Blended learning in higher education.* San Francisco: Jossey-Bass.

Holmberg, B. (1989). *Theory and practice of distance education.* London: Routledge.

Moore, M. (1990). Recent contributions to the theory of distance education. *Open Learning*, 5(3), 10–15.

Moore, M.G. (1991). Editorial: Distance education theory. *The American Journal of Distance Education*, 5(3), 1–6.

Peters, O. (1994). Distance education and industrial production: A comparative interpretation in outline (1973). In D. Keegan (Ed.), *Otto Peters on distance education: The industrialization of teaching and learning.* London: Routledge.

Peters, O. (1998). *Learning and teaching in distance education: Analyses and interpretations from an international perspective.* London: Kogan Page.

Peters, O. (2003). Learning with new media in distance education. In M.G. Moore & W.G. Anderson (Eds.), *Handbook of distance education.* Mahwah, NJ: Lawrence Erlbaum.

Peters, O. (2007). The most industrialized form of education. In M.G. Moore (Ed.), *Handbook of distance education.* Mahwah, NJ: Lawrence Erlbaum.

Shale, D. (2002). The hybridization of higher education in Canada. *International Review of Research in Open and Distance Learning*, 2(2) [Online]. Retrieved on July 7, 2004 from: http://www.irrodl.org/content/v2.2/shale.html.

Shale, D. & Garrison, D.R. (1990). Introduction. In D.R. Garrison & D. Shale (Eds.), *Education at a distance: From issues to practice.* Melbourne, FL: Krieger.

Wedemeyer, C.A. (1971). Independent study. In R. Deighton (Ed.), *Encyclopedia of Education IV.* New York: Macmillan.

# 3

# Organization and Technology of Distance Education

## Dr. Gary E. Miller
Executive Director Emeritus, Penn State World Campus
Pennsylvania State University

## Introduction

Distance education during the industrial period developed at the intersection of three powerful forces: social change, technological development, and the need for educational institutions to adapt to changing social needs. Among these three forces, technology has been both a cause of change—due to its impact on society—and a means by which distance education responded to those changes. Technology also affected how institutions organized the distance education function over time. To understand better the interactions among technologies, organization, and the role of distance education, it is good to take a long view.

*One response in the U.S. was to create new communication lines to farms. It was called Rural Free Delivery (RFD) and it was the information highway of the 19th century.*

## The Development of Distance Education Programs

*Organizing the University for Correspondence Study*

In North America, distance education began as a response to the workforce and economic developments of the 19th-century Industrial Revolution. In the 1880s, North America was a generation into the Industrial Revolution and in the midst of dramatic social changes. The western frontier was closing (the U.S. frontier would close officially in 1891) and new industry was spurring rapid urban growth, driven by immigration and by the movement of young people from poor rural areas to the cities in search of prosperity.

New forms of higher education—the utilitarian public college and university movement—arose to respond to the workforce needs of the new industrial economy. However, the government became concerned about the migration of people from farms to the cities. The country needed a strong agricultural system to support continued urban growth, but young people found rural life to be increasingly isolated. One response in the U.S. was to create a new communication line to farms. It was called Rural Free Delivery (RFD), and it was the information highway of the 19th century. RFD meant that farmers no longer needed to go into town to collect their mail: it would be delivered at home, greatly increasing the speed of communication for farm families.

RFD was still experimental in 1892 when three institutions—the University of Chicago, followed quickly by the Pennsylvania State College and the University of Wisconsin (MacKenzie et al., 1968, p. 29)—launched the first systematic correspondence study programs in the United States. Correspondence study had its roots in Europe, where foreign language instruction by correspondence was offered as early as 1856 (p. 24). However, the programs launched in 1892 stimulated a national movement for correspondence study in public universities.

*Guiding Principles*

Institutions offered both credit and noncredit courses via correspondence study and, by the 1920s, some universities, led by the University of Nebraska, began to offer high school courses by correspondence. In all cases, the programs were marked by several guiding principles:

- Broad Access: Most programs were offered to anyone, anywhere, without regard to political boundaries.
- Time Independence: Courses were not based on campus semester calendars. Instead, students could enroll at any time and have six months or more to complete a course.
- Formal, Individualized Interaction: Correspondence courses assumed individual interaction between a student and instructor based on written assignments.

While these principles benefited students, they also were made possible—and in some cases dictated—by the delivery technology itself.

*Organization of a Correspondence Study Program*
While the delivery infrastructure for correspondence study—the postal
system—was ubiquitous and free, this form of distance education
required that institutions create a substantial administrative and support infrastructure within the institution. Elements of this system
included several functions that would become core to future distance
education programs. Course development support for faculty in correspondence programs consisted mainly of editors and graphic artists. As
other media took their place alongside printed materials, instructional
designers were added to the team. Correspondence programs also
required a publishing and distribution system for the printing, ware-
housing, and mailing of course materials and commercially published
texts. Other support systems were needed to accommodate the unique
needs of the delivery system and distant students; these included a
system to register, advise, and otherwise support students who had no
physical connection to the institution, and a mechanism for hand-
ling written lessons and proctored examinations. It also required a
marketing/recruiting strategy quite different from that used to recruit
traditional students; business practices that allowed students to register,
pay tuition, and begin taking a course at any time during the year; and
a budget model that allowed the institution to recover new costs
associated with distance education from this new revenue stream.

In most institutions, this required a centralized instructional delivery
unit that adapted for distance education students many of the services
provided to campus-based students. It also required new policies that
did not assume physical contact between the student and faculty or
student and institution for a wide range of support services. The result
was what today would be called a 'virtual campus,' a structure that was
rarely recognized as a separate academic unit but that, instead, worked
with faculty and academic units across the institution to extend their
academic programs to distant students.

These requirements, in turn, dictated the organizational structure
of correspondence study at the university level. Some programs—
those focused on agriculture and home life—were integrated into the

Cooperative Extension Service function. However, most institutions housed correspondence study in university-wide General Extension or Continuing Education units, with the Director of Correspondence Study (or Independent Study by Correspondence, as it came to be called) reporting to a Vice-President/Vice-Provost for Extension or Continuing Education. These units housed the centralized support services—instructional design, registration and records, student services, publishing and distribution, marketing, etc.—and worked with individual faculty and academic units across the institution to develop and deliver individual courses, certificate programs, and, eventually, full degree programs. Programs tended to operate as cost centers, fully responsible for both academic and delivery costs and expected to recover costs through tuition revenue and sale of materials. Faculty participation tended to be outside the normal teaching workload, with faculty members paid extra to develop and teach distant students.

*Inter-institutional Collaboration and Communities*
While correspondence study arguably made all participating institutions directly competitive for the same student, in fact the field developed a strong inter-institutional professional community. It was not unusual for an institution to purchase correspondence course materials from another institution, for instance. In 1938, the International Council for Correspondence Education (ICCE—now the International Council for Open and Distance Education) was founded, creating the first global professional organization for correspondence study institutions and professions. In 1955, the U.S.-based National University Extension Association (NUEA—now the University Continuing Education Association) established a Division of Correspondence Study, putting this mode at the same level as other types of continuing education. In 1962, the Division of Correspondence Study developed a self-evaluation guide for correspondence study departments and, for the first time, a national catalog of university-based correspondence study programs and courses (MacKenzie et al., 1968, pp. 206–207).

*Other Organizational Patterns for Correspondence Study*
Several other structures have also emerged over time to support correspondence study. In 1929, the University of Nebraska became the

first U.S. state university to offer supervised correspondence study at the high school level. By 1965, at least 42 universities that were members of NUEA offered correspondence courses at the high school level (MacKenzie et al., 1968, p. 32). These typically were integrated into the higher education correspondence program. Several states— Oregon, North Dakota, and Montana are examples—also developed correspondence study programs for both adults and high school students; these tended to be managed directly by the State Department of Education or the State Board of Higher Education (p. 34).

A variety of proprietary correspondence study programs also emerged in the first half of the 20th century. The Distance Education and Training Council (DETC) was founded in 1926 "to promote sound educational standards and ethical business practices within the correspondence field" (DETC website). DETC became a recognized accrediting agency for proprietary programs.

*Telecourses*

In the 1950s, a section of the public airwaves was set aside for educational use, spurring the development of educational television stations and networks in North America. In the United States, several land grant universities, some of which already had invested in correspondence study, as well as major urban community colleges licensed educational television stations and began to use them to deliver both formal and informal education. In addition, several U.S. states and Canadian provinces created coordinating agencies for educational broadcasting; examples include TV Ontario, Access Alberta, and British Columbia's Open Learning Agency in Canada; and Kentucky Educational Television and Wisconsin Public Television in the United States.

Community colleges, in particular, used public television (and, eventually, cable TV) to create a new kind of distance education: the telecourse. Typically, a community college telecourse included 28–30 half-hour television programs (designed so that two programs could be broadcast each week over a 14- or 15-week semester), a standard textbook, and a study guide that summarized key concepts and included assignments and additional references. Institutions often offered periodic face-to-face study meetings during the semester. After the introduction of low-cost videocassettes in the 1980s, telecourses were also offered as enhanced correspondence courses, with the media materials delivered by mail. By the mid-1980s, the telecourse had become a major force in distance education.

*Guiding Principles*

Telecourse delivery tended to be limited by the broadcast or cablecast 'footprint' of the broadcast television station or cable television outlet over which they were delivered. At many institutions, telecourses were offered as 'blended' courses in which the use of video replaced the classroom lecture, but typically did not totally eliminate classroom sessions. As a result, most institutions that offered telecourses were guided less by the goal of broad geographic access and more by the desire to give students within a defined geographic area convenience and flexibility. They also entailed a greater attention to instructional design, as the use of broadcast television programs both required greater attention to how content was presented and permitted new, more visual ways to illustrate key concepts. In many respects, the organization of a telecourse progam paralleled what would be needed later to support online learning.

*Organization of a Telecourse Program*

Telecourses required that an institution have—or have access to—media production and distribution facilities. These included a television production studio to create course materials and either or both a television broadcast and/or a cable delivery facility. Initially, the financial investment in technical infrastructure was significant. However, over time, as the number and quality of telecourse packages available for license grew and as more local cable television franchises provided local educational access channels at no cost to the institution, the entry cost for this kind of distance education dropped, and many institutions were able to offer telecourses to local students.

Because telecourses tended to be offered over local media outlets, students were not far from campus. As a result, telecourses tended to fit into existing administrative and student support systems. Typically, they were offered by the continuing education administrative unit that also offered evening and off-campus programs. Academic advising, library support, books, etc., were also handled through existing on-campus services. Where institutions offered telecourses using non-broadcast videocassettes, these courses typically were simply added on to an existing correspondence study program, with the major new element being the additional cost of duplicating and mailing tapes.

*Inter-institutional Collaborations*

The high cost of production and, initially, the limited broadcast area for delivery drove institutions to seek out opportunities for collaboration, both for the development of telecourses and for their distribution to other institutions. Major community colleges—

> Community colleges, in particular, used public television (and, eventually, cable TV) to create a new kind of distance education: the telecourse.

including Coastline Community College, Dallas Community College District, and Miami-Dade Community College—formed the Telecourse People, which marketed the collected telecourse libraries of participating colleges to other institutions. The University of Mid-America provided an umbrella under which land grant universities in the U.S. Midwest collaborated to develop telecourses and to market them to other institutions. In Michigan, Wayne State University, working with the United Auto Workers, created the To Educate the People Consortium to develop and distribute inter-disciplinary tele-courses designed for the working adult.

In 1978, the Public Broadcasting Service shifted from land-line distribution of its national programming to satellite delivery. This created, for the first time, a national distribution network for tele-courses. PBS organized the Adult Learning Service within its structure to facilitate the sharing of telecourses nationally. Each public television station became a distributor of telecourses to its local colleges and universities. Institutions could license use of PBS-distributed tele-courses, which would then be broadcast over their local station. This system essentially eliminated the need for local institutional media infrastructure: any institution could offer a telecourse with an invest-ment as low as $300 per course, plus $15 for every student who enrolled locally.

In the early 1980s, Walter Annenberg, founder of *TV Guide*, offered the Corporation for Public Broadcasting (the corporation established by the U.S. government to guide the use of federal funds for public broadcasting) $150 million to stimulate the development of high-quality telecourses that could be offered over PBS. The result was a surge in the development of telecourses with very high television production standards that further enhanced the popularity of this kind of distance education.

### *The Open Learning Movement: Emergence of Specialized Institutions*

> Throughout the Industrial Era, new, innovative institutional models evolved in response to new workforce needs and changing social dynamics.

Throughout the Industrial Era, new, innovative institutional models evolved in response to new workforce needs and changing social dynamics. Examples include technical colleges, community colleges, civic 'red brick' universities in the United Kingdom, and other public universities that grew out of the need to prepare teachers and other professionals to support a changing society. Distance education spawned a similar innovation: the open university movement.

The open university movement began in the 1960s when Great Britain established the first Open University in an attempt to bring into higher education adults and lower-income individuals who had been excluded from the elitist British higher education system. Over the next decade, many other countries developed national open universities to democratize access to education.

### *Guiding Principles*

While distance education previously had developed within traditional colleges and universities, the Open University reflected a commitment to creating a fully autonomous institution totally organized around the needs of nontraditional students (Moore & Kearsley, 2003). These 'single mode' distance teaching institutions would be learner-centered. Not only instruction but all support services would be designed specifically to meet the needs of nontraditional students, reflecting an understanding that, for many adults, education is not only an academic but a cultural and personal challenge. The underlying principle guiding the development of these institutions was to make education accessible for all and, in the process, to improve society. As the Open University of the United Kingdom's mission statement puts it, "The Open University is open to people, places, methods and ideas . . . It promotes educational opportunity and social justice by providing high-quality university education to all who wish to realize their ambitions and fulfill their potential" (Open University website).

*Organization of an Open Learning Institution*

The success of the Open University of the United Kingdom stimulated the development of other open universities around the world. Most of these were created as national institutions, designed to empower wider participation in higher education. In the United States and Canada, where higher education is organized at the state/provincial level, new institutions were developed at that level, either as fully independent institutions or as separate institutions within a state/provincial system of higher education. Examples include Athabasca University in Canada's Alberta Province and, in the United States, Empire State College (New York) and Edison State College (New Jersey).

Regardless of the political framework in which they are chartered, most are capable of serving distant students beyond their political boundaries.

*Inter-institutional Collaborations*

Inter-institutional collaborations among open learning institutions tended to be focused on sharing courses and course materials. An example is the International University Consortium (IUC), led by the University of Maryland University College and the Maryland Center for Public Broadcasting. IUC was a collaboration among institutions to share and, in some cases, collaboratively develop, open university materials. The British Open University of the UK had a long-standing interest in expanding to North America. However, its curriculum was highly interdisciplinary, with single courses the equivalent of a full year of study. As a result, it was difficult for the OU to catch hold, and few North American institutions were prepared to partner with them. IUC was created to adapt these highly produced, but also highly interdisciplinary, materials to the North American curriculum. Eventually, IUC included not only institutions in the U.S. and Canada, but in Australia, Hong Kong, and Venezuela. In addition to adapting British Open University materials, IUC worked with its member institutions to develop new courses collaboratively with international, cross-cultural faculty teams, such as "The Literature of the Americas."

*Teleconferencing: Point to Multi-point Distance Education*

> The underlying principle guiding the development of these institutions was to make education accessible to all and, in the process, to improve society.

Another form of distance education that emerged in the 1970s was interactive teleconferencing: the delivery of credit courses and noncredit conferences and workshops as live, interactive media events through a variety of telecommunications services, ranging from the telephone to the Internet. These technologies have enabled a wide range of distance education initiatives that share several common principles and elements.

*Guiding Principles*

While *access* is a guiding principle of all types distance education, teleconferencing defines access in very specific ways. Teleconferences are 'real-time' events that require participants to be in particular places at particular times. However, the places may be very widely distributed. With the exception of telephone conferencing (except in situations where access to telephony is limited), teleconferencing almost always involves a relationship between an *originating* organization and one or more *receiving* organizations. For example, a university may originate a graduate course in engineering that is received by employees in a specially equipped training room at their worksite: the relationship is not only between the student and the instructor, but between the institution and the employer.

> While access is a guiding principle of all types of distance education, teleconferencing defines access in very specific ways.

The fact that teleconferencing takes place in real-time may also affect the instructor's role.

A teleconferencing program may be offered outside the normal campus teaching schedule (as is the case with correspondence study or tele-courses), or it may extend to distant sites a traditional on-campus course that is part of the faculty member's normal teaching load. The historical distinctions between distance education and campus-based teaching begin to blur in this environment.

*Elements of a Teleconferencing Program*
The three main elements of teleconferencing are delivery technology, building and maintaining relationships with receiving organizations, and content development. These tend to drive how institutions organize for teleconferencing.

The delivery technologies used for teleconferencing have expanded over time, but all remain available and used in different situations:

- Telephone: While some institutions in developing countries have used ham radio and other audio technologies, the telephone is generally the most basic delivery technology for teleconferencing. It allows a faculty member or conference leader to convene multiple sites through an audio bridge. Sites may be individuals in their homes or groups of participants gathered around a speakerphone.
- ITFS and Related Fixed Educational Video Frequencies: This system was the original videoconferencing technology and requires special video origination and receiving equipment to be installed in all participating locations. In many cases, it has since been replaced by the other kinds of videoconferencing described below. It was used mainly for long-term relationships between universities and employers or to interconnect campuses in multi-institutional systems, etc.
- Dial-up Videoconferencing: As telephony moved to fibre optics and broader bandwidth technologies, it became possible to connect multiple sites through dial-up videoconferencing systems over telephone lines. This required special equipment at receiving sites, which have become increasingly portable over time.
- Satellite: Since the 1970s, it has been possible to extend real-time events (courses, seminars, workshops) from one point to many other sites via satellite, with access expanding greatly as the

number of satellite receivers has grown. Typically satellite tele-conferencing is one-way video and two-way audio, with receiving sites interacting with the originating site by telephone.

• Internet-based Conferencing: Since the 1990s, the Internet has become an increasingly common technology for audio- and video-conferencing, allowing individuals to participate from wherever they have Internet access.

*Organization*

The key elements of a teleconferencing program vary depending on the type of program being delivered. However, several elements are common to most forms. They include the technology (originating class-room or studio, access to delivery system—telephone lines, satellite, etc.—and compatible technology at the receiving site); faculty members, staff to coordinate use of the technology, access to a registration and records system (through either the residential system or continuing education) and relationship management. The last item is critical to the success of a teleconferencing program, as all teleconferencing assumes a relationship between the originating institution and a variety of receiv-ing sites.

Similarly, teleconferencing has spurred a variety of organizational structures, depending on the programmatic mission of the telecon-ferencing function at a particular institution. Several examples will illustrate:

• Graduate Program Delivery: Many institutions have used teleconferencing to extend professional graduate programs to worksites. Typically, these extend resident-instruction courses to off-campus audiences, and many are organized at the academic unit level. Faculty members within the academic unit manage the relationship with the receiving sites, which typically are employers with which the academic unit has multiple relationships.

• Noncredit Education and Training: Institutions offer a variety of noncredit programs via teleconference. Typically, these use a centralized distance education office that coordinates with multi-ple academic units and with receiving sites that may be different for each program.

- Institutional Networks: The U.S. Cooperative Extension Service is an example of a centralized university office that operates statewide (with offices in most counties of its state) and maintains receiving sites at County Extension offices in order to deliver specialized programs.

*Collaborations*

Teleconferencing, more than any other form of distance education, relied on organizational collaborations in pre-Web technologies. Several examples illustrate the variety of structures that arose to support teleconferencing:

- American Educational Satellite Program (AESP): In 1973, the University of Kentucky organized the Appalachian Educational Satellite Program, which used a still-experimental ATS satellite system to provide continuing professional education for teachers and other public service professionals at 15 sites in the Appalachian region of the United States. The receiving sites were located at higher education institutions, school districts, and other community-based organizations.
- National University Teleconferencing Network (NUTN): The Public Broadcasting Service in the U.S. initiated satellite distribution of its national program schedule in the late 1970s, creating a national delivery capability for satellite-based videoconferencing. The National University Teleconferencing Network operated as a membership organization of universities that used this system to create a national network of originating institutions and receiving sites, organized through the continuing education offices of member institutions. Any institution or external organization could organize a teleconference; NUTN would license access to the event by its member institutions, which would then charge a fee for local participants. Founded in 1982, NUTN membership grew to more than 200 campuses.
- Contact North/Contact Nord: Founded in 1986, this Ontario consortium provides access to formal education and training and nonformal educational opportunities for residents of Northern Ontario. It collaborates with aboriginal peoples, Francophone

residents, and local communities through a network of 89 'access centers.'

- American Distance Education Consortium (ADEC): This consortium of 65 land grant universities, historically black colleges and universities, Hispanic serving institutions, and tribal colleges was funded as AG*SAT to use satellite teleconferencing to deliver agricultural programs to institutional sites nationally. In recent years, it has diversified its use of technology to include Internet2, commodity Internet, satellite uplinks, downlinks, satellite-based Internet, digital television, and audioconferencing.

**Future Issues**

Teleconferencing helped begin the transition of distance education from the Industrial Era to the Information Era. By the 1990s, society was a generation into the Information Revolution. Many institutions saw real-time teleconferencing as the future of distance education. However, that was not to be the case. The first Web browser was released in 1993. Within a few years, many institutions were experimenting with online learning, both for distance education and on campus. Unlike other technologies that had been used for distance education, the Internet evolved as part of the basic infrastructure of higher education institutions. As learning applications became more widely available, the most significant technological and cost entry barriers were erased, and online distance education attracted a wide range of institutions. Allen and Seaman (2007) reported that, over the five-year period beginning in 2001, nearly three-quarters of all U.S. institutions of higher education offered courses in which at least 80 percent of the course is online.

*Principles of an Online Distance Education Program*

Online learning has removed both time and geography as defining elements of the learning environment. In that sense, it is more like correspondence study than any other form of distance education, embracing again the principle of wide access and learner control. The major differences (other than the technology itself) are: delivery and response are immediate, so online courses can be offered at a distance within a traditional semester timeframe; and, while correspondence study permits only limited, formal interaction, students in an online course can interact freely and spontaneously with content, the instructor, and each other, allowing the creation of a learning environment that shares many elements with a face-to-face course. As a result, all of the elements that support a correspondence study program described earlier apply to online distance education.

*Organizational Impact*

There is no single organizational model for online distance education. This is most likely the result of the interaction of several factors: the ubiquitous nature of the Internet, which allows innovation at many points within an institution; the number and variety of institutions involved in online distance education; and the impact of existing academic and student policies, information systems, and business models on the development of online learning at individual institutions. However, three general organizational models seem to predominate:

- Centralized Delivery: This model is similar to correspondence study and involves a single administrative unit—usually housed in the continuing education or extension function—to coordinate nonacademic aspects of delivery on behalf of multiple academic units.
- Decentralized Delivery: Individual academic units are responsible for all aspects of development and delivery, with central support limited to technology infrastructure.
- Coordinated: In multi-campus systems, especially, a coordinating council serves to help overcome internal policy, infrastructure, and support issues.

## Future Issues: The Implications for Online Distance Education

Online education quickly overcame and, in some cases, replaced earlier forms of distance education, creating a single technological platform to help higher education institutions adapt to the needs of the Knowledge

Society. The potential to mingle on-campus and distant students in the same online course creates pedagogical, operational, and administrative challenges.

Pedagogical challenges include how to create a common sense of community among students of very diverse backgrounds and interests. Increasingly, Web applications facilitate a degree of collaboration and active creation of knowledge that are not feasible in a typical classroom, but have become necessary workplace and even civic skills.

Operational challenges include how to ensure that distant students have equitable access to informal contact with faculty members and with support services provided on campus. In this new environment, what are the co-curricular responsibilities of an institution to all students, regardless of their location?

Administrative issues include the need to develop budget policies and procedures that do not assume co-location of the student and institutional support services. Many issues related to infrastructure and support services require institutions to reconsider fundamental budget issues—how funds are distributed to support student learning and faculty support—and student information system issues—how students are defined and how their progress is tracked through administrative computing systems. Online learning—both at a distance and on campus—challenges a basic assumption that historically underpins many institutional policies: that the student and the institution are geographically co-located.

> Online learning—both at a distance and on campus—challenges the basic assumption that historically underpins many institutional policies: that the student and the institution are geographically co-located.

## Conclusion

Throughout the industrial period, distance education was defined by the interactions—and tradeoffs—between three key principles:

- Access: Extending the reach of education and training opportunities to individuals and groups who otherwise did not have effective access to education. Mail service to individual homes allowed for the widest, most democratic access to education through correspondence study. Throughout the 20th century, electronic technologies enhanced the quality of content delivered at a distance and, in some cases, allowed institutions confidently to extend more complex programs—professional graduate degrees, for instance—to groups of students far from campus. The result, by the end of the industrial period, was an overlapping network of technologies and services that served different audiences with different needs.

- Independence: Allowing the student the freedom to determine when and where to study. Correspondence study provided the greatest degree of independence. While teleconferencing required students to be in particular places at particular times, it granted a degree of independence not otherwise available at the time for graduate education; students could study at a great distance from a campus and integrate learning into their work and family lives.

- Interaction: Formalizing communication between student and instructor, student and course content, and among students. Interaction was most formalized and structured in correspondence study. Teleconferencing, while it limited independence, allowed students the opportunity for spontaneous, real-time interaction with their instructor and with each other.

For most of the 20th century, distance education flourished among the institutions that were created specifically as a response to the Industrial Revolution: public universities, community colleges, and open universities. Teleconferencing developed at the beginning of a transition from the Industrial Age to the Information Age, bringing into the field professional graduate programs from private universities, such as Stanford University in the United States. The rise of Web-based distance education after 1993 would complete the transition, bringing many new institutions into distance education. At the same time, online technologies came to be used for both on-campus and distance education, blurring the traditional lines between the two methods and moving distance education into the mainstream of higher education.

*For most of the 20th century, distance education flourished among the institutions that were created specifically as a response to the Industrial Revolution: public universities, community colleges, and open universities.*

While the immediate issues change over time, distance education continues to evolve at the intersection of social change, technological development, and the need for our institutions to adapt to changing social needs.

## TERMS AND DEFINITIONS

**Correspondence study:** An early form of distance education in which both subject matter and all interactions are formalized in written documents.

**Industrial Revolution:** A major shift in culture that began in the late 18th and early 19th centuries as a result of innovations in manufacturing, transportation, and agriculture, which transformed social and economic structures from an agrarian to an industrial base.

**Information Revolution:** A major shift in culture that began in the 1930s and saw its full flowering in the late 20th and early 21st century as a result of innovations in technology and communications, transforming social and economic structures from an industrial to a technological base.

**Interaction:** Three different types of interaction are core to all distance education programs: the interaction of the learner with content, the learner's interaction with the instructor, and the learner's interaction with other learners (Moore & Kearsley, 2005, p. 140).

**Rural Free Delivery (RFD):** An initiative of the United States Postal Service in the 1890s to improve the quality of rural life by delivering mail to individual homes in rural areas. RFD stimulated the development of catalog merchandising, correspondence study, and other services designed to reach farm families.

**Single mode institution:** An institution in which all resources are devoted exclusively to distance education (Moore & Kearsley, 2005, p. 4).

**Teleconference:** A distance education format that uses communications technology—telephone, satellite, or the Internet, as examples—to connect multiple sites for live, real-time interaction among instructor and students at all locations.

**Telecourse:** A media-based distance education course package in which the traditional lecture component is delivered by video or audio programs, complemented by one or more texts and, often, a study guide.

## QUESTIONS FOR REVIEW AND REFLECTION

1. In what ways are the influences of the Industrial Revolution and the Information Revolution the same in terms of their impact on the evolution of distance education? In what ways are they different?
2. What elements of a correspondence study program are important to the organization of an online distance education program?
3. What is the continuing impact of teleconferencing on distance education?
4. What was the societal goal in the development of the Open University?
5. How did the public broadcasting structures of different countries affect distance education?
6. What are the implications of online learning for traditional universities?
7. In what ways did inter-institutional collaborations change as new forms of distance education arose?
8. What are the implications of blurring the traditional lines between distance education and campus-based education that is being brought about by online learning?

### Significant Contributor

**Dr. Otto Peters** has had a virtually unrivaled, global impact on distance education. Entering the field in the 1960s, when it was beginning to be affected by telecommunications technology, Dr. Peters provided both administrative and scholarly leadership when distance education was being transformed, in both industrialized and developing countries, from a 'correspondence study' model to a media-based national strategy for workforce development. As a pioneering administrative leader, scholar and professional leader, he shaped the direction of university-based distance education in Europe and the world during a career that spanned four decades. He is considered to be the founder of the theory of industrialized education. In 1975, after a decade as a distance education scholar at the University of Tubingen, Dr. Peters became the founding Rector of the Fern-Universität in Hagen, the national distance teaching university of Germany. As Rector from 1975 to 1985, he traveled the world to study distance education systems in other countries and cultures. Under his leadership, FernUniversität grew into an internationally respected provider of distance education that now serves 55,000 students annually. As Rector, Dr. Peters maintained an active research program in the theory and practice of distance education. He conducted an extensive research project, University Study for Persons Working for a Living, and published *The Pedagogical Structure of Distance Education* (1973). Following his term as Rector, Dr. Peters held a FernUniversität chair in the Methodology of Distance Education.

## References

Allen, E. & Seaman, J. (2007). *Online nation: Five years of growth in online learning.* Needham, MA: Sloan Consortium.

About the OU: Our mission. Retrieved May 6, 2009, from: http://www.open.ac.uk/about/ou/p2.shtml.

Bramble, Q.J. and Ausness, C. (Eds.) (1974). An experiment in educational technology: An overview of the Appalachian Education Satellite Project. *Technical Report Number 2.* Eric Document ED103007.

DETC History. Retrieved October 1, 2009, from: http://www.detc.org/the association.html#history.

History of the Open University. Retrieved May 6, 2009, from: http://www.open.ac.uk/about/ou/p3.shtml.

MacKenzie, O., Christensen, E.L., & Rigby, P.H. (1968). *Correspondence instruction in the United States.* New York: McGraw-Hill.

Moore, M. & Kearsley, G. (2005). *Distance education: A systems view* (2nd edition). Belmont, CA: Wadsworth.

Network of Access Centres Connecting Northern Ontario. Retrieved May 15, 2009, from: http://www.contactnorth.ca/index.php?sv=&category=Menu&title=Access Centres.

Poley, J. (2009). *About ADEC: Background on the American Distance Education Consortium.* Retrieved May 6, 2009 from: http://www.adec.edu/admin/adec-background.html.

The NUTN Experience. Retrieved May 15, 2009, from: http://144.162.197.249/about_us/experience.html.

# 4

# TEACHING AND LEARNING IN DISTANCE EDUCATION BEFORE THE DIGITAL AGE

## Dr. Margaret Haughey

Vice-President Academic
Athabasca University

## Introduction

Models of teaching and learning in distance education are usually extensions of the current theories about the relationship between teaching and learning in use at the time. Prior to the

> *The culture of the times shaped what learning meant . . .*

Digital Age, a number of different models of teaching and learning had been developed, all with their implications for contemporary distance education. These influenced the foundational distance education model, which is the focus of this chapter.

As far back as the Greeks and Romans, it was accepted that while going to school and learning with the support of a tutor was preferred for younger students, adults learned through private study and then tested their ideas in public discussion and debate. The culture of the times shaped what learning meant—to be able to quote extensively and at will from all the major classical writers and to debate the meanings of passages and link their author's argument to the issue at hand. Adult education in these times, then, used the letter to exchange ideas among scholars and the book, on vellum scrolls, to share ideas among a readership. With the addition of a study guide, these remained the main tools of Western correspondence education until the mid-20th century. In ancient China, there was much the same system, with the addition of the examination. Studying for the examination meant private study of the texts often with the assistance of a written guide.

Any man who was successful in a series of rigorous government examinations based on the works of classical Chinese writers and philosophers could obtain a civil service position. Such scholars were revered in Chinese society, and emperors often appointed a Chief Soldier and a Chief Scholar and gave them equal rank.

For a considerable period of time through the Middle Ages and into the Renaissance, the mark of a learned man (most cultures did not consider such learning suitable for girls since they were not expected to participate in public debate) was his ability to discuss ideas and recall passages from the Canon, all the major classical writings. This definition of learning extolled memory and the ability to recite from memory; it praised argument, disquisition, and public oratory. Sir Francis Bacon, a philosopher during the time of Elizabeth I (the mid-1500s), is generally thought to have been the last man to have read the entire Canon and to have a holistic knowledge of the theories of the world. Already the number of important publications in different languages made this difficult. Following the development of the printing press, books and their contents gradually became more accessible to a broader society and knowledge was no longer an elite commodity. Knowledge became increasingly specialized. Mathematics and the sciences become more important. Learning, then, over all these centuries, was a means to becoming knowledgeable about a subject. It occurred through reading and studying texts, often with written or oral guidance, and was demonstrated through writing and debate. Then the notion of what learning was for changed.

Initially, schooling focused on preparing young boys for their place in society. For girls, schooling involved a private tutor and for those children not fortunate enough to be able to afford schooling, the apprenticeship was the means to knowledge. Ways of learning then included various forms of rote learning aimed at memorization of facts and passages from classical literature, the delineation of argument and debate with one's peers in speech and writing, and public oratory. It is not surprising that

*Over the course of the Victorian era, essentially the 19th century, the tutor was replaced by the school and the classical curriculum was replaced by a public curriculum set by the local authorities.*

when the Industrial Revolution occurred and parents and children went to work in factories, the notion of schooling for such children was focused on preparing them for the world of work. The schoolroom became the commonplace, and the disciplinary methods of the workplace were used to ensure that students learned their place as well as their lessons. Over the course of the Victorian era, essentially the 19th century, the tutor was replaced by the school and the classical curriculum was replaced by a public curriculum set by the local authorities. The examination replaced public discourse in law or politics as the criterion for entry into adult work. Private study through access to books continued but the focus was on pleasure rather than erudition. How, then, did these forms of learning influence distance education?

### Distance Education, pre-1970

Prior to the 1970s, distance education was characterized as correspondence education and was based on independent study using books, and materials delivered and returned by mail. A series of lessons was prepared and sent to students who studied on their own and mailed their assignments to the institution who marked and provided feedback. In many of the commercial establishments who ran these programs you were not sent the next lesson until the previous assignment had been received. The tone of the work was neutral or passive and the materials were essentially a series of exercises with little or no psychological or motivational support for the student. In 1858 the University of London began providing programs for external study. Syllabi, texts and prior examination questions were sent to those seeking to obtain what was known as an external degree. The student had to pass the examination, set and marked in London. Correspondence tuition was set up by the University Correspondence College to support the University of London students. In many ways the University of London prefigured the OU UK not only in its format but because it provided opportunities to obtain a higher education degree for those such as women and racial minorities who were barred from higher education by political or personal circumstances.

Among their many outcomes, the two world wars ushered in modern distance education. Not only did they bring great destruction and loss of life, but many of the survivors had been dislocated from their homes and communities and had missed several years of schooling. France, the Netherlands, and West and East Germany set up correspondence schools to address this need. Glatter (1969) reported that in 1968 the French CNED had over 124,000 students while the Netherlands had 723,000 registrants. In East Germany, 37 percent of all technical college and 25 percent of all university students were enrolled in correspondence education. Correspondence education based on a personal study model was used by elementary and secondary education students who could not access classroom instruction and adult students who needed to combine work and study. In Canada Queen's University offered a combination of summer campus courses and winter correspondence courses for teachers seeking to complete their degrees. Other universities, such as the University of Alberta, offered undergraduate-level courses by correspondence but did not grant credential credit for the experience.

In North America the second half of the 20th century saw many changes in the ways people thought about learning and in the development of curriculum and provision of education. The post-war conservatism of the 1950s gave way to the excitement of the 1960s. In education, the launch of the Sputnik satellite in 1957 led to immediate concerns in the USA about the need for a reformed curriculum with more science and technology. It was also the age of educational radicalism when authors such as Jonathan Kozol, John Holt, Carl Rogers and Ivan Illich challenged the mass education orientation of public secondary and post-secondary schooling. Increasingly, post-war governments recognized that post-secondary education was essential for their economic growth and the development of their citizens. At the same time there was increased pressure on the system because growing numbers of adults desired post-secondary schooling. For example, in the 1960s only about 5 percent of the UK population went on to post-secondary education (Harry, 1983). The old system of elite universities which continued after the Second World War needed to be transformed but time was short; a new system of education was required. One version of that system was based on the open education movement, of which the open universities are the major proponents.

These new institutions faced enormous challenges: they had to prove to the government that they were fiscally viable, to the resident universities that they were credible peers, and to the public that their graduates could compete with those from the other universities in obtaining employment. They had to design a new form of teaching which would engage faculty who were used to the free flow of exchange in classrooms. They had to employ a range of professionals in the

*The old system of elite universities which continued after the Second World War needed to be transformed but time was short; a new system of education was required. One version of that system was based on the open education movement, of which the open universities are the major proponents.*

areas of curriculum development and course design, both relatively new to tertiary education. They had to envisage a system which would enable this to occur within the fiscal and organizational constraints and yet meet the educational and political visions for these new institutions. The components of the models they developed are the focus of this chapter.

## Design of Open Universities

The first open university, the Open University of the United Kingdom (OU UK), began in 1969. The design of the open universities was strongly influenced by the education issues in the decade or so that preceded their development. The curriculum development movement which had challenged the previous behavioristic notions of providing only what students required for their future endeavors had spawned the open classroom movement in Britian, where students were placed in enriching learning environments with a large variety of resources and encouraged to choose what they wanted to study. Teachers worked with the students to ensure the development of educational abilities. Some of this related to the work of Dewey and his concern for the development of a democratic society which gave students the opportunity to study what they wanted and not what was deemed appropriate for them. Tony Bates, who worked at the OU UK for many years, described his understanding of the process: "The first UK Open

University courses were based on instructional systems design" (Bates, 2008, p. 224). Later, he added that "industrially organized post-secondary institutions tend to design teaching and learning in ways that suit an industrial economy" (p. 229). The distance education theorist who is most closely associated with this perspective is Otto Peters, the founding Rektor (President) of the FernUniversität, Germany, who described distance education as an industrialized process. He explained his view in this way:

> Its structure is determined to a considerable degree by the principles which govern the industrialization of the working process in the production of goods . . . This means the principles of rationalization, division of labor, the assignment of fragmented tasks to specialists, mechanization and automation.
>
> (Peters, 1993, p. 93)

Peters (2008, p. 297) suggested that such an approach could be viewed as more modern and up to date than previous forms of education since it was more reflective of societal trends and could accommodate the needs of working adults, noting:

> it is significant to see that these open universities represent a new type of university that is in accordance with marked political and educational trends: the democratization of university study, mass higher education, lifelong education, adult higher education, professional qualifications, collaboration with the labour market, and globalization.

Writing about ten autonomous multimedia distance teaching universities, Greville Rumble and Keith Harry (1983, pp. 222–223) argued that these universities employed:

> a conscious and systematic approach to the design of learning materials for independent study; the use of a wide range of media and other resources to teach . . .; the centralized design and production of materials, combined with localised learning (the last two features leading to a division of labour); the provision of two-way communication between students and tutors who generally operate at a distance from the student (correspondence tuition, telephone tuition) but with the possibility of occasional meetings (face to face tuition) . . .; the introduction of a

number of quasi-industrial processes . . .; [and] extensive and well-defined administrative areas.

Yet while these are often identified as the common points for distance education universities, there were also differences among the universities: some had open admission (Athabasca University, OU UK) while others had traditional entrance criteria; some had a wide selection of undergraduate courses (Chinese Central Television University) but many focused on professionally oriented degree programs; and some had a wide range of programs from general education courses to graduate education (Allama Iqbal Open University, Pakistan). Even in the development of courses there were wide variations between the OU UK, with a highly complex course development process involving large numbers of internal staff, and Athabasca University, which had worked with other institutions in the design of some of its courses and had a much more streamlined version (Stringer, 1980). One commonality among the institutions, however, was the predominance of print. While many used television and radio, only the Chinese Central Television University and the OU UK made substantial use of these resources. The FernUniversität, on the other hand, (initially) chose not to use any audio-visual materials, based on the belief that its print was of superior design.

The philosophy of the OU UK was based on the open education movement and encapsulated by it first chancellor, Lord Perry, in his inauguration address: "Open to people, open to places, open to ideas and open to methods." However, while the openness to people and places through the reduction of geographic, educational, financial and life circumstance barriers was widely supported, other forms of openness were harder to realize, given the size and complexity of the institution. A number of decisions shaped the design used at the OU UK. The courses were to be paced with set beginning and end points, similar to the timetable of their residential counterparts. The students were to study in their own time and were not required to attend lectures. It was expected that there would be very large numbers of learners, essential for the institution's viability, and reflecting the recognized demand for an alternative post-secondary option for working adults. To achieve the objective of being open to places, essentially to be independent of the need to attend lectures, a model involving individualized instruction was adopted.

Lord Perry (1976) noted in his reminiscences that in his view the concept of the course team was the single most important contribution of the OU UK to tertiary education. In this he was not meaning the use of a team approach as much as recognizing the change from teaching as a craft done by a single individual to teaching as a multi-faceted endeavor involving specialists in a wide range of areas, usually reflected in the members of the course team. There were three major components to the new design: learning resources, individualized study with a face-to-face support, and the coordinated development and production of components encapsulated by Bates in his reference to instructional systems design. This latter component refers to the entire system that needed to be developed to ensure that students received their materials and obtained feedback on their work in a timely way. At another level, it also included how the actual courses were designed and developed.

**The Systems Approach**

It was essential for an institution that planned to serve over 100,000 students annually in its first 20 years to use a model which ensured not only that there were systems in place to handle myriad decisions but that these decisions fitted within the institution's policies and procedures. At the OU UK the systems allowed for coordination and quality assurance of the course design and development processes, and the production and dissemination of materials as well as the registration and coordination of students and the hiring and support of a wide range of academic, professional and support staff.

*Developing Courses*

> The course team's task was to identify, write and develop all the materials needed by the student.

The course development model adopted by the OU UK was the course team. The team was led by an academic, a continuing faculty member with expertise in the area, who with a small team of internal and external colleagues had drawn up a course syllabus which had received internal academic approval. The course team's task was to identify, write and develop all the materials needed by the student. Members of the course team also included educational technologists who focused on the pedagogical design, contract academics as subject experts, a BBC (British Broadcasting Corporation) producer, librarians and a course manager who provided administrative support to the team. The tasks of the team included

> (1) writing particular sections of the course; (2) planning and presenting broadcasts in conjunction with the BBC . . .; (3) deciding on set books and recommended readings; (4) designing tests and exercises; (5) developing home experiments; (6) writing supplementary materials including notes for tutors; and (7) reading and commenting on drafts written by other course team members.
>
> (Harry, 1983, p. 178)

The last point should not be underestimated. Drafts were expected to go through three committee readings and the quality and clarity of the materials were seen as direct reflections of the time and thought which had gone into this process. The documents subsequently went through an editing and design process before being produced in the relevant medium. This entire process, which usually took between 24 and 36 months, was monitored closely by a Project Control office to ensure that delays did not affect production deadlines since many courses were in production at the same time. Tight (1985, p. 48) commented that it was likely that course teams as a model for development existed prior to the OU UK but "What the Open University has done is to pick on a particular model and adopt it wholesale. In this, as in a number of other aspects of its practice and ideology, the Open University can appear at times to have developed little since the late 1960s."

Tight saw two potential problems with the course team format: the sheer number of people involved in the team and the expectation that despite the numbers and differing roles it would be a collegial process. Since its initial development, the course team has been a topic of strong disagreement among OU staff on these issues (Hawkridge, 1980, p. 75). Today, the number of members on the team has been substantially reduced and there is clearer role differentiation but the university still remains concerned at the length of time it takes to develop and revise courses as more courses go online. In turn, faculty feel pressured to meet production guidelines which in their mind take precedence over academic discussion.

*Learning Resources*

The development of resources was based partly on the open classroom idea of a rich learning environment referred to earlier, partly on encouraging learners to use resources immediately available to them and partly to expand the use of printed guides to include audio-visual materials. Resources for a course might include a textbook or books, written by some of the major course authors, a variety of audio-visual materials and a study guide which integrated the information in the textual and audio-visual resources. The most important resource was the 'main text,' a printed book in paperback format of around 100 pages with relevant illustrations, diagrams and photographs. They were designed to integrate "the additional reading materials, with assignments and with radio and television programes to form *units of work*, each requiring one week of study. The main text contained self-assessment questions to help the student determine his progress" (Harry, 1983, p. 177). Keith Harry also described the other resources:

> The student also receives printed supplementary materials which may consist of broadcast notes to accompany radio and television programmes, off-prints, computer-marked and tutor-marked assignments and other information which needs to be revised regularly and is therefore not suitable for inclusion in the main texts, which are normally produced for use over a period of at least four years. The students are expected to buy certain specified *set books*, which may be readers compiled specially for the course, and receive a list of recommended readings which may be borrowed from public libraries.
>
> (Harry, 1983, p. 177; italics in original)

In addition, students studying science and technology subjects received kits which enabled them to undertake experiments at home, and do fieldwork associated with their courses. Each one had to be designed to meet the course objectives and integrate with the other course elements.

The OU UK had made arrangements with the BBC to make and broadcast educational materials that provided pertinent resources for their courses. These ranged from discussions of major concepts involving presentations by academics to programs which provided supplementary material to enrich the student's learning. The present Open Source site (www.opensource.ou.uk) provides some online examples from these resources. Like today's learning objects, these resources were designed to meet both the pedagogical objectives of the OU UK and the media standards required of public radio and television productions.

*Individualized Instruction*

Another major argument which surrounded the use of the course team model was about the extent to which this model prefigured a particular orientation to university education. The individualized instruction movement had two competing orientations: that of learner-centered personal growth with the teacher as the consultant following Carl Rogers; and a more behaviorist alternative based on the work of Skinner. The orientation of behaviorist psychology was to provide effective education in a cost-efficient manner that produced better workers. One of the earliest initiatives was led by Fred Burke and Mary Ward from the San Francisco State Normal School (1912–1915). In an effort to improve the level of teaching, provide more variety for the motivated pupils, and ensure that all essential concepts were included, they developed a series of booklets for grades 1–8 which were a runaway success until the State Board stopped the experiment. One of the then current manifestations of the same approach was the Keller Plan (1968), which was used in university teaching. It combined programmed instruction, individual progress based on achievement (mastery learning), learner persistence and formal support from peers who acted as tutors and also marked the tests of more junior students. Another influence on the design of course materials was the adoption of Bloom's taxonomy. First published in the mid-1970s, it had a strong influence on the subsequent structuring and orientation of instructional materials.

*Learner Support*

In writing about the OU UK in 2003, Alan Tait, now an OU UK pro-vice-chancellor, noted that "It was not until the establishment of the Open University UK in 1969 that modern distance education was formed by the development of a range of learning and teaching media along with an integrated student support system" (2003, p. 1). In this comment, Tait is defining a model for the OU UK which is at odds with the instructional systems design approach identified earlier. In his view, the OU UK chose this approach because it was cognizant that its population was not made up of the average 18–24-year-old under-graduate student but rather working people who had not previously considered post-secondary education, and included all people who sought to enter. He summarized this orientation as: "That is to say students chose the university and not the other way around" (p. 2). For Tait, the genesis for key elements in this approach were the University of London External Degree system, the National Extension College (the successor to the original University Correspondence College) and the thinking of Michael Young, its director. Tait identified R.H. Beevers, the original director of Student Support, and his successor, David Sewart, as being integral to the model developed at the OU UK. Sewart (1981) stressed a service perspective rather than the product orientation that was more prevalent in the literature. He emphasized the centrality of the learner to the process, the importance of helping the student mediate between the materials provided and their own understandings. Learners worked with resource materials, with their peers, and with their tutor in integrating their new knowledge with their own understandings and their lifestyles.

Tait (2003) outlined what he saw as the important aspects of this model. The characteristics of the learner support system for the OU UK included:

- Each student had a personal tutor, in a group with no more than 25 or so other students, in order to allow personal knowledge, support and understanding to grow up through the lifetime of a course.
- The tutor gave teaching feedback and the mark for work com-pleted during the course, thus having a pivotal role in supporting

student learning and progress (and which gave rise to the serious development of the teaching skill known now as correspondence teaching).

- All students were offered the opportunity but not the obligation to take part in face-to-face tutorials, and more recently computer-mediated tutorials, managed by their own tutor (online courses still remain only a tiny minority within the overall provision of the OU UK).
- A network of some 260 study centres were established throughout the UK in order to provide such tutorial opportunities, supported by 13 regional centres, thus ensuring that the student felt 'nearer' the university, whose headquarters are in central England.
- A limited amount of residential school experience on a conventional campus was essential, at a minimum one week.
- From 1971 to 1997 all undergraduate students—i.e., the great majority—had access to a personal tutor-counsellor who offered them support and advice throughout their career with the university whatever course they were on, providing for what was called 'continuity of counselling.'

The model was premised on the importance of the student–instructor dialogue and strongly emphasized the integral role of the tutor in conversation with the student and the need for students to be in a community of learners (Tait, 1996). In general tutors were to help students learn how to study, help them learn more about their own understandings, and help them learn how to consider critically what they read rather than just absorbing it. This orientation to learning can been seen in Mary Thorpe's (1979, p. 15) comment:

> I think we should begin from the assumption that course materials are not the course; rather the course is an annual process of interaction between students, the materials, the tutors and that, in this sense, tutors and students 'produce' courses as well as course teams.

The result was that courses included a number of tutor-marked assignments where tutors provided feedback through commentary which was expected to be helpful and encouraging as well as responding to what the student had written. Tutors were available to meet with learners and regular study center meetings were set up in local or regional centers. Each learner had an assigned tutor-counsellor who provided program and course advice throughout the duration of the program and helped in addressing distance education issues. Students who registered for the Foundations course had more allocated contact time with tutors in their first year. Mills (1978), in discussing ICCE papers on student support and advisory services in various countries, reported a study by Flinck (1975) where Swedish students were asked to contact their tutors by telephone and these data were compared with that gathered from another study where tutors were instructed to make regular calls to students at certain points during the course. Flinck found that while the students seldom called the tutors, when the tutor called the student both reported "considerable benefit and usage" (p. 75). Orton (1978) reported on a study completed at Queen's University in 1975. Over a three-year period, students were invited to make telephone contact with instructors in selected courses. About 31 percent of students phoned their instructors and about the same percentage of instructors phoned students. This issue of independence and interaction was highlighted by John Daniel and Clement Marquis (1979) in their paper "Interaction and independence: Getting the mixture right." Their main conclusion concerning the tutoring function was "that remote learning systems would do well to place greater emphasis on written interaction" (p. 39).

Tait (1996) juxtaposed his understanding of the OU UK model with that of Peters, commenting that while the industrialized nature of distance learning was its most common description, Peters by 1989 (p. 4) had begun to have reservations about this description, noting, "the dangers of a technological model of distance study, the over-emphasis on technical devices, the inevitable reduction of possible learning objectives, the fragmentation and compartmentalization of the learning process, the dominance of technical rationality at the cost of 'critical rationality.'" However, while Peters's reservations came about because he saw the world moving into a post-industrial era (1993), and hence his basic premise of reflecting the modern stayed intact, Tait's model was based on a philosophy in which learner support is the expectation that "learners interact not only with the learning materials but with each other and with a tutor" (1996, p. 59). He saw this as not only providing a means to personalized learning but representing "ways of meeting fundamental human needs for social interaction in the educational context" (pp. 59–60). Tait saw his views as reflected in the work of Holmberg and Moore, two other important theorists whose work influenced this era.

Borje Holmberg, a Swedish scholar, formerly head of Hermods, a correspondence education system reporting to the Chancellor of the Swedish Universities and now a commercial publishing house, and then for many years at the University of Hagen in Germany, was one of the first to recognize that correspondence materials lacked any personal relationship with the student. He proposed a conversational model, one where the relationship between the course writer and the student was a psychological contract—essentially, you do your best to learn and I will do my best to support you. He provided a set of guidelines for course authors which stressed the importance of using a conversational orientation such as using personal pronouns rather than the impersonal 'the student.' Within the constraints of the paper format, he described ways to engage the student in internal and written dialogue that provided support, encouragement and feedback on their work.

Michael Moore worked at the OU UK during these early years but most of his career has been at the University of Pennsylvania. His theory of transactional distance supposed shifting relationships among the structure of the course, the amount of interaction required and the autonomy of the student such that the tighter the structure the less the autonomy and the whole being mediated by the extent of interaction with a more conversational and dialogic interaction, such as through the feedback on written assignments, being preferred.

## Conclusion

The development of modern distance education owes its roots to the OU UK, but while this was not the only distance education institutional model developed, as Rumble (1986) and others have documented, its structure embodies many of the challenges faced by distance educators in the 40 years since it was established. First, it took up the challenge of providing opportunities for public higher education for large numbers. In doing so, it sought to use contemporary processes to design a system that would be of high quality and yet be able to serve the very large numbers of students expected. Hence, for the development of its course materials it introduced production systems into an educational organizational model based on craft processes. This in itself created several tensions by moving from a traditional hierarchical structure to a systems organization with multiple integrating parts, each of which was essential to the functioning of the overall system. One was the redefined role of academics from sole course creators responsible for course creation and provision to the course team format with multiple contributors where decisions were to be arrived at collegially. Another was the much greater control exerted by the need to have materials ready for students and the resulting timelines, clash of differing types of expertise and production criteria which were felt to impinge on academic autonomy.

Second, it sought to attract and retain as learners those already in the workplace and those who had had no prior aspirations for post-secondary education. The structural response was to design a learner support systems model that responded to the needs of such adult learners through a much more complex system than the original University Correspondence College model of the University of London. Over the twenty years between the inauguration of the OU UK and the beginnings of the Digital Age, the challenges to distance education provision continued. Two major debates arose around aspects of the course development and student support models. Discussions on the meanings of 'openness' raised many questions about the use of pre-set content and whether the materials were really open to ideas, such as raised in David Harris's (1988) text on the micropolitics of courses. It was part of a larger discussion in the literature about the importance of developing independent learners and providing them with choice. Identifying ways of encouraging deep versus superficial learning was integral to these debates.

Third were the complexities of economies of scale. Indeed, as the OU UK moved from very large numbers in its foundation courses to smaller enrollments in more advanced courses, it found itself forced to consider the fiscal realities of course designs that involved extensive multimedia resources. In addition, models which provided study groups and face-to-face meetings were more difficult to organize when there were fewer learners living farther apart. Daniel and Marquis (1979) addressed the question directly. For them, adult learners were able to accomplish their aims under a variety of approaches but "the costs of interactive activities tend to increase in direct proportion to the number of students" (p. 32). Hence, although it receives less press, the models in use have to reflect the fiscal realities of openness, in this case a very large student population and multiple courses and program offerings involving multimedia resources, learner interaction and study support. The particular combination chosen is one that has to remain elastic to changes in both technologies and finance. Although Daniel (1996) had proposed that economies of scale were essential to the fiscal viability of distance education institutions, the OU UK model was heavily tested as the numbers of learners far outpaced expectations. The amount of BBC-produced materials for radio and television was reduced partly because learners did not want to be tied to the 6 a.m. broadcast times eventually allocated to educational programming and not everyone could receive the programs or wanted to go to a study center. Access to tutors by telephone was added with much discussion about the loss of the visual component of the discussion.

While OU UK group study and summer schools declined in importance as learners sought to retain flexibility, the use of audio- and video-conferencing models took hold in North American distance learning programs. In the OU UK design, the course development and student support models are two aspects of an integrated system. The third component is the learner. Tutors were expected to work in partnership with learners. Courses should be designed to provide students with multiple sources of information and elements of choice: the learner can dig deeper and has opportunities to go beyond the essential material if the topic is of particular interest. If less interested, the learner can work through the topic quickly and focus on others of more interest. Learners can seek help or not; it is the learner's choice. Providing flexibility for the learner means more than open access to courses. It

> *Providing flexibility for the learner means more than open access to courses. It means ensuring that adult learners have the means to be successful whether they consult with friends, workmates or their tutors.*

means ensuring that adult learners have the means to be successful whether they consult with friends, workmates or their tutors. While technologies may change, retaining this flexibility in a distance education system remains a major challenge.

## TERMS AND DEFINITIONS

**Curriculum:** A program of courses offered by an education system or institution, usually around a discipline or disciplines, or a field of study. According to Joseph Schwab (1978), curriculum emerges in the confluence of four common places of education: the students, instructors, subject area and milieu.

**Digital Age:** An era characterized by the use of computers, hand-held communication devices, the Internet, and the movement of digital information and objects. This access to digital knowledge has changed social and economic structures that existed in support of the Industrial Age. This term is linked to the term Information Age, defined as a shift from traditional industry that drove the Industrial Revolution to a social and economic system based on the movement and manipulation of information.

**Higher education:** Education beyond the secondary level at the college or university level; distinct from post-secondary study, which includes any study or training beyond high school education, including apprenticeships and technical training.

**Independent study:** Usually used in contrast to group and paced courses, independent study opportunities allow learners flexibility and choice around content, pace and/or assessment strategies.

**Instructional design:** The creation of a systematic and sequenced set of learning principles, educational media and activities that engage learners in an experience such that desired learning outcomes will be realized.

**Open university:** The term 'open' in reference to university programs and courses describes a wide range of education realities. In general, it denotes a flexibility and accessibility not normally found in traditional offerings. This can refer specifically to admission requirements, flexible schedules, and accessible locations—or some combination of these and other conveniences. The OU UK seeks to be "open people, places, methods and ideas" (http://www3.open.ac.uk/about/).

**Tutor:** This label was given to instructors in distance education because of the one-on-one, private nature of the exchange between context expert and learner. The definition of tutor refers to one charged with instruction and guidance on a given topic or subject.

## QUESTIONS FOR REVIEW AND REFLECTION

1. What constituted the 'Canon' in early days of education, and who is believed to have mastered the entire work?
2. Prior to the 1970s, how was distance education characterized and on what was it based?
3. How did the curriculum development movement challenge behavioristic notions of learning requirements in higher education?
4. What process might leaders of open and distance institutions use to influence and inform governments, in order to realize necessary policy and monetary support?
5. What two problems did Tight (1985) identify in the course team approach? How might these problems, should they occur, be remedied?
6. What structures did open universities put in place to provide public higher education to large numbers of people? Has it worked? Who may still be left out of the public higher education system?

**Significant Contributor**

**Diana Laurillard** is Professor of Learning with Digital Technologies at the London Knowledge Lab, Institute of Education, leading externally funded research projects on developing a learning design support environment for teachers, and on developing software interventions for learners with low numeracy and dyscalculia. This work relates closely to her role as a founding member of the cross-institutional Centre for Educational Neuroscience (IOE, Birkbeck, UCL). Previous roles include: Head of the e-Learning Strategy Unit at the Department for Education and Skills, where she developed the first cross-sector e-learning strategy on Harnessing Technology; Pro-Vice-Chancellor for Learning Technologies and Teaching at the Open University; and Visiting Committee on IT at Harvard University. Current roles include: National Teaching Fellowship Scheme panel, boards of the Observatory for Borderless HE, the Centre for Applied Research in Educational Technologies at the University of Cambridge, and the Supervisory Council for FernUniversität in Hagen. Professor Laurillard has given many international keynote addresses, has published in many academic journals and books, and her book *Rethinking University Teaching: A Conversational Framework for the Effective Use of Learning Technologies* (RoutledgeFalmer, 2002) is one of the most widely cited in the field. All her work is focused primarily on improving the quality and reach of formal education, at all levels, through the most effective use of learning technologies. The Conversational Framework encapsulates our collective theoretical knowledge of what it takes to learn, in formal education. It can be deployed to challenge the extent to which both conventional and digital teaching methods meet learners' needs, and thereby leads to more effective use of these methods.

## References

Bates, T. (2008). Transforming distance education through new technologies. In T. Evans, M. Haughey, & D. Murphy (Eds.), *International Handbook of Distance Education*. London: Emerald.

Daniel, J. (1996). *Mega-universities & knowledge media*. London: Croom Helm.

Daniel, J.S. & Marquis, C. (1979). Interaction and independence: Getting the mixture right. *Teaching at a Distance*, 14, 29–44.

Flinck, R. (1975). Two-way communication in distance education. In E. Ljosa (Ed.), *The system of distance education*. Papers to the 10th International Conference of the Council on Correspondence Education, May.

Glatter, R. (1969). Aspects of correspondence education in four European countries. *Comparative Education*, 5(1), 83–98.

Harris, D. (1988). The micro-politics of openness. *Teaching at a Distance*, 3, 13–16.

Harry, K. (1983). The Open University, United Kingdom. In G. Rumble & K. Harry (Eds.), *The distance teaching universities*. London: Croom Helm/ St Martin's Press.

Hawkridge, D. (1980). Witches and wizards in open university course teams. *Teaching at a Distance*, 17, 75–76.

Mills, R. (1978). Student support and advisory services in distance and adult education. *Teaching at a Distance*, 11, 73–79.

Orton, L.J. (1978). Inproving two-way communication in correspondence teaching. *Teaching at a Distance*, 11, 80–91.

Perry, W. (1976). *Open University: A personal account by the first Vice-Chancellor*. Milton Keynes: The Open University Press.

Peters, O. (1989). The iceberg has not melted: Further reflections in the concept of industrialization and distance teaching. *Open Learning*, 4(3), 3–8.

Peters, O. (1993). Distance education in a postindustrial society. In D. Keegan (Ed.), *Theoretical principles of distance education*. London: Routledge.

Peters, O. (2008). Transformation through open universities. In T. Evans, M. Haughey, & D. Murphy (Eds.), *International Handbook of Distance Education*. London: Emerald.

Rumble, G. (1986). *The planning and management of distance education*. London: Croom Helm.

Rumble, G. & Harry, K. (1983). General characteristics of the distance teaching universities. In G. Rumble & K. Harry (Eds.), *The distance teaching universities*. London: Croom Helm/St Martin's Press.

Schwab, J. (1978). *The teaching of science: The teaching of science as enquiry*. Cambridge, MA: Harvard University Press.

Sewart, D. (1981). Distance teaching: A contradiction in terms? *Teaching at a Distance*, 19, 8–18.

Stringer, M. (1980). Lifting the course team curse. *Teaching at a Distance*, 18, 13–16.

Tait, A. (1996). Conversation and community: Student support in open and distance learning. In R. Mills & A. Tait (Eds.), *Supporting the learner in open and distance learning*. London: Pitman.

Tait, A. (2000). Planning student support for open and distance learning. *Open Learning*, 25(3), 287–299.

Tait, A. (2003). Reflections on student support in open and distance learning. *The International Review of Research in Open and Distance Learning*, 4(1), 1–9.

Thorpe, M. (1979). When is a course not a course? *Teaching at a Distance*, 16, 13–18.

Tight, M. (1985). Do we really need course teams? *Teaching at a Distance*, 26, 48–50.

# PART II
# A New Era

# 5

# DISTANCE EDUCATION IN A POST-FORDIST TIME

## Negotiating Difference

### DR. HEATHER KANUKA
Professor and Director
University of Alberta

### CHARMAINE BROOKS
PhD Candidate
University of Alberta

## Introduction

Can the essence of a university education be preserved in post-Fordist times given the inherent tensions between providing flexible access, quality learning experiences and cost-effective distance learning offerings? We engage this question by first outlining the construct of post-Fordism, followed by a summary of the post-Fordist debate in higher education. We move to describe and connect constructivist learning theory with the post-Fordist framework, including an overview of the industrial, production and process issues that revolve around distance education. This will then be followed with a brief section on constructivist learning theory and its potential role within a post-Fordist era. We conclude that in a post-Fordist framework, distance education can achieve any two of the following: flexible access, quality learning experience and cost effectiveness—but not all three at once. The on-campus university experience has been a prominent face of the Zeitgeist for centuries, with professors being the "visible embodiments of the realised humanity of our aspirations, intelligence, skill, scholarship" (Arrowsmith, Green-Lewis, & Soltan, 2008). The very idea of seeking to restore the interpersonal relationships between professors and students from the time of Socrates has been perceived by many as the spirit and essence of a university education. The core of this vision, the student–professor interrelationship, first began to show signs of erosion with the age of industrialism, alongside the need for a move to a cost-effective, transmissive mass education.

During the last two decades we have begun to hear more about a desire and need for an engaged and interpersonal relationship between students and professors. How to provide this in a manner that is both accessible and cost effective for the average student has been, and continues to be, a challenge. Pundits, futurists and technologists have shared their vision, imagination and Net-based tools for re-engaging students and professors, while continuing to provide an education to the masses, cost effectively. The imperative for students to be on-campus with their arsenal of books has been presented as an ante-diluvian vision of how students achieve a degree; course content can be retrieved online, delivered at home, or at work, or wherever. Indeed, we are told the classic large undergraduate class offerings of 200-plus students, where the interpersonal student–professor interrelationship is nothing more than a lecturer at the podium, can now be facilitated with student–professor interaction, cost effectively, through Net-based communication tools (e.g., Twigg, 2003).

Net-based educational opportunities emerged in the early 1990s, most often with a promise of ameliorating problems within the post-secondary sector, but also as an educational revolution (National Academy of Sciences, 2002). For example, according to Drucker (1997, 1999), the physical presence of universities will cease to exist within ten years: post-secondary education will either be delivered by technology or will become non-existent. There will be no campus, and there will be no need for students to meet face-to-face with their professors. Richard Katz, Vice-President of EDUCAUSE, boldly claims some colleges and universities might disappear. Some might acquire other institutions. One might even imagine a Darwinian process emerging with some institutions consuming their competitors in hostile takeovers in a quest for economies of scale. That is certainly conceivable given what we have witnessed in the last ten years with the growth of transnational corporations, and most recently in the finance sector.

Such forecasts of an educational (r)evolution, and the ensuing demise of traditional on-campus learning, were being discussed in the early 1990s. And yet, almost 20 years later, traditional, on-campus student enrollment in the post-secondary sector continues not only to survive but to thrive. And so the question has to be asked: Why? Or more specifically, what is the draw of the on-campus university? Responses to this question by advocates of on-campus post-secondary institutions argue that it is the *visible* embodiment of intelligence, skill, and scholarship that is the draw to the on-campus experience:

> The best teachers embody their learning in every aspect of their lives and they turn those lives outward for students to see—in writing, in conversation, and (best of all) in the dense daily life of the great household of a residential college. The importance of embodying knowledge in this manner has long been a central theme of the collegiate way.
>
> (O'Hara, 2008)

And so we have not witnessed a revolution as described by many futurists and pundits a decade ago; nor have we witnessed an amelioration of the problems in the post-secondary sector as a result of Net-based distance learning. What we have seen, however, is an enduring belief—for more than two decades now—that we can provide flexible and accessible quality learning experiences that are cost effective for a mass population through the use of Net-based communication tools. Part of the persistence in this belief stems from the impact of a post-Fordist mode of capital accumulation that is characterized by flexible modes of mass production according to the *just-in-time* principle aimed at being more responsive to changes in consumer demand.

In this chapter we discuss the complex relationships between providing flexible access, quality learning experiences and cost-effective distance learning offerings in relation to a post-Fordist framework. We begin with an introduction of the construct of post-Fordism, followed by a summary of the post-Fordist debate in higher education. This will then be followed with a section on constructivist learning theory and the role it plays in a post-Fordist framework, as well as an overview of the industrial, production and process issues that revolve around distance education. This will be followed with a brief section on constructivist learning theory and its potential role within a post-Fordist era. We conclude that in a post-Fordist framework, distance education can achieve any two of the following: flexible access, quality learning experience and cost effectiveness. How post-secondary institutions move forward in an increasingly competitive, globalized world will depend on their ability to respond to market-driven imperatives while not compromising the core values and mission of higher education.

## Background: Introducing Post-Fordism

From the latter part of the 20th century, the dominant system of economic production and consumption in most industrialized countries was, and continues to be, post-Fordism. As its name implies, post-Fordism is contrasted to Fordism—the production system in Henry Ford's automotive factories where workers performed individual tasks repetitively on a production line. While there are widely varying understandings and definitions of what exactly Fordism is, most would agree that its essence involves a production model that has low product innovation, low process variability and low labour responsibility (Badham & Mathews, 1989). In relation to education, "the ubiquitousness of Fordism has established itself as a grand narrative of modernity with bureaucracy and industrialisation supporting the national and international proclivities for a mass education" (Stevens, 1996, p. 255). Most historians, theorists, researchers and practitioners within the field of distance education concur that up to the 1980s, the dominant paradigm for distance education within the post-secondary sector was Fordism, as described by Campion and Renner (1992, p. 10):

*The need by firms for flexible knowledge workers, in turn, had an impact on education systems.*

> The Fordist strategy for distance education suggested a fully-centralised, single-mode, national distance education provider, gaining greater economies of scale by offering courses to a mass market, thereby justifying a greater investment in more expensive course materials. Rationalisation of this kind allows for increased administrative control and a more extreme division of labour as the production process is fragmented into an increasing number of component tasks.

As consumer demand began to change in the early 1970s—specifically a demand for products that appealed to the consumers' individual preferences—so too did distance education. In the corporate sector these changing consumer demands resulted in the formation of production firms that were compelled to create systems of labor and machines that could respond to the unique demands of the market. This is referred to as *flexible specialization*, and is core to the post-Fordist framework. Advances in technology made the production of diverse products possible, economically feasible and simple. But the flexibility and skill of the worker were also central to making flexible specialization possible. In particular, firms were required to have workers that had flexible skill sets, as well as time flexibility to provide just-in-time products. The need of firms for flexible knowledge workers, in turn, had an impact on education systems. Reflecting these changes in the market, distance education also became less standardized and more specialized and flexible (Campion & Renner, 1992, pp. 10–11):

> The post-Fordist strategy is characterised by high levels of all three variables: product innovation, process variability and labour responsibility. It is opposed to neo-Fordism and to Fordism, dispensing with a Taylorist division of labour and rigid managerial control and deliberately fostering a skilled and responsible workforce. A post-Fordist model of distance education would be decentralised and retain integration between the study modes. Academic staff would, however, retain autonomous control of their administered courses, and in so doing, would be able rapidly to adjust course curriculum and delivery to the changing needs of students.

The notion of using a post-Fordist framework to describe the corporate sector is not new, but using it widely as a framework for distance education is, relatively, new (emerging in the early 1990s). Upon initial reflection, it may seem counter-intuitive to use a framework originally based on car production for public education systems, especially given the different governance structures (Monahan, 2005). Acknowledging the many significant differences between public education systems and private companies, the notion of a flexible, mass production with empowering structures for the laborers is the strand of the post-Fordist framework that has been applied to both organizations. Within the field of distance education, Rumble published a series of papers that criticized the application of the Fordist framework in the mid-1990s (e.g., Rumble, 1995a, 1995b, 1995c). Campion (e.g., 1996a, 1996b) responded to these papers, and there was a special issue on post-Fordism in *Distance Learning* in 1995 (Volume 16, Number 2).

Earlier discussions by Giddens (1994) emphasized post-Fordism as changes in educational systems that are fundamentally connected to the reflexivity of the increasingly educated populous, and their need to have greater autonomy of action. Campion and Renner (1992) observed a move toward the dismissing of modern notions of progress and a return to such notions as flexibility, decentralization, democratic participation, and emancipation—rejecting notions of empiricism and instrumental rationality. In particular, the flexible production and the grassroots decision-making that underpin post-Fordism result in greater autonomy of action. The relationship between a reflexive and knowledgeable populous and a post-Fordist model, then, resulted from an increasingly educated public who needed to engage with the unremitting onslaught of information in order to prosper (Evans, 1995). In relation to open and distance education, in particular, the post-Fordist framework presents itself as modest, flexible organizations using Net-based communication tools to distribute learning opportunities (Campion, 1992). Not long thereafter, those concerned with distance education were viewing "Fordist principles of distance education production . . . as ideologically unpalatable and threatening to less technocratic and more humanist qualities of openness" (Stevens, 1996, p. 248) and becoming increasingly dysfunctional in the production of open and distance learning materials (Raggatt, 1993). Within a post-Fordist framework, the focus is on the individual as a consumer (Stevens, 1996)—serving the needs of individual lifestyles and status in a manner that supersedes that of production (Edwards, 1995). This kind of 'functional flexibility' is viewed as more "just and democratic, and therefore not as negative as Fordism" (Stevens, 1996, p. 256).

Also important to note is that this kind of customization of education discourse is occurring at the same time as the accountability discourse which creates some natural tensions in education generally, but especially in distance education:

Globalization of knowledge, knowers, and the concomitant alternative ways of knowing provided by ICT has provided an exponentially more complex, dense, and sometimes chaotic system of filters that determine validity, reliability, generalizability, verifiability, importance, meanings, and implications of what is learned and how it is learned and subsequently reconstructed by learners.

(Kompf, 2005, p. 226)

### Ruminating about Post-Fordism in Distance Education

Beginning in the early 1990s, attitudes about open and distance education were also beginning to change. Rather than viewing distance education as a second-rate, off-campus, correspondence experience sometimes described as 'instructional industrialism' (Evans & Nation, 1989), distance education was beginning to be viewed opportunistically as a flexible and affordable way to engage in a quality learning experience using collaborative communication tools. By the mid-1990s, the post-Fordist concept had become framed within distance education as a flexible, global enterprise due primarily to one Net-based technology: computer mediated communication—which was eventually embedded within course management systems (e.g., WebCT, BlackBoard, Lotus Notes, Desire2Learn, etc.). While course management systems (CMSs) originated within a Fordist framework—they were uniform, mass produced and delivered—they eventually transitioned to a neo-Fordist model with the emergence of the various options (Edwards, 1995). More recently, it has been argued that social software, or Web 2.0 tools, has moved us to a post-Fordist framework, offering flexible processes, dynamic innovation and authority of content by the learners (McGee & Green, 2008).

In spite of the advances in technologies, criticisms have been, and continue to be, leveled against the applicability of a post-Fordist framework achieved through Net-based communication technologies, especially with respect to how they uncritically romanticize skilled production and create opportunities to invade others' spaces and territories. Evans (1995, p. 266) advises us to recognize and use reflexivity cautiously: "future forms of open and distance education should not be seen as matters of 'access' or 'invasion' . . . but rather as being open to dialogue or interaction between the participants." Campion (1995) asserts further that when institutions of open and distance education measure their success by the size of their student populations, there is an inevitable move back to the Fordist model, with bureaucratic practices being the norm. Rumble (1995b, p. 26) also acknowledges that "The management of student progress is, however, very bureaucratic. To the extent that the Open University is Fordist." In response to the difficulty of applying a post-Fordist framework to open and distance education, whereby an aim is to provide flexible and quality learning opportunities to the masses, Campion (1995, p. 202) concludes that "the pressure for Fordist bureaucratic solutions is high, and yet such an orientation would appear to fly in the face of the dominant economic arguments for flexibility and entrepreneurialism."

After a critical analysis of the debate surrounding Fordism (including post- and neo-), Stevens (1996, p. 248) concludes that institutions of open and distance education need to move from the identification of production models to theoretical underpinnings, and the process—with a reorientation away from the former characteristic of distance education "as a mere form of provision." The learning theory with which many distance educators have aligned themselves in the post-Fordist period has been *constructivism*—as it too focuses on process. As such, the post-Fordist framework and constructivism were integral in advancing open and distance education. In particular, emerging views of cognition around the same time were suggesting that learning could be effectively enhanced between and among learners to make sense of information and ideas, with the instructor acting as a facilitator or *guide on the side*, rather than *sage on the stage* (Brown, Collins, & Duguid, 1989). Prior to Net-based communication tools, the type of interaction fundamental to constructivist learning was difficult to achieve in distance education courses.

## Introducing Constructivism

Characteristic of the industrial, Fordist distance education models was standardized courseware for a mass market, designed by subject matter and media experts, widely accessible (in terms of time, place and situation) and affordable to the ordinary consumer (Renner, 1995). As the cycle in the marketplace began to move to a "multi-skilled, adaptable and innovative worker encouraged to take on high levels of functional flexibility, responsibility and autonomy" (Renner, 1995, p. 287), so too did distance education. Around the same time, there were new computer technologies (e.g., desktop publishing) allowing for production of high-quality materials developed by instructors who could customize course content and structure to meet their students' diverse needs better, as well as affordable communication tools (e.g., Net-based group fora) presenting opportunities for interactive learning between and among students and instructors. Under this new open, post-Fordist model, systems of production were viewed as providing "an exemplary model of productivity, flexibility and democracy through an agenda of decentralisation and a return to craft-based academic skills" (Renner, 1995, p. 289). The theoretical framework for learning most closely aligned with these shifts is constructivism.

From a post-Fordist perspective, the accelerating global competition between post-secondary institutions in combination with increasing student enrollment and learner expectations forced higher education institutions to improve access by removing time, place and situational barriers, in ways that were cost effective. These kinds of flexible and open learning opportunities were consistent with cognitive constructivist learning theory (Kanuka & Anderson, 1999). Retrospectively, and in keeping with the changes in the market from Fordism to post-Fordism, providers of post-secondary education also viewed technology-mediated learning as an option to remove time, place and situational barriers—while retaining the ability to provide a quality learning experience, specifically, the quality of the interactions between peers and instructors. Prior to the emergence of Net-based technologies, there was initial reluctance in higher education communities to adopt and/or integrate technologies, such as teleconferencing. This resistance stemmed from limitations such as physical space restrictions and high cost, as well as pedagogical considerations. Specifically, the inability of pre-Internet communication technologies to provide the amount and quality of interpersonal interaction, with ease of access and cost effectiveness, that were considered essential to the facilitation of higher levels of thinking and learning (i.e., developed in small group discussions, Socratic dialogue, collaborative/cooperative learning, brainstorming, debriefing, case studies, problem-based learning, etc.) —and in keeping with the growing adoption by educators of constructivist learning theory.

The growing uptake of constructivist learning strategies by educators (Kanuka, 2001) over the last two decades has occurred alongside the move to a post-Fordist paradigm within which institutions of higher education are operating. Increasingly, institutions of higher education are faced with: (1) a greater demand for accountability by the public for what is being taught and by the accreditation bodies for what is being learned; (2) increasing diversity of the student population; (3) changing student attitudes and expectations; and (4) a growing expectation by the government and public that universities will assume greater responsibility for funding their own operations. Higher education must now shift from reporting what resources they have and what they are doing with them to how much their students have learned and what they can actually do. Higher education institutions are being asked to be accountable for their graduates and ensure they are not only knowledgeable within their field of study, but capable and competent practitioners. This requires a moving of thinking about learning as *information transmission* to include learning activities and experiences that require the students actually to do something with information, while demonstrating competence. This shift is consistent with the basic tenets of constructivism whereby knowledge is actively constructed, contextual, embedded in prior experiences and reflective (Kanuka, 2002).

With the widespread use of ubiquitous and cost-effective Net-based technologies, along with a promise of Net-based communication tools to support the basic tenets of constructivist learning theory, the prevailing attitude that open and distance education was a second-rate learning experience began to dissipate. The type of student–student and student–instructor interactions considered central to facilitating constructivist learning theory could be widely accessible and facilitated flexibly through new communication technologies, such as text-based, asynchronous computer mediated conferencing. In certain applications, these technologies were also proving to be cost effective, and accessible to learners who were experiencing time, place, or situational barriers (Bates, 1995), while supporting the development of higher-order thinking skills (Bullen, 1997; Newman, Webb, & Cochrane, 1995). For these reasons, many post-secondary institutions began integrating communication and instructional technologies into their teaching programs. Hence, the relationship between constructivism and post-Fordism is in many ways aligned with the role of educational technology as a facilitator of constructivist pedagogy. According to Renner (1995, p. 298), "constructivist developments within the field of educational technology are reminiscent of Post-Fordism."

Finally, constructivism is also consistent with post-Fordism in that it rejects the domination of efficient production over effective learning offerings. But herein lies a distinct difference between constructivism and post-Fordist frameworks: the emphasis on product versus process. Post-Fordism is a market framework for producing *products* that are flexible, meeting the unique needs of the *consumer*. Constructivism is a learning framework about facilitating the learning *process* that is flexible, meeting the needs of the *learner*. Viewing the learner as a consumer, while not entirely unfitting, is problematic within credential institutions. The problem is as follows: like businesses that *sell* products, it must be acknowledged that post-secondary institutions are in the business of *selling* information to students—*ergo*, students are *customers* who purchase an education (the product). The product being sold is a credential. The *consumer* and *product* relationship that occurs in a business model is difficult to apply to a credentialed education model because the *customers* (students) must provide evidence that they have earned the credential. Hence, the offering institution/business must provide a service (teaching and courses/curriculum) and a product (a credential) but the customers/consumers of the service must *earn* the product before receiving it. Indeed, the *customer* may well never receive the *product* they *purchased*. The product must be earned, thus the transaction is not a simple matter of commerce/trade. Complicating this further is the more recent focus on the *process* of the learning experience (e.g., constructivist learning theory) rather than on the *product* (e.g., efficient transmission of information). Accordingly, while applying a post-Fordist framework to distance education offerings is possible, many educators have concerns revolving around the application of a market and consumer model to credentialed educational offerings and question the appropriateness of doing so.

Thus, while a rudimentary synopsis on the application of a post-Fordist framework to a constructivist distance learning experience seems commonsensical, some distinct differences arise when putting these propositions into practice.

### Conclusions: When the Rubber Hits the Road

Technologically mediated open and distance learning has been viewed as responding to the post-Fordist consumer demand on flexibilization (Field, 1995), in a manner that is cost effective, with a quality learning experience—quality being understood as an engaged and interpersonal experience between students and professors (Arrowsmith, Green-Lewis, & Soltan, 2008). However, Field also reminds us that there is a misplaced faith in assuming that open and distance learning is a means to achieve these goals. Stevens (1996) warns that flexibility may also result in a form of social exclusion and marginalization, and notes that post-Fordism has not been successful as a paradigm for distance education. The problem stems from the application of a concept that emerged from an economic situation and applying it to an education situation.

Distance education, although it appears to mimic a producer–consumer economic relationship, must also attend to the *process* of learning in order to assure the quality of the *product*, education. Reversing the focus creates a consumerist culture which "may abrogate academic responsibility to market-place power" (Campion, 1993, p. 59). A product-focused, credential-driven program will result in the commodification of distance education and the move of knowledge to an informational commodity (Lyotard, 1979). In turn, universities may move from valuing emancipatory and humanist forms of knowledge to valuing the efficient production of learning opportunities. The danger in this, as Stevens (1996, p. 260) states, is that "Knowledge is achieved through values of teaching and learning—education—not through market-place values. Distance education as a form of education, first and last, cannot be successfully accommodated within the paradigms of industrial sociology." It must be noted further that Edwards (1995) has argued that while open learning represents post-Fordism, distance education is Fordist, and is crippled due to a lack of openness.

Atop the above rationale, to date there is no unequivocal evidence to show that the use of technology improves the quality of the learning experience (Abrami et al., 2006; Bernard et al., 2004; Rourke, 2005). At best, reviews of the research reveal that, depending on the context, technologically mediated distance learning can be better, or worse. When Net-based communication technologies emerged there was anticipation, premised on a post-Fordist framework, that technologically mediated learning (whether blended or fully online) could: (1) provide flexible access to the masses, (2) be cost effective, and (3) be provided in a manner that improves the quality of the learning experience. Two decades of research is revealing that technologically mediated distance learning can achieve any two of these goals, but not all three, at the same time. The reasons for this are varied. One put forward is that post-Fordist models that continue to rely on CMSs (i.e., flexible, mass offerings that are cost effective) focus on the delivery of instruction (they are transmissive) and do not, indeed cannot, address the learning design (McGee & Green, 2008). Specifically, even though it has been argued that there are Net-based discussions capable of providing opportunities for a student–professor interpersonal relationship, it is not sustainable (at least not cost-effectively) with large enrollment classes—a key characteristic of education systems designed for the masses.

A perfunctory overview of mega-universities (Daniel, 1996) that offer Net-based distance learning reveals they can offer flexible, accessible and cost-effective learning opportunities achieved through the division of tasks, re-skilling and cooperation—and what Drucker (1999) refers to as the knowledge worker model of management. Moreover, universities that serve the masses and aggressively use information and communication technologies can increase efficiency and productivity. Yet, as Rumble (1995b) observes, the industrial model which accommodates mass education denies the art and craft of teaching through de-skilling. While Internet-based models

> The problem with existing providers of distance education is that their operations are often governed by a Fordist framework. This problem revolves around the incompatibility of industrial paradigms for high-quality distance education programs.

provide some interactivity and make a move towards learner-centered strategies, the emphasis remains on providing instruction to the masses. Indeed, Rumble argues further that while distance education can be offered cost effectively, it is also the case that it is only cost effective when it is inflexible and vertically integrated. Cost effectiveness is realized through the homogeneity of a CMS and the consistent look and feel of course design. The problem with existing providers of distance education is that their operations are often governed by a Fordist framework. This problem revolves around the incompatibility of industrial paradigms for high-quality distance education programs. It has been argued that industrialized theory fails to provide a "suitable foundation for distance education" (Stevens, 1996, p. 264).

The fact of the matter is this: as humans we are complicated. How we learn perhaps best represents how complicated we are, with factors such as level, pace, timing, motivation, characteristics, culture, ethnicity, gender, age, income and so forth all influencing our learning. This makes pedagogy a complicated construct, requiring informed awareness of, and attention to, individual needs—including a close interpersonal relationship between students and professors. In turn, providing a close, interpersonal relationship requires an investment in human capital. Investing additional funding in human capital results in less cost-effective educational offerings. Herein lies the first barrier to achieving a quality learning experience that is cost effective and accessible for the masses.

In the area of open/flexible learning, this too presents a problem and the potential for undesirable outcomes. As one might imagine, many of the students who do not have self-regulation skills and/or minimum requirements may not have any prospect of succeeding. We know from research conducted on successful undergraduate university/college experiences that there are a number of conditions that foster student learning and development (e.g., Astin, 1991, 1993; Chickering, 1993; Feldman & Newcomb, 1969; Kuh, Schuh, Whitt & Associates, 1991; Pascarella & Terenzini, 1991; Tinto, 1993). Perhaps the best-known research in this area is by Pascarella and Terenzini, who found that the best predictors of whether a student will graduate are academic preparation and motivation (Pascarella & Terenzini, 1991). We also know that the surest way to increase the number of successful students ('successful' being most often defined as those who persist) who benefit in desired ways from their post-secondary experiences, are satisfied with the institution, and graduate, is to admit only well-prepared, academically talented students (Kuh, 2001).

The most obvious course of action based on this research is to admit only well-prepared students. Of course, the problem with this approach is that admitting only the most talented and well-prepared students is neither a solution nor an option within an open learning framework. And herein lies a second problem: admitting students who are not well prepared in distance education courses results in high non-completion rates (Moore & Kearsley, 1996; Tinto, 1993). Most administrators of post-secondary institutions know this, but students are a valuable source of revenue—and large enrollments ensure economies of scale, necessary for providing cost-effective learning offerings. On this issue O'Hara (2008) draws on the model of *predatory lending*, and applies it to education, referring to the practice of admitting unprepared students as *predatory admissions*.

Knowing what we do about successful students, post-Fordist shifts advocating open and distance learning, then, have at least the appearance of being driven more by a desire for providing a cost-effective education than they are by any noble prospect of providing a flexible, accessible, quality learning experience: "Efficiency is the name of the game, with reduced resources per student the supreme goal, both from the side of provision and from the supplements student must contribute" (Martin, 2008). On the instructor side, the lifelong learning phrase "oscillates between the dream of fulfilling self-transformation beyond the privileges of youth, and the nightmare of indiscriminate de-skilling and re-skilling according to the dictates of a 'flexible' labour market" (Martin, 2008). And herein lies yet another problem: in order to remain cost effective, open and distance education is forced to use economies of scale, with a division of labor via the unbundling of the teaching responsibilities, resulting in the de-skilling of the teaching process.

What we have today, in Western and industrialized countries, is a dynamic tension between welfarist modes of regulation and the post-Fordist mode of capital accumulation that is characterized by flexible modes of mass production according to the *just-in-time* principle aimed at being more sensitive toward changes in demand than was the Fordist *just-in-case* principle. The importance of flexibility and access is, today, greater than it used to be. The fields of open and distance education are certainly no exception to experiencing the pressures of providing accessible and flexible learning opportunities, while con-

> *[P]edagogy [is] a complicated construct, requiring informed awareness of, and attention to, individual needs—including a close interpersonal relationship between students and professors.*

tinuing to offer a quality commodity that is also cost effective for a mass market. How higher education institutions negotiate the *product* and *process* aspects of the learning experience in a culture of accountability, choice and increasing accreditation will become a direct reflection of their values and vision.

In this chapter we described the relationships between providing flexible access, quality learning experiences and cost-effective distance learning offerings, and the role of constructivist learning theory in this post-Fordist era. Internet-based technologies can serve to support constructivist pedagogical approaches and flexible, high-quality learning experiences for some, but always at a significant cost. Ultimately the industrial model, although it also strives to serve a mass market in a cost-effective manner, cannot reflect the complexity of the learning or the mandate of higher education. We conclude this chapter with a concession that in this post-Fordist era, open and constructivist distance education can achieve any two of the following: flexible access, a quality learning experience and cost effectiveness—but not all three at once.

## TERMS AND DEFINITIONS

**Constructivism:** A theory about knowledge and learning whereby learners actively construct their own knowledge by anchoring new information to pre-existing knowledge.

**Distance education:** As defined by Michael Moore, then director of the American Center for the Study of Distance Education, Penn State: "Distance education is planned learning that normally occurs in a different place from teaching and as a result requires special techniques of course design, special instructional techniques, special methods of communication by electronic and other technology, as well as special organizational and administrative arrangements" (Moore and Kearsley, 1996, p. 2).

**Fordism:** The system of mass production and consumption characteristic of highly developed economies during the 1940s–1960s.

**Open education:** Access to education through the removal of barriers, including time, place, and situational (e.g., grades and level of prior education completed).

**Pedagogy:** The art and science of teaching, whereby teaching is understood as interventions (e.g., instructional strategies and methods) by teachers to bring about learning.

**Post-Fordism:** Flexible production based on flexible systems and an appropriately flexible workforce.

## QUESTIONS FOR REVIEW AND REFLECTION

1. How is the relationship between constructivism and post-Fordism aligned with the role of educational technology as a facilitator of constructivist pedagogy?
2. How are the post-Fordist framework and constructivism integral to advancing open and distance education?
3. Why is it impossible for cost effectiveness, a quality education and access to occur at the same time?
4. Why must higher education shift from reporting what resources they have and what they are doing with them ('inputs') to how much their students have learned and what they can actually do ('outputs')?
5. What are the relationships between providing flexible access, quality learning experiences and cost-effective distance learning offerings, and the role of constructivist learning theory in this post-Fordist era?
6. What are the characteristics of a Fordist education?
7. What are the characteristics of a post-Fordist education?
8. What is the difference between education that focuses on 'process' and one that focuses on 'product'?

9. What are the basic tenets of constructivist learning theory?
10. Prior to the emergence of Net-based technologies, why was there reluctance in higher education communities to adopt and/or integrate technologies?

Significant Contributor

**Michael G. Moore** is known in academic circles for leadership in the scholarly study of distance education. He published the first statement of theory about distance education in English in 1972, and has achieved a number of other firsts in this field. While teaching the first course in this subject at University of Wisconsin in the mid-1970s he helped found the national annual conference there. Moving to Penn State in 1986, he founded the first American journal (*The American Journal of Distance Education*), established the first full sequence of taught graduate courses, a national research symposium, an online international network and a national leadership institute. Before joining Penn State, he had worked for nine years at the British Open University and has practical experience of teaching in all technologies and of most client groups, has supervised several dozen doctoral degrees and is, at present, experimenting with Web 2.0 technologies in teaching his Master's degree online. Moore has over 30 years' unbroken service as an editor of distance education journals, has served on the editorial boards of all the main journals, on program committees for the International Council for Distance Education and similar organizations, published over 100 articles and monographs, and given speeches and presentations in over 30 countries. Books include *The Handbook of Distance Education*, now in its second edition, and the second edition (with G. Kearsley) of *Distance Education: A Systems View*, with translations available in Portuguese, Chinese, Korean and Japanese. His interest in distance education began during a seven-year career in East African rural development in the 1960s. Since then he has participated in numerous projects in Latin America, Asia and Africa, including consultancy work for UNESCO and other United

Nations agencies, the International Monetary Fund and the World Bank. He has contributed to distance education policy at UNESCO and the Commonwealth of Learning and, during a period of full-time employment from 1996 to 1998, at the World Bank. He was a member of the 1994 ANC/SAIDE Commission on Distance Education in South Africa and continued as a consultant there through the mid-1990s. He introduced distance education in the late 1980s to leading universities in Mexico; in Brazil he was an adviser from 1996 to 2002 to the Federal Ministry of Education as well as the state of Minas Gerais; and more recently he has been a consultant to the government of Mozambique. Notable projects in economically more advanced countries include introduction of distance education in the principal universities in Finland and training-of-trainers in the armed forces of Norway, Sweden and Denmark. He served as North American Vice-President of the International Council for Distance Education from 1988 to 1992. Honors include induction into the United States Distance Learning Association's Hall of Fame in 2002. In the academic year 2008/9, he had sabbatical leave appointments as Visiting Research Fellow at the University of Cambridge, and as Visiting Professor at the United Kingdom's Open University.

## References

Abrami, P.C., Bernard, R., Wade, A., Schmid, R., Borokhovski, R.T., Surkes, M., Lowerison, G., Ahany, D., Nicolaidou, I., Newman, S., Wozney, L., & Peretiatkowicz, A. (2006). A review of e-learning in Canada: A rough sketch of the evidence, gaps and promising directions. *Canadian Journal of Learning and Technology*, 32(3), 1–70.

Arrowsmith, W., Green-Lewis, J., & Soltan, M. (2008). Teaching beauty. *Inside Higher Education*, 4(21). Retrieved January 12, 2009 from: http://insidehighered.com/views/2008/04/21/beauty.

Astin, A.W. (1975). *Preventing students from dropping out* (1st edn). San Francisco: Jossey-Bass.

Astin, A.W. (1991). *Assessment for excellence*. New York: Macmillan.

Astin, A.W. (1993). *What matters in college: Four critical years revisited*. San Francisco: Jossey-Bass.

Badham, R. & Mathews, J. (1989). The new productions debate. *Labour and Industry*, 2(2), 194–246.

Bates, A.W. (1995). *Technology, open learning and distance education*. London: Routledge.

Bernard, R.M., Abrami, P.C., Lou, Y., Borokhovski, E., Wade, A., Wozney, L., Wallet, P.A., Fiset, M., & Huang, B. (2004). How does distance education compare to classroom instruction? A meta-analysis of the empirical literature. *Review of Educational Research*, 74(3), 379–439.

Brown, J.S., Collins, A., & Duguid, P. (1989). Situated cognition and the culture of learning. *Educational Researcher*, January–February, 32–42.

Bullen, M. (1997). A case study of participation and critical thinking in a university-level course delivered by computer conferencing. Unpublished doctoral dissertation. University of British Columbia, Vancouver, Canada.

Campion, M. (1992). Revealing links: Post-Fordism, postmodernism and distance education. In T.D. Evans & P. Juler (Eds.), *Research in distance education* (2nd edn), Geelong: Deakin University Press.

Campion, M. (1993). Post-Fordism: Neither panacea nor placebo. *Open Learning*, 8(2), 59–60.

Campion, M. (1995). The supposed demise of bureaucracy: Implications for distance education and open learning—more on the post-Fordism debate. *Distance Education*, 16(2), 192–216.

Campion, M. (1996a). Open learning closing minds. In T.D. Evans & D. Nation (Eds.), *Open education: Policies and practices from open and distance education*. London: Routledge.

Campion, M. (1996b). Post-Fordism not a poison either! *Open Learning*, 11(1), 41–54.

Campion, M. & Renner, W. (1992). The supposed demise of Fordism— Implications for distance and higher education. *Distance Education*, 13(1), 7–28.

Chickering, A.W. (1993). *Education and identity* (2nd edn). San Fransisco: Jossey-Bass.

Daniel, J.S. (1996). *Mega-universities and knowledge media: Technology strategies for higher education.* London: Kogan Page.

Drucker, P. (1997). Interview. *Forbes*, March, n.p.

Drucker, P.F. (1999). *Management challenges for the 21st century.* New York: HarperCollins.

Edwards, R. (1995). Different discourses, discourses of difference: Globalisation, distance education and open learning. *Distance Education*, 16(2), 241–255.

Evans, T. (1995). Globalisation, post-Fordism and open and distance education. *Distance Education*, 16(2), 256–269.

Evans, T.D. & Nation, D.E. (1989). Dialogue in practice, research and theory in distance education. *Open Learning*, 4(2), 37–43.

Feldman, K.A. & Newcomb, T.M. (1969). *The impact of college on students.* San Francisco: Jossey-Bass.

Field, J. (1995). Globalisation, consumption and the learning business. *Distance Education*, 16(2), 270–283.

Giddens, A. (1994). *Beyond left and right: The future of radical politics.* Cambridge: Policy Press.

Green-Lewis, J. & Soltan, M. (2008). Teaching beauty. *Inside Higher Education*, 4(21). Retrieved January 12, 2009 from: http://insidehighered.com/views/2008/04/21/beauty.

Kanuka, H. (2001). Assessing higher levels of learning in Web-based post-secondary education. *Academic Exchange Quarterly*, 5(4), 106–111.

Kanuka, H. (2002). A principled approach to facilitating diverse strategies for Web-based distance education. *Journal of Distance Education*, 17(2), 71–87.

Kanuka, H. & Anderson, T. (1999). Using constructivism in technology mediated learning: Constructing order out of the chaos in the literature. *Radical Pedagogy*, 1(2). Retrieved January 12, 2009 from: http://radical pedagogy.icaap.org/content/issue1_2/02kanuka1_2.html.

Kompf, M. (2005). Information and communications technology (ICT) and the seduction of knowledge, teaching, and learning: What lies ahead for education. *Curriculum Inquiry*, 35(2), 213–233.

Kuh, G.D. (2001). Assessing what really matters to student learning: Inside the National Survey of Student Engagement. *Change*, 33(3), 10–17, 66.

Kuh, G.D., Schuh, J.H., Whitt, E.J., & Associates (1991). *Involving colleges: Successful approaches to fostering student learning and development outside the classroom*. San Francisco: Jossey-Bass.

Lyotard, J. (1979). *The postmodern condition: A report on knowledge*. Minneapolis: University of Minnesota Press.

Martin, S. (2008). Pedagogy of human capital. *Culture and politics after the Net*. Retrieved January 12, 2008 from: http://www.metamute.org/en/Pedagogy-of-human-Capital.

McGee, P. & Green, M. (2008). Lifelong learning and systems: A post-Fordist analysis. *Journal of Online Learning and Teaching*, 4(2). Retrieved January 12, 2008 from: http://jolt.merlot.org/vol4no2/mcgee0608/htm.

Monahan, T. (2005). The school system as a Post-Fordist organization: Fragmented centralization and the emergence of IT specialists. *Critical Sociology*, 31(4), 583–616.

Moore, M. & Kearsley, G. (1996). *Distance education: A systems view*. California: Wadsworth.

National Academy of Sciences (2002). *Preparing for the revolution: Information technology and the future of the research university*. Washington, DC: The National Academic Press.

Newman, D.R., Webb, B., & Cochrane, C. (1995). A content analysis method to measure critical thinking in face-to-face and computer supported group learning. *Interpersonal Computing and Technology*, 3(2), 56–77.

O'Hara, R.J. (2008). The global war on Taylorism. *Higher Education News from the Collegiate Way*. Retrieved January 12, 2009 from: http://collegiateway.org/news/2008-gwot.

Pascarella, E.T. & Terenzini, P.T. (1991). *How college affects students: Findings and insights from twenty years of research*. San Francisco: Jossey-Bass.

Raggatt, P. (1993). Post-Fordism and distance education—a flexible strategy for change. *Open Learning*, 8(1), 21–31.

Renner, W. (1995). Post-Fordist visions and technological solutions: Educational technology and the labour process. *Distance Education*, 16(2), 284–301.

Rourke, L. (2005). Learning through online discussion. Unpublished Ph.D. dissertation. University of Alberta, Edmonton, Canada.

Rumble, G. (1995a). Labour market theories and distance education I: Industrialisation and distance education. *Open Learning*, 10(1), 10–21.

Rumble, G. (1995b). Labour market theories and distance education II: How Fordist is distance education? *Open Learning*, 10(2), 12–28.

Rumble, G. (1995c). Labour market theories and distance education III: Post-Fordism the way forward? *Open Learning*, 10(3), 25–42.

Stevens, K. (1996). Have the shifting sands of Fordism resulted in ground lost or ground gained for distance education? *Distance Education*, 17(2), 247–266.

Tinto, V. (1993). *Leaving college: Rethinking the causes and cures of student attrition* (2nd edn). Chicago: University of Chicago Press.

Twigg, C.A. (2003). Improving learning and reducing costs: New models for online learning. *EDUCAUSE Review*, 38(5), 28–38.

# 6

# BEYOND BOUNDARIES

## The Evolution of Distance Education

### DR. DOUG SHALE
Director, OIA (retired)
University of Calgary

## Introduction

Historically, the hallmark of distance education has been a philosophical commitment to extending access to education to those who would not normally have such an opportunity. Given this commitment, the overarching challenge for distance education has been to bridge the spatial separation of the learner from a teacher. In the more remote past, the separation has largely been due to the geographic locations of participating individuals. Over time, this separation has also become due to other kinds of personal circumstances on the part of the learner—generally scheduling commitments that prevent a student from going to a location where the teacher is situated (for example, shift workers and those who have to work away from home intermittently).

So from this point of view, the development of distance education has really been about: (1) administrative and organizational ways and means of situating an educational institution to commit itself (at least to some extent) to doing distance education; and (2) ways and means of bridging the separation of teacher and student.

Extending access to educational opportunities has appeared in various forms in different countries—for example, in the Chataqua movement in the U.S., in the advent of night schools in some American institutions, and in extension departments of various kinds of educational institutions. However, let us agree to begin this overview of distance education with what has become widely—and perhaps notoriously—known as correspondence study.

Let us also agree to restrict the overview to university-level education because the context for education at this level is fundamentally different from grade school and technical/vocational education. Perhaps this difference accounts for why the literature of distance education is so predominantly about universities.

Whatever the educational level, correspondence study has relied on the transcription of teaching material to printed form from what would have been presented by a teacher in a face-to-face situation. In the earlier forms of distance study this printed teaching material was sent out by mail to students (hence 'correspondence education'). Students would read and study this material and reply to prescribed exercises designed into the correspondence material. And, of course, mail also provided the means for communication between students and teacher (but not for exchanges among students).

What has happened to distance education over time? How has it changed? And how does it fit in the contemporary world where technology is causing a fundamental change in how universities teach and students learn?

### An Organizational View of Distance Education

One could argue that the correspondence form of distance education is still commonplace, albeit gussied up either with respect to the organizational forms that support it (for example, independent distance education providers such as the UK Open University and the many variants of this model) or with respect to the methods used to 'deliver' the learning material and to support the students as they work through it.

From an organizational point of view, the introduction of the external studies model used most notably in Australia and New Zealand (but in other countries as well) was a major advance in establishing and maintaining a university-based distance education function. External studies was a quasi-independent entity operating under the auspices of a host university as an integrated extension of the university's academic remit. The supreme academic council of the university responsible for vetting and approving a university's academic programming and practices had (and has) absolute power over which courses and programs were offered out of the external studies unit—and how they were offered.

Historically such academic bodies have had considerable reservations about the academic quality of courses and programs offered by correspondence. This almost invariably leads to imposing conditions on correspondence study such as regulations about how a degree earned through external studies should be indicated on students' transcripts (implying a sort of second-rate credential), or regulations about not allowing regular on-campus students to take correspondence courses for credit toward their degrees. And often conditions were prescribed around how such offerings ought to be made (for example, the requirement that students appear on campus for a summer school experience was commonplace for external studies offerings).

> *[T]he reward structures in universities do not much favor teaching—and certainly did not favor distance teaching.*

In some universities the reservations about distance/correspondence study were so ingrained that distance study was non-existent or too marginal to matter. Partly because of these reservations, it was very difficult to interest the teaching faculty in offering and supporting distance study. In addition the reward structures for faculty clearly mitigated against service and teaching (a situation that seems to prevail even today). Paradoxically, in that context the organizational solution to committing to and supporting distance study institutionally was to create a free-standing unit (generally called 'external studies') with a mandate to 'facilitate' the creation and continuance of distance study programs.

Academic 'ownership' of all courses and programs—including those delivered at a distance—resided with the academic departments, as did academic authority. Faculty members in the academic departments were responsible for producing the correspondence courses, for supporting the courses by tutoring through the mail, and for setting and marking exams. However, as noted above, the reward structures in universities do not much favor teaching—and certainly did not favor distance teaching. As a result there was generally considerable reluctance on the part of academic staff, and hence academic departments, to participate in distance study.

In many instances, the solution to this dilemma was to include a requirement in an individual's contract that would have them commit a designated amount of time to producing and delivering correspondence courses (in addition to their on-campus teaching and research responsibilities). This seems to have met with varying levels of success but there were some universities that did quite well for a time by this organizational model (for example, the University of New England and Murdoch University in Australia).

A key factor in running a successful distance education operation within a university has been the budget allocation process. Money allocated to departmental budgets tended to get used for what the department would regard as priorities—and distance education typically would not be one of those. On the other hand, money allocated to—and dispersed by—an external studies unit was more or less guaranteed to be expended for the intended purpose. However, university budget allocation processes are strongly determined by the academic units because they get a big say in how money is distributed institutionally. So while money in the external studies budget can be protected and allocated solely to external studies, the amount of money in that budget is a reflection of what the academic body considers to be its priorities.

Some universities still operate on variants of the external studies model and apparently are reasonably satisfied and successful with that. However, even some of the most venerable of the external studies operations have been subjected to drastic overhaul because of the inherent irreconcilable contradictions in offering education in the two modes. In a number of instances, the overhaul has been focused on 'repatriating' the distance teaching functions to their respective academic homes. The jury would still seem to be out on how successful those attempts as a whole have been. Under the correspondence model of distance education it is difficult to imagine that

> *A key factor in running a successful distance operation within a university has been the budget allocation process.*

> *[E]ven some of the most venerable of the external studies operations have been subjected to drastic overhaul because of the inherent irreconcilable contradictions in offering education in the two modes.*

the problem of coexistence has been satisfactorily resolved. However, with the advent of computer-based telecommunications technologies the situation is changing drastically (this is a theme we will pick up later in the chapter).

### The Dedicated Distance Teaching Universities

In the late 1960s and particularly through the 1970s, the ubiquity of radio and television strongly influenced the next major organizational development in distance education—influenced undoubtedly by the traditional academies' inability to come to terms with a consistent combined approach to offering on-campus and distance education. This development was the establishment of dedicated distance education universities—the Open University in the United Kingdom being the classic example.

Originally touted as a 'university of the air' the OU UK rapidly became renowned for its innovative approach to producing richly (and expensive) multi-mediated course packages by means of a course team comprising: a subject matter expert (usually a professor); an instructional designer; a media specialist/graphic designer; and an editor—plus or minus some others. The intention at the outset was that each course package should include supporting television programming as part of the educational experience—thus giving form to the political aspirations that the OU should be a 'university of the air.'

The course team concept (which was adopted by some other distance education providers) had a volatile start and much was written about the ills of course teams and how to remedy these ills. Nonetheless, versions of the course team are found today, particularly where sophisticated media are required to support a course package.

These large-scale, materials-oriented 'open universities' also were known for the methods they used to produce, distribute and support course packages. And, in fact, the industrial-like approach they developed has sometimes been claimed to be one of the criteria that define distance education.

Because of its innovative nature, the OU UK gave some care to implementing safeguards and procedures demonstrably to assuage doubts within the UK academic community regarding the quality of its courses and degrees. One way in which it did this was to implement a compulsory summer school—in similar fashion to the external studies schools. Another method was to engage in systematic research activities and to publish information meant to address issues of quality.

The OU UK also invested in an extensive student support system. The most prominent feature of this support system was the network of regional centers the Open University established throughout the UK.

No doubt stimulated by the success of the OU UK, so-called open universities sprang up all around the world. Some were fairly modest in scale while others, the mega-universities for instance, were staggering in their size (as indicated by the numbers of students enrolled).

A major force driving the establishment of the open universities was an ideological bent toward higher education at a time when people should have an opportunity to participate in it and thus improve their lots in life. Many of the open universities (including the OU UK) touted themselves as institutions offering people a second chance to earn a degree. Since distance study primarily attracted adults as students, serving the needs of adults distance education came to characterize itself by the constituency it served.

This philosophy was in accord with the notion of extending access to higher education through distance education methods. As a result, many of these institutions—now free from the fetters imposed on external studies units struggling for life in the traditional academy— formulated very liberal 'open admission' policies. These extended, inter alia, from very relaxed admission standards to recognition of prior university study credit to a liberalization of the amount of time allowed for completion of courses and programs.

This gave rise to the recasting of 'distance education' to 'open and distance learning' (or ODL, as it is often called). Interestingly enough, 'open-ness' and 'distance education' are not necessarily co-dependent conditions and it is arguable as to whether they represent a unified, unique entity (for example, distance study through external studies units had very restrictive admission requirements and was open only in respect to allowing students to study from their homes).

There have been many distance teaching universities established since the advent of the OU UK. Some have become distinctive because of their size (for example, the Chinese Radio and Television University and the mega-universities). More recently others have distinguished themselves by the nature of their specialized mandates.

### Telecommunications and Distance Education

Another major force that strongly characterized the development of open universities was the technology used to deliver and support teaching and learning. The correspondence approach had inherent serious short-

> *[R]adio and television were often touted as cheap transmission vehicles for educational purposes.*

comings particularly in countries with limited or underdeveloped communications and postal infrastructure. Slow, unreliable, intermittent service was a hurdle not easily overcome. This is undoubtedly partly why there was such wide (and public) interest in using radio and television for distance study. Also radio and television were often touted as cheap transmission vehicles for educational purposes. Whether they were educationally efficacious was an issue not often inquired into—it was largely simply assumed or asserted.

The use of radio and/or television in conventional universities required the involvement of professional staff generally situated in a department that could provide technical assistance and advice on how to use such technology. This is why at various points along the way in the 1970s and 1980s we see distance education at conventional universities being offered in conjunction with university media departments. In some cases, state and provincial authorities were charged with distributing educational programming in collaboration with educational institutions (in Canada there was a raft of these— provincially based—set up in response to a federal requirement that television cable companies would receive operating licenses only if they guaranteed that a channel would be reserved for educational purposes).

However, at this time there were many complications (and costs) in using radio and television as a primary vehicle of instruction and relatively few universities (whether distance or campus based) tried to go down this route. Most continued to rely on a print-based learning package. If radio or television was used, it was primarily supplementary to the course package.

When satellites came on the scene in the 1970s various countries and universities explored the possibilities of audio-teleconferencing using satellite telecommunication. Perhaps the best-known efforts were experimental programs offered at the University of the South Pacific (USP) and the University of the West Indies (UWIDITE). The wide geographic coverage possible with satellite-enabled voice transmissions was a particular godsend to these two university systems because of the many widely dispersed countries included in their ambit. Time differences among the countries (and a Dateline difference in the case of USP) compounded the challenge.

The experimental nature of these ventures constrained the success they enjoyed. In particular the cost of leasing satellite use was initially underwritten by the respective satellite project. Expanding and/or continuing the use of satellite technology beyond the trial period required a significant commitment of resources from the universities. Also, at the time when communications satellites were becoming prominent, the technology for audio-conferencing was still quite limited (with only asynchronous transmission capability) and cumbersome, requiring a specialized technical support group to operate the technology. As a consequence audio-teleconferencing—whatever the supporting transmission technology—did not displace correspondence study and was not particularly embraced by conventional universities looking to establish a distance study facility.

The situation changed with the introduction of videoconferencing (and at the same time wire-line and cable transmission capabilities permitted a considerably extended and more affordable reach). The technology of videoconferencing (perhaps because of the inherent 'sexiness' of the medium) was picked up and embraced on many fronts—universities included. Videoconferencing proved to be most useful for occasional business meetings and presentations, but less useful for courses or programs that had to run at regular times for extended periods (largely because of costs, scheduling constraints and limited availability of willing instructors). Nonetheless, videoconferencing did seem to have a discernible effect on the advancement of distance education (if only in respect of the amount of attention it attracted).

Prior to the advent of two-way (full duplex) teleconferencing and interactive videoconferencing, the technology used to deliver education

*Prior to the advent of two-way (full duplex) teleconferencing and interactive videoconferencing, the technology used to deliver education at a distance did not fundamentally change the nature of the 'distant' educational experience.*

at a distance did not fundamentally change the nature of the 'distant' educational experience. Instruction was essentially materials based and communication was asynchronous and delayed (although it should be noted that many institutions tried to address this issue by providing access to course tutors—for example, Athabasca University in Canada).

The opportunities for enhanced interaction and spontaneity of discussion—in addition to providing a more 'natural' teaching/learning experience— proved to be a means to address the issue of the academic quality of distance education. First of all the nature of the educational event became more like the norm in higher education—free-flowing exploration of information and ideas. But perhaps more importantly, the technology allowed for easier participation on the part of the regular on-campus teaching faculty—teaching through interactive video-conferencing came more closely to simulate the familiar face-to-face classroom experience.

The impact of this progression in distance education from one-way, delayed and constrained communication to spontaneous, real-time voice- and image-based interaction is reflected in Garrison's (1985) conceptualization of three generations of technology use in distance education.

The evolution of real-time, interactive media and its incorporation in teaching and learning represents a progression in education at a distance—at least from the point of view of more easily reaching target audiences economically. The instructional efficacy of the technology, however, remains an open question—see, for example, Clark (1983), who argued that from a learning effectiveness point of view, it does not matter which technology is used. Moreover, it can be said that the use of multimedia in classical distance education has suffered from the absence of a rubric that would guide the effective use of media. There have been no formal standards or conceptual frameworks to inform the appropriate selection and effective use of technology to support learning. As a result, for example, television has been a dominant presentation vehicle and most of the programming is best described as 'educational TV.' As such, its instructional impact has been passive rather than integral to the learning process.

Without question, though, the emergence of Web-based technology is having a revolutionary impact on the creation of multi-mediated instruction and its distribution—as well as being a time-responsive, inexpensive means of communication among teachers and students. Web-based technology is ubiquitous, relatively easy to use and extremely versatile—so much so that one could say it is in common use for teaching purposes on university campuses. And, of course, the dedicated distance education providers are using the technology as well (interestingly, generally with a continuing commitment to packaged materials).

### Future Issues—the Convergence of Distance and Traditional Education

Even the relatively advanced technology of interactive videoconferencing was a challenge to conventional universities to implement for distance delivery of their courses. There needed to be a specialized organizational unit supporting the linkage between teacher and students. This was costly and somewhat cumbersome organizationally because professors had to be trained and supported in the technology—and they had to be convinced that the effort and encumbrance was worth their while given other demands on their time and energy.

However, the emergence of the Web has changed all that. Individuals now have sufficient capabilities through the Web essentially to function independently. This facility has had substantial repercussions—not just in facilitating distance education, per se, but in generating and distributing regular on-campus courses.

It takes no great insight to foresee an increasing use of the Web and for more and more distributed instruction and learning to occur. As this happens clearly the traditional universities will come closer to engaging in the kind of mandate assumed by distance education providers—namely, making education more readily available outside the constraining conditions of the on-campus lecture format. What are the possible implications of this for distance education?

Dedicated distance universities, ideologically, have been committed to extending educational opportunity to as many people as they can reach. The sheer volume of 'business' they have to contend with requires that they continue to adhere to a philosophy of 'massifying' education. 'Economies of scale' still factor prominently in the world of distance education (hence the mega-universities). One implication of this is that faculty-to-student ratios need to be very large in distance education, exacerbating what has historically been regarded as the Achilles heel of distance study—weak and insufficient interaction with students.

Another implication that arises from regarding higher education as an industrialized activity is the sense (usually only implied) that education is a commodity that can be packaged up by an educational institution (not a professor—an institution) and transmitted to students who then 'consume' the product on the way to becoming educated. We can see the effects of this point of view in the unsuccessful past efforts to effect exchanges of courses among institutions. For example, the Commonwealth of Learning had, as one of its founding objectives, facilitating the free exchange of distance education courses among countries of the Commonwealth. The concept apparently never worked much beyond a simple collection and cataloging of materials. (It should be noted that this is different from the production of general education materials that have been generated and distributed by the COL.)

The notion that a course package (however constituted) is sufficient to induce learning has been the source of much misconception in distance educators (the failure of the course exchange idea being a good example). This notion is also at the heart of the 'parity of esteem' issue raised so notably by Jevons (1984). The issue is a nagging one and continues to dog distance education in a variety of ways. In many circles distance education is still marginalized. Despite grandiose claims by a variety of prognosticators that the traditional universities would be put out of business by technologically distributed education (going all the way back to Edison, who claimed that movie technology would obviate the need for any and all teachers), there is absolutely no indication that this is the case. (Niche filling such as provided by the University of Phoenix hardly qualifies for consideration as competition (in the context delineated in this chapter).)

In fact, there is evidence that there are still contrary pressures on distance education providers. One of the more notable and apparent failures was the demise of the Technical University of British Columbia in Canada. We have already noted the fates of a number of previously quite successful distance education operations (namely several external studies offices in Australia). The records of the then Open Learning Institute of British Columbia (also notable because it was founded on the premise that it would offer courses acquired elsewhere, most notably the OU UK—but could not do so) and Athabasca University in Alberta indicate the shaky ground both occupy. Athabasca University was reportedly at risk of closure in the mid-1980s when faced with a 30 percent budget cut imposed by the provincial government (later moderated), while the rest of the post-secondary system was charged with only a 21 percent reduction. The magnitude of this threatened budget cut called into question the continuing existence of Athabasca University. It was reputedly a punitive action on the part of the government of the day, reflecting the low esteem in which the university was held at that time.

Conclusion

Different claims have been made by different people who would have distance education declared a unique form of education—and therefore beyond the critical bounds and standards at the heart of the 'parity of esteem' issue. For example, in the earlier days of distance education, the isolated circumstances in which learners had to learn was transmogrified into the virtue of 'independent learning' (Holmberg, 1985) —somehow conflating personal independence of thought and action with physical isolation in which it was not possible to confer or collaborate with like-minded persons. This view of student isolation is unfortunate because it is antithetical to the philosophical view that learning is a social dynamic requiring people to interact. Failure to recognize this issue has blinded distance education to considerations that could address the issue.

In the late 1970s and the early 1980s there was an assertion that distance education was a discipline (for example Keegan, 1986)—by virtue of the amount of interest in distance education, the amount being written about it and the number of so-called scholarly publications being produced. In retrospect (and even at the time for many of us working in the field) such claims were a real stretch and a rather lame attempt to make a virtue out of the limitations inherent in distance education at that time. It should be clear now that such claims are simply not on and can only perpetuate a misconception of what distance education is and can continue to be.

Notwithstanding the threats and circumstances mentioned above, there does not seem to be any particular reason to conclude that conventional universities will, in their turn, put dedicated distance education providers out of business. In fact, enrollments in distance courses and programs are too substantial to be glib about. In many countries the economics of providing so much educational opportunity is sufficient impetus to keep the distance education enterprise alive and thriving. The dynamic seems likely to differ in, say, developed countries, where there is already a considerable higher education infrastructure—as compared to the environments in which one finds the mega-universities. But even there, it seems likely there will continue to be considerable demand for the particular opportunities available from distance education institutions.

If both distance education and traditional education are converging by dint of each using the same delivery technology, can we expect the educational transaction and outcomes to be the same?

Flawed though it often is, the traditional educational transaction is predicated on the philosophy that knowledge is induced through shared experience—not transmitted, as is the case for most distance learning experiences. This shared experience and the associated dialectical exchange with students and professors and among students are integral parts of good teaching and effective learning in the on-campus experience. Consequently there is a predisposition to requiring the same ethos be present and active in the distance delivered versions of courses delivered by a campus-based university.

How can this occur? It was mentioned earlier that there has been no apparent formalized rubric to guide the design of distance education courses and the use of technology in producing and supporting these courses. Is the conventional academy any better off in this regard? If not, then the traditional university would likely proceed as the distance education provider has—with the same resulting emphasis on 'telling' students what to think rather than helping them know how to think. And, therefore, there would be no qualitative difference between distance and campus-based courses.

However, given the predisposition of traditional universities to require some semblance of interaction among professors with students and among students, the climate is at least favorable for working on a framework for effectively using technology to 'induce' knowledge in students. Moreover, what is good for on-campus students in this regard would similarly be good for potential distance students—and vice-versa. We are already seeing some conventional universities attempting to develop a framework for effective teaching supported through effective use of technology—namely, blended learning.

The essential feature of blended learning is the creation and sustainment of a community of inquiry outside the confines of a classroom (see Chapter 2, this volume; also Garrison and Vaughan, 2008). In this context effective teaching and use of technology is a consequence of how well we have managed to create and sustain communities of inquiry.

Distance education universities are inherently constrained in how they can approach a blended learning approach. How do you create and sustain communities of learning when students are necessarily distant from each other and from their university? Also, how does one reconcile the need to serve large groups of students with the need to cultivate the feeling of immediacy and intimacy that is integral to a community of inquiry? It is not easily done but efforts can and should be made. In any event, successfully creating and sustaining communities of inquiry may be the qualitative difference in distributed learning emanating from distance education universities and distributed learning coming from on-campus universities.

## TERMS AND DEFINITIONS

**Dedicated distance education university:** A university specifically established to offer courses and programs to students who are not able to pursue an education at a conventional on-campus university. The specific mandate of these universities precludes them from having students 'resident' at the university.

**Distributed learning:** A synonym for distance delivered education.

**Duplex and simplex teleconferencing:** Early forms of teleconferencing that allowed only one person at a time to speak. A protocol had to be used to 'hand over the microphone' to the next person wishing to say something (usually people would say, "over"). Full duplex allowed for people to converse in the more natural way of alternating turns by attending to verbal cues. One person speaking did not cut out another person's speech.

**External studies:** An organizational unit established within some universities in Australia and New Zealand charged with responsibility for establishing and maintaining a distance education operation.

**Open and distance learning:** A term adopted by institutions for a range of features meant to extend access to educational opportunity to people who would otherwise be excluded. The term was intended to indicate that 'openness' is dependent on much more than just delivering courses at a distance.

## QUESTIONS FOR REVIEW AND REFLECTION

1. What would you regard as the major shortcomings of the correspondence form of distance education (if none, please give an argument in support of your position)?

2. List the various approaches taken by universities delivering distance education to bridge the geographic separation of teacher and students. State what you would regard as the major advantage and disadvantage of each approach.

3. What advantages would the dedicated, independent distance universities have over campus-based universities delivering distance education in extending educational opportunities to otherwise disadvantaged students?

4. What was the point of requiring distance education students to attend summer school sessions at the OU UK?

5. What is the 'parity of esteem' issue all about and why is it critical that practitioners in distance education address the matter?

6. Given the challenge of getting the teaching faculty in a campus-based university interested in doing distance education, why not

just establish a separate unit with its own academic staff who would be charged with the task of creating and supporting distance delivered courses? (The University of Queensland tried this approach in the early 1980s. What do you think were the results?)

7. What advantages do you see to campus-based universities becoming more involved in distance education through a commitment to teaching through blended learning, problem-based learning and the like?

8. Do you think that distance education institutions will lead to obsolescence of campus-based institutions (provide an argument for your point of view)?

9. Do you think that distance education providers could be put out of business by campus-based universities' increasing interest in teaching students with technologies such as the Web (provide an argument to support your point of view)?

10. If you could draw on the features of distance education and campus-based universities, what would you see as an ideal educational experience?

### Significant Contributor

**Sir John Daniel** became President of the Commonwealth of Learning in 2004. This followed appointments at the Télé-université (Directeur des Etudes, 1973–1977), Athabasca University (Vice-President for Learning Services, 1978–1980), Concordia University (Vice-Rector, Academic, 1980–1984), Laurentian University (President, 1984–1990), the UK Open University (Vice-Chancellor, 1990–2001) and UNESCO (Assistant Director-General for Education, 2001–04). His non-executive appointments have included the presidencies of the International Council for Open and Distance Education, the Canadian Association for Distance Education and the Canadian Society for the Study of Higher Education. He also served as Vice-President of the International Baccalaureate Organization. The best known of Sir John's 250 publications is his book *Mega-Universities and*

*Knowledge Media: Technology Strategies for Higher Education* (Kogan Page, 1996). He was knighted by Queen Elizabeth for services to higher education in 1994 and holds 30 honorary doctorates, fellowships and professorships from universities and professional bodies in 16 countries.

## References

Clark, R.E. (1983). Reconsidering research on learning from media. *Review of Educational Research*, 53, 445–459.

Garrison, D.R. (1985). Three generations of technological innovation in distance education. *Distance Education*, 6(2), 235–241.

Garrison, D.R. & Vaughan, N.D. (2008). *Blended learning in higher education*. San Francisco: Jossey-Bass.

Holmberg, B. (1985) *Status and trends of distance education*. Sweden: Lector.

Jevons, F. (1984). Distance education in a mixed institution: Working towards parity. *Distance Education*, 5(1), 24—37.

Keegan, D. (1986). *Foundations of distance education*. London: Croom Helm.

Renwick, W., King, S., & Shale, D. (1991). *Distance education at the University of the South Pacific*. Vancouver: The Commonwealth of Learning.

Renwick, W., Shale, D., & Rao, C. (1992). Distance *education at the University of the West Indies*. Vancouver: The Commonwealth of Learning.

Shale, D. (2002) The hybridization of higher education in Canada. *The International Review of Research in Open and Distance Learning*, 4(2). Retrieved June 2009 from: http://irrodl.org/index.html.

# 7

# TEACHING AND LEARNING IN POST-INDUSTRIAL DISTANCE EDUCATION

## DR. KAREN SWAN
Stukel Distinguished Professor of Education Leadership
University of Illinois Springfield

> In a world in which knowledge production is collective and communication occurs across an array of different media, the capacity to network emerges as a core social skill and cultural competency. A resourceful student is no longer one who personally possesses a wide palette of resources and information from which to choose, but rather, one who is able to successfully navigate an already abundant and continually changing world of information.
>
> (Henry Jenkins, 2008)

## Introduction

Post-industrial distance education, as previously noted, is quite different from its Industrial Era predecessor. This chapter explores those differences. Indeed, especially as it is practiced at the post-secondary level, post-industrial distance education is different enough that it is most commonly referred to as 'online learning' to distinguish it from Industrial Era 'distance education.' In the discussions which follow, I will accordingly use the term 'online learning' to refer to post-Fordist distance education and 'distance education' to refer to its Industrial Age predecessor.

Henry Jenkins (2006) writes that media are characterized not only by the technologies they employ but by the cultural practices that surround their use. Similarly, what distinguishes online learning from the distance education of the previous era is not just the digital technologies from which it takes its name, but, more importantly, the pedagogical approaches they enable. Where distance education was materials and teacher-centered, online learning is student-centered; where distance education focused on independent study, online learning focuses on collaboration; where distance education was grounded in behaviorist and cognitive psychology, online learning is grounded in social constructivist learning theory. In this chapter I will explore why, and more importantly how, online learning is embracing both emerging digital technologies and social constructivist epistemologies. I will argue that a particular confluence of emerging technologies, cultural practices, and serendipity has resulted in online teaching and learning that is characterized by social constructivist and inquiry-oriented approaches.

I will first discuss the emerging technologies that not only support online learning, but have the potential to enable significant changes in teaching and learning. Emerging technologies themselves are at the center of important cultural transformations around our use of media (Jenkins, 2006; Keen, 2007; Postman, 1994; Stephens, 1998; Surowiecki, 2005). Those transformations obviously contribute to the cultural surround affecting online pedagogies. Another important cultural influence is the relatively recent rediscovery and enthusiastic embrace of social constructivism by the education community. This trend and its implications for online learning are addressed in the second section of this chapter. Equally important from a pedagogical point of view is the way constructivism resonates with age-old academic ideals, and this is where serendipity and confluence come in. Because online learning evolved from early experiments with computer-mediated discussion, and because those early online discussions resonated strongly with traditional notions of the importance of interaction, inquiry and critical thinking in post-secondary education, online learning has taken on a distinctly social constructivist character. Indeed, the most widely accepted model of online learning is known as the Community of Inquiry (CoI) model. In the third section of this chapter, I will explore the CoI framework and research findings supporting it.

Teaching in Technologically Mediated Environments

*Pedagogical Affordance and Emergent Digital Technologies*

All technologies are selective. They facilitate, emphasize, and enhance particular kinds of experience, while inhibiting, limiting, and sometimes even excluding others (Gibson, 1979; McLuhan, 1964). This is particularly true of communication technologies and cognitive processes, such as teaching and learning. As Gavriel Salomon (1981) reminded us, it also has important implications for pedagogy. Media, and the technologies that enable them, he contended, have unique characteristics that matter, or that can be made to matter, in teaching and learning.

> *Indeed, the point is that the traditional model of higher education takes advantage of the unique characteristics of print technologies, and has, moreover, until now been constrained by them. The emergence of digital technologies removes many of those constraints at a period in time when social constructivist pedagogies are gaining favor among the education community.*

We have witnessed and are witnessing today the emergence and rapid acceptance of a variety of digital technologies which, as McClintock (1999) argues, have already changed what is pedagogically possible. (For a further discussion of possibilities, see Chapters 8 and 10, this volume.) What is different about these technologies is that, unlike the presentation, push-type, technologies which enabled distance education, the new digital technologies supporting online learning are interactive, generative and uniquely participatory (Jenkins, 2006; Tapscott & Williams, 2006). They are thus particularly supportive of social constructivist pedagogies. Let us briefly explore a few broad examples and their implications for teaching and learning.

*Access to Information*

The World Wide Web (WWW) begat online learning as we know it, so it is appropriate that we begin here. The growth of the WWW has made enormous amounts of information on just about everything available to anyone with a computer and a broadband connection. In 2007, for example, Thomas Boutell estimated that there were

108,810,358 distinct, publicly accessible websites, containing approximately 29.7 billion pages of information. Obviously, such numbers are constantly and quite rapidly expanding. They make the notion that the purpose of higher education is the acquisition of scarce or privileged knowledge somewhat absurd, especially in the context of the open courseware movement (Massachusetts Institute of Technology, 2004). These numbers do, however, highlight the problem of information overload, and the need to be able to separate the wheat therein from the chaff. The growth of the WWW, then, provides educators with the opportunity, perhaps the imperative, to change their pedagogical focus from the transmission of knowledge to one enabling students both to make sense of an overabundance of information and to use it to generate knowledge themselves.

*Multimedia Integration*

Concurrent with the growth of the WWW has been the growth of digital multimedia and the ready availability of relatively inexpensive multimedia tools. Digital multimedia makes it possible to access, evaluate, manipulate, create and share ideas in a variety of media formats. According to YouTube (2008), for example, hundreds of thousands of user-created videos are uploaded to their site every day, and hundreds of millions of videos are watched. Virtually every news organization in the world today provides news and information not just in textual form, but in a wide variety of video, graphical, and interactive formats. The critical use and/or production of multimedia calls for intellectual skills and ways of knowing that are quite different from the manipulation of text and numbers privileged by higher education (Stephens, 1998). The growth of digital multimedia thus challenges such privilege, as well as our conventional notions of what it means to be literate (Snyder, 1998; Tyner, 1998). Indeed, the growth of digital multimedia challenges educators not only to expand their pedagogical repertoires to include multimedia, but, in particular, to facilitate its critical understanding and generation.

*Collaboration*

Most recently, technological innovation has produced a suite of digital applications collectively (and perhaps unfortunately) labeled Web 2.0.

While these applications will be explored in depth in Chapter 8, it is relevant here to consider their pedagogical affordances. Such affordances are many, but the unique support of a range of Web 2.0 applications for the collaborative creation and organization of digital content is particularly relevant to the current discussion. Web 2.0 tools, for example, have enabled the ongoing development of Wikipedia, the online encyclopedia written collaboratively by volunteers from around the world. At the time of writing, Wikipedia had at least 75,000 active contributors working on over 10 million articles in 260 languages read by more than 684 million visitors a year (Wikipedia, 2008). Its success and the success of a host of similarly Web 2.0 enabled projects has led some scholars (Jenkins, 2006; Surowiecki, 2005; Tapscott & Williams, 2006) to argue that large-scale collaboration, and not the individual labors of an elite few, will drive knowledge creation in the 21st century. Although there are obvious problems with such arguments (Keen, 2007), Web 2.0 technologies clearly and explicitly support the social construction of knowledge, and so favor collaborative pedagogical approaches over individualistic and/or authoritative ones.

At the beginning of this section, I argued that the unique characteristics of online technologies significantly change what is pedagogically possible. I identified three such unique characteristics and the kinds of pedagogical change they enable. Much greater access to information enables a change in pedagogy from knowledge transmission to knowledge generation. Multimedia integration makes possible a more media-inclusive understanding of what it means to be literate. Support for large-scale collaboration facilitates a change from authoritative and individualistic to collaborative and more democratic teaching and learning strategies

Please note my use of the word 'possible' here. You may have noted that higher education has not really abandoned its centuries-old authoritative, lecture- and text-based model of knowledge transmission; a model, I might add, itself made possible by the development of print technologies (Eisenstein, 1980). Indeed, the point is that the traditional model of higher education takes advantage of the unique characteristics of print technologies, and has, moreover, until now been constrained by them. The emergence of digital technologies removes many of those constraints at a period in time when social constructivist pedagogies are gaining favor among the education community. This latter trend and its implications for online learning are explored in the following section.

### Constructivism and Online Learning

'Constructivism' is the name given to theories of learning grounded in an epistemological alternative to objectivist theories of knowledge. Central to such alternatives, and to constructivism in general, is the notion that meaning is imposed on the world rather than extant in it. Both objectivism and constructivism agree there is a real world we experience. However, while objectivists believe that meaning exists in that world to be discovered by us, constructivists believe that we impose meaning on it (Duffy & Jonassen, 1992). They hold that meaning is constructed in our minds as we interact with the physical, social, and mental worlds we inhabit, and that we make sense of our experiences by building and adjusting the internal knowledge structures in which we collect and organize our perceptions of and reflections on reality. Social constructivists further contend that (almost) all knowledge construction is facilitated through social interaction (Vygotsky, 1978), with some social constructivists, by extension, viewing cognition as distributed among the thinking individual, interacting others, and cognitive tools (Brown, Collins, & Duguid, 1989).

While constructivism, then, is first and foremost a learning theory and not a theory of instruction, particular conceptualizations of learning suggest corresponding pedagogical approaches. According to constructivists, no matter how we are taught, all learning occurs in our minds as we create and adjust internal mental structures to accommodate our ever-growing and ever-changing stores of knowledge (Piaget, 1957). Constructivists thus believe that all learning is an active process, that it is unique to the individual, and that it is, accordingly, intimately tied to individual experience and the contexts of that experience, no matter how or where it takes place. Such beliefs have obvious pedagogical implications. Most importantly, they shift the pedagogical focus from knowledge transmission to knowledge construction; that is, from teaching to learning.

Why is there no word in English for the art of learning? Webster says that the word pedagogy means the art of teaching. What is missing is the parallel word for learning.

(Papert, 1993, p. 82)

Constructivist ideas are certainly not new. John Dewey (1938), for example, was a constructivist, although he would not have called himself so. One could even quite reasonably argue that Socrates was a social constructivist because he believed in the development of knowledge through dialogue. Epistemological approaches, however, wax and wane in the academy, and, I suppose, in the world. For most of the second half of the last century, objectivist epistemologies have held sway. Beginning with the rediscovery of Vygotsky (1978) in the early 1980s, however, constructivism in general and social constructivism in particular has been on the rise. Its ascendancy is epitomized by the U.S. National Research Council's publication of *How People Learn* (Bransford, Brown, & Cocking, 2000), a semi-official text which summarizes research findings on learning and their educational implications from a constructivist perspective.

The central pedagogical tenet of *How People Learn* is that educators' concern should not be focused on instructional design per se, but rather on the design of learning environments. Although such contrast may appear merely semantic, it is not. Moreover, it is especially significant to this discussion. *How People Learn* urges replacing a traditional focus on the design and delivery of instruction and instructional materials with design approaches which focus on the creation of environments that foster and support active learning in collaborative communities. Such distinction is clearly similar to what differentiates distance education from online learning. Moreover, conceptualizing the design and delivery of online courses in terms of the development of learning communities seems both natural and useful. In the remainder of this section, I will, therefore, structure my reflections on constructivist pedagogies and online learning relative to the four characteristics of constructivist learning environments that Bransford et al. (2000) identify as particularly important. Constructivist learning environments, they argue, are learner-centered, knowledge-centered, assessment-centered, and community-centered.

*Learner-Centered Learning Environments*

Learner-centered learning environments are focused on learning. They are grounded in the constructivist notion that because all learning is unique to the individual, individuals bring unique understandings, cognitive organization, and ways of knowing to the learning experience. It follows that the same instruction will be differentially perceived, understood, and internalized by different students. Learner-centered teaching is thus concerned more with what and how students are actually learning than with what and how it is being taught. Learner-centered teaching moreover builds on students' conceptual and cultural knowledge by linking learning to their knowledge and experiences, while exploring and valuing the multiple perspectives and divergent understandings unique individuals necessarily maintain (Bransford, Brown, & Cocking, 2000). This is not to say that learner-centered teaching is not concerned with diagnosing and remediating learner misconceptions; as noted above, it is very concerned with what and how students learn. Constructivism suggests, however, that the remediation of misconceptions takes place through accommodation. That is, because remediating misconceptions requires deconstructing and remaking conceptual understanding, teachers must help students to make their thinking visible, to test their ideas against experience and explore their limitations, and to reconstruct more viable understandings based on that experience and their reflection on it.

Online learning poses many challenges to the development of learner-centered environments. For example, most online courses must be developed before any students join them, making it difficult to adopt learning activities to learner characteristics. Moreover, the reality that online interactions are necessarily mediated by digital technologies, and most often by asynchronous ones, makes the negotiation of meaning more challenging. At the same time, the very characteristics of the online medium which create such challenges offer unique affordances to learner-centeredness. For example, computer-based learning applications have a long history of support for individualized instruction and can be quite easily incorporated into online courses. Indeed, when Carol Twigg (2001) gathered together innovative virtual educators to discuss paradigm changes that might enhance the effectiveness of online learning in large undergraduate courses, their overall conclusion was that individualization, which they termed *personalization* (arguably a more constructivist term), was key to innovation. Twigg and her colleagues concluded that quality courses should use computer-based learning technologies to facilitate initial assessments of students' knowledge and skills and manage individualized student learning trajectories within an array of interactive learning materials based on continuous assessment and feedback. Such personalized approaches clearly focus on student learning and do so in an ongoing manner. Personalized approaches also address the conceptual knowledge students bring to their online experiences, as well as the diagnosis and remediation of any misconceptions they might acquire, and are particularly supportive of the acquisition of foundational disciplinary knowledge. Many would argue, however, that computer-based, individualized learning is not really personal in that it does not value students' unique knowledge and experience, that it is culturally insensitive, and that it is antithetical to the consideration of multiple perspectives and the social construction of knowledge.

Well-developed asynchronous online discussions, in contrast, can be uniquely supportive of multiple voices and the social construction of knowledge. Researchers have found online discussion to be more equitable and democratic (Eastmond, 1995; Harasim, 1990), more reflective (Garrison, 2003; Hiltz, 1994; Poole, 2000), and in surprising ways more personal (Gunawardena & Zittle, 1997; Walther, 1994) than traditional classroom discussions. They are more democratic because their asynchronicity provides time for all participants to con-tribute, while making it very difficult for anyone, instructors included, to dominate. They encourage reflection because they produce an organized transcript which students can consult in crafting their own contributions, which they can, in turn, consider and refine before posting. Indeed, the discussion transcript might be viewed as an explicit representation of the social construction of knowledge as it grows like a crystal from the contributions of many. Asynchronous discussions can be quite personal when they invite students to share personal experiences and beliefs; when they encourage linking such personal knowledge to course concepts they are particularly effective from a social constructivist point of view. Although I will argue in the next section that it is asynchronous discussion which made online learning social constructivist in nature and so distinguished it from distance education, many would argue that asynchronous discussion is often too learner-centered and too social. Indeed, several researchers in the field have noted the common inability of online discussions to move beyond the exploration of multiple ideas to convergence on negotiated understanding and its application (Garrison & Arbaugh, 2007).

*Knowledge-Centered Learning Environments*

Knowledge centered learning environments support students' construction of deep understandings of particular topics and disciplines (Bransford, Brown, & Cocking, 2000). Constructivism likens knowledge-centered learning to learning a landscape by living in it and exploring it from a variety of perspectives (Spiro & Jheng, 1990) and so argues for the design of learning environments that encourage sense-making and learning with understanding through in-depth explorations of big ideas. It puts less emphasis on breadth and the acquisition of a large number of ill-connected facts and procedures, and concentrates instead on learning in context, on the development of complex knowledge, on authentic problem-solving, and on the authentic practice of particular disciplines. The constructivist argument is not that students do not need to learn facts and procedures, but rather that facts and procedures are learned only when they are integrated within the rich corpora of individual understanding.

As with learner-centeredness, the online medium provides unique affordances and constraints to the development of knowledge-centered learning environments. On the one hand, because the WWW is clearly an information environment, online learning seems ideally positioned for knowledge-centered learning. The way in which courses are created and placed online not only allows for the design and refinement of well-structured, knowledge-centered materials and activities, but, as previously noted, supports a greater variety of ways for integrating diverse media than traditional lecture and text environments. Moreover, the WWW itself offers unprecedented access to information and authentic contexts (McClintock, 1999) which can be easily incorporated into course materials and activities. At the same time, the nature of the online medium makes it possible for students to visit and revisit such diverse course materials and activities in ways and at times of their own choosing (Spiro & Jheng, 1990).

On the other hand, as Shank (1998) reminds us, information is not knowledge. The abundant possibilities for presentation and creation of knowledge, the near-infinite access to information, the freedom learners have to access and navigate course materials, in short, the enormous knowledge-creation potential of online environments, paradoxically challenges knowledge-centered course design. If knowledge is constructed in individual minds and does not exist outside them, it is impossible to know what information, what kinds of presentations, and what sorts of learning activities in what combinations and sequence best support knowledge construction for particular learners at particular times. Even if we could know such things, we could not enforce them in the non-linear, multi-task online universe. We can, however, explore the cognitive effects of much smaller intellectual landscapes.

We can presume that knowledge-centered online learning environments will be those which support students' deep exploration of big ideas through multiple and varied learning activities, that such activities will be generative, employ a range of media and include opportunities for reflection, discussion, assessment, and feedback, that as much as possible they will be authentically situated and problem or project based. My personal preference would be to conceptualize knowledge-centered learning environments in a sort of recursive framework (for example, at the program, course, and concept level) with an emphasis on the development of small digital learning objects (DLOs) centered on single concepts (Rothkopf, 2008) meeting the criteria outlined above. Not only could instructors and course designers draw from some set of such concept-oriented mini-environments in developing larger course environments, but they could offer students bounded learning choices, multiple paths for meeting course objectives. At the program level, not only could DLO sets be shared and reused, but better articulated learning outcomes might underwrite the development of multiple paths for meeting program objectives.

*Assessment-Centered Learning Environments*
Assessment-centered learning environments put particular emphasis on the ongoing provision of meaningful feedback to learners (Bransford,

Brown, & Cocking, 2000). While most theories of learning and instruction recognize the importance of assessment and feedback, constructivists believe that knowledge construction, hence learning itself, emerges from our ongoing reflections on feedback from environmental interactions. Constructivism thus suggests self-assessment is integral to learning, and so believes that opportunities for self-assessment should occur continuously and be embedded within learning activities. Constructivist theory further suggests a pedagogy which encourages students continuously to interrogate and reconstruct their knowledge and to evolve and change their understandings in response to feedback. Thus, constructivist approaches contend that good formal assessment practices are those which value revision and the processes of knowledge construction. Because constructivism views knowledge as complex and evolving mental structures, constructivist approaches further maintain that good formal assessment practices evaluate for deep understanding and the ability to apply knowledge to novel situations.

In many ways, the online environment offers considerable support for the development of assessment-centered learning. To begin with, online learning necessitates ongoing assessment simply because assessment and feedback are its main avenues for teacher–student interaction. Most online course platforms provide very complete records of student work, including user logs and discussion transcripts, and make these available from a range of perspectives, including something like individual e-portfolios. They also support multiple and varied forms of assessment, including assessments involving a variety of media, peer assessment, and revision sequences. Most course platforms also provide tools for embedding assessments within student work thus linking feedback to performance, and for managing and grading course assignments in ways that are transparent to students. Moreover, as previously noted, computer-based assessments can be easily embedded in online courses to give automated and instantaneous feedback to students, making it possible to provide far greater opportunities for self-assessment with little cost to instructors.

However, assessment and feedback, especially at the deep understanding level prized by constructivism, can be particularly taxing for online instructors. As previously noted, the lack of regular face-to-face meetings makes frequent, regular feedback critical. Online instructors typically need to develop and assess many more assignments over the course of a semester than face-to-face instructors, who have the opportunity to assess and remediate student understandings informally in the classroom. In addition, online learners expect a much faster turnaround on their assignments than traditional students. While this is good for learners, it is hard on instructors. While automated assessments are easily managed online, some research suggests that students learn better from personal feedback tailored specifically to their needs (Kashy et al., 2003), especially when learning involves higher-order understanding and the application of knowledge (Riccomini, 2002). One solution to this conundrum may be found in Bill Pelz's (2004) first principle of effective online pedagogy: "Let the students do (most of) the work" (p. 33). Pelz suggests having students lead discussions based on text chapters, locate and discuss relevant Web resources, check and grade their own homework, and provide initial feedback on assignments to each other. The instructor, he argues, can then concentrate on thoughtfully providing necessary structure, direction, support, and corrective feedback when necessary, and on making final evaluations.

*Community-Centered Learning Environments*
Community-centered learning environments support the development of community on two levels (Bransford, Brown, & Cocking, 2000). At the first level, community-centered learning environments support the social construction of knowledge within relatively small, tight-knit learning communities. At the second level, community-centered learning environments connect to students' larger community and the larger society and culture. On the first level, constructivism implies that learning is strengthened by environments which support and value the participation of all students, whose social norms encourage collaboration, the negotiation of meaning, and the search for understanding, and in which multiple perspectives are respected and incorporated into collective meaning-making. On the second level, constructivism suggests that learning is enhanced when it is related to students' interests and experiences, when it is situated in authentic 'real-world' problem-solving, and when it is linked to and resonates with the greater culture and society at large.

At first glance, it might seem that online learning is particularly ill-suited to the development of community-centered learning environments at the first level identified above. Indeed, some communication theorists have argued that the lack of the vocal and visual cues available in face-to-face learning diminishes the quality of social interactions online to such an extent as to render the social construction of knowledge all but impossible (Picard, 1997; Rice, 1992; Short, Williams, & Christie, 1976). Researchers experienced in online teaching and learning, however, contest this view. What are important, they contend, are not media capabilities, but personal perceptions (Gunawardena & Zittle, 1997; Rourke et al., 2001; Swan, 2002a, 2002b; Walther, 1994). Their research demonstrates that participants in online courses often feel less psychological distance between themselves and their classmates than they do in traditional, face-to-face classrooms. However, the development of community is something that must be consciously engineered and supported in online courses (Shea et al., 2005), much more so than in face-to-face classrooms (Rovai, 2002).

The second level of community-centeredness, making connections to students' larger community and culture, is less well documented, perhaps because it seems much more straightforward. The interconnectedness of Internet sites and their frequent updating makes it quite easy, to a greater or lesser degree, to situate learning in authentic, real-world problems and link it to local communities and cultures. Indeed, links to the Internet, as previously noted, make it possible to explore a variety of world cultures to an extent that would not otherwise be possible. As in any learning environment, online discussions and learning activities can be designed to engage students' interests and experiences. Unlike other venues, however, online discussions and activities can involve more experienced others from around the world. Anecdotal accounts suggest such strategies are very effective in supporting learning, but more research in these areas is clearly indicated.

## Serendipity: An Aside and Transition

In the previous section, we saw how emerging digital technologies remove many of the constraints on educational activity that have historically encouraged teacher- and instruction-centered practices. We saw how contemporary educational theory favors constructivism's learner- and learning-centered approaches. We explored some ways in which online environments can be designed to be learner-centered, knowledge-centered, assessment-centered, and community-centered, using digital technologies to implement constructivist pedagogy.

As previously noted, more than a few communications scholars at the time doubted the capacity of purely text-based digital communications to convey enough 'social presence' to support the development of learning communities (Short, Williams, & Christie, 1976; Rice, 1992; Picard, 1997). As also previously noted, however, researchers actually working with online discussion reported the exact opposite: that participants in online discussions strongly perceived each other's presence (Walther, 1994; Gunawardena & Zittle, 1997). Online educators, moreover, noted the ways in which online discussion seemed to embody the academic ideal of Socratic inquiry, and so online learning evolved with online discussion as its centerpiece. Indeed, a group of Canadian researchers investigating online discussion developed an inquiry-oriented model of online learning that is probably the most commonly referenced among online educators (Garrison, Anderson, & Archer, 2000; Garrison & Anderson, 2003). Their Community of Inquiry (CoI) framework is discussed in the next and final section of this chapter.

### Community of Inquiry Framework

> Not only has the CoI model sparked large amounts of research, it remediates a lack of theory development in online distance education.
>
> (Akyol et al., 2009, p. 131)

The CoI framework (Garrison, Anderson, & Archer, 2000) is a process model of online learning. It is grounded in a collaborative constructivist view of higher education and assumes that effective online learning requires the development of a community (Rovai, 2002; Shea, 2006) that supports meaningful inquiry and deep learning. The CoI framework has been quite widely used to inform both research and practice in the online learning community and an increasing body of research supports its efficacy for both describing and informing online learning (Arbaugh et al., 2008; Swan, Garrison, & Richardson, in press).

Building from the notion of social presence in online discussion, the CoI framework represents the online learning experience as a function of the relationship between three presences: social presence, teaching presence, and cognitive presence (see Figure 7.1). The CoI framework suggests that online learning is located at the intersection of these three presences; that is, all three presences are necessary for learning in an educational context to take place. In this section, the elements of each of these of these presences and their implications for online learning pedagogy are discussed.

*Social presence*

Social presence refers to the degree to which learners feel socially and emotionally connected with others in an online environment. A number of research studies have found that the perception of interpersonal connections with virtual others is an important factor in the success of

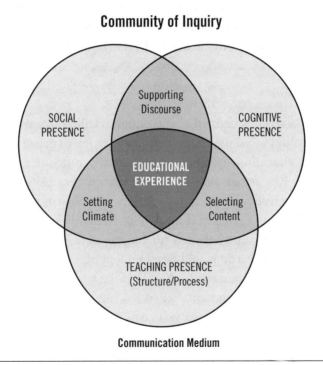

**Figure 7.1** Community of Inquiry Framework

*Source:* Garrison, Anderson, & Archer, 2000

online learning (Picciano, 2002; Richardson & Swan, 2003; Swan, 2002a; Swan & Shih, 2005; Tu, 2000). Garrison and Anderson (2003) identified three elements that contribute to the development of social presence in online courses: affective expression, open communication, and group cohesion. Research suggests that these elements are strongly affected by teaching presence—both instructor behaviors (Shea et al., 2005; Shea & Bidjeramo, 2008) and course design (Swan & Shih, 2005; Tu & McIssac, 2002) (see next section).

*Affective expression* refers to participants' ability to express their personalities in virtual environments through sharing experiences, beliefs and values, self-revelation, humor, and the use of paralinguistic affective indicators. Course activities that provide opportunities for affective expression are obviously a necessary condition for its development, but it is critical that instructors value and encourage these behaviors in students and model their use themselves. It is also critical that course designers and instructors establish and maintain *open communication*, a climate in which students feel free to express themselves, and provide opportunities and support for the development of *group cohesion* through interactive and collaborative activities.

*Teaching Presence*

Teaching presence is defined as the design, facilitation, and direction of cognitive and social processes for the realization of personally meaningful and educationally worthwhile learning outcomes (Anderson et al., 2001). Researchers have documented strong correlations between learners' perceived and actual interactions with instructors and their perceived learning (Jiang & Ting, 2000; Richardson & Swan, 2003; Swan et al., 2000); and between teaching presence and student satisfaction, perceived learning, and development of a sense of community in online courses (Shea et al., 2005). In fact, the body of evidence attesting to the critical importance of teaching presence for successful online learning continues to grow (Garrison & Cleveland-Innes, 2005; Murphy, 2004; Swan & Shih, 2005; Vaughan & Garrison, 2006; Wu & Hiltz, 2004) with the most recent research suggesting it is the key to developing online communities of inquiry (Shea & Bidjeramo, 2008).

Garrison and Anderson (2003) identified three elements that contribute to the development of teaching presence in online courses—design and organization, facilitating discourse, and direct instruction—all of which deserve careful attention. The first element, *design and organization*, cannot be neglected in an online learning environment, especially as regards the clarity and consistency of course organization and clear statement of goals and objectives. The selection of worthwhile collaborative and other learning activities is also especially important. *Facilitating discourse* is particularly focused on facilitating online discussion, where it is important to be supportive and present, but not overly so (Vandergrift, 2002). There will, of course, be times when it is necessary to intervene directly in online discussions to correct misconceptions, provide relevant information, summarize the discussion, and/or provide some metacognitive awareness. This is the third element of teaching presence, *direct instruction*, which also includes any lecture-like material included in online courses, as well as instruction included in feedback to students.

*Cognitive presence*

Cognitive presence describes the extent to which learners are able to construct and confirm meaning through course activities, sustained reflection, and discourse (Garrison, Anderson, & Archer, 2000). In the CoI framework, cognitive presence is seen as consisting of four phases of practical inquiry, adapted from Dewey (1933), which begins with a *triggering event* and extends through *exploration* and *integration* to culminate in *resolution*. Researchers have been able to find evidence of practical inquiry in online discussion, but several studies have found that online discussion rarely moves beyond the exploration phase, where participants share information and brainstorm ideas (Garrison & Arbaugh, 2007; Kanuka & Anderson, 1998; Luebeck & Bice, 2005; Murphy, 2004).

*In studies where students were challenged to resolve a problem and explicit facilitation and direction provided, students did progress to resolution.*

While various explanations have been explored, it is most likely that much of this has to do with the nature of the assignments and instructional direction (teaching presence) provided (Garrison & Arbaugh, 2007). In studies where students were challenged to resolve a problem and explicit facilitation and direction provided, students did progress to resolution (Akyol & Garrison, 2008; Meyer, 2003; Murphy, 2004; Shea & Bidjeramo, 2008; Wang & Chang, 2008). It may also be that ideas explored in online discussion are integrated and resolved through other course assignments.

## Conclusion

In this chapter, we have seen how the confluence of emerging technologies, trends in educational theory, the historical origins of online learning, and the way constructivist approaches resonate with academic ideals led to the adoption of distinctly social constructivist pedagogies in online learning. We reviewed current best understandings concerning the design of learning activities, and accordingly looked at ways in which online environments can be designed to be learner-centered, knowledge-centered, assessment-centered, and community-centered. We also examined the Community of Inquiry (CoI) model of online learning and some ideas suggested by it for collaborative constructivist approaches. You may have noticed, however, that two things were not discussed.

The first has to do with emerging technologies. Although I discussed how emerging technologies remove constraints on educational activity, I did not deal with their integration in the design of learning environments or CoI pedagogy. To do so adequately would take an entire chapter, and, indeed, emerging technologies are covered in the next chapter. I would encourage you, none the less, to keep the frameworks reviewed in this chapter in mind as you read the next.

The second has to do with constraints. I discussed the affordances of emerging technologies and online learning, but I did not talk about the constraints. These are worth considering. For example, we remarked on the difficulty of moving online discussion to integration and resolution; it would be much less difficult in a face-to-face environment. Neil Postman (1994, pp. 4–5) reminds us that it is also important to consider who benefits and who is marginalized by our embrace of new technologies—"[I]t is a mistake to suppose that any technological innovation has a one-sided effect. Every technology is both a burden and a blessing; not either–or, but this and that". I urge you to consider 'that'.

## TERMS AND DEFINITIONS

**Cognitive presence:** The extent to which learners are able to construct and confirm meaning through sustained reflection and discourse in a critical community of inquiry.

**Community of Inquiry framework:** A theoretical model consisting of three overlapping presences (social, cognitive, teaching) that provides a coherent representation of a collaborative, constructivist educational experience.

**Constructivism:** A philosophy of learning based on the axiom that individuals construct meaning and understanding as they experience and engage the world. Learning is seen as a process of creating and adjusting mental models to accommodate new experiences.

**Emerging technologies:** This expression refers to leading developments of objects, devices, apparatus, and materials for use in the extension of human abilities and activities. Technology is said to be emerging to the extent that is novel and/or disruptive.

**Social construction of knowledge:** The concept of social construction was popularized by the sociologists Berger & Luckman in 1966. The concept has since been applied to all social human activity and the products of that activity. Individuals interacting together form, over time, mental representations of the way things work. Knowledge is then constructed from the experiences and interactions individuals have in relation to the world and each other. These models build and are tested and evaluated over time, eventually becoming embedded into the fabric and structure of society's knowledge.

**Social presence:** The ability of participants in a community of inquiry to project themselves socially and emotionally, as 'real' people (i.e., their full personality), through the medium of communication being used.

**Teaching presence:** The design, facilitation, and direction of cognitive and social processes for the purpose of realizing meaningful and educationally worthwhile learning outcomes.

**Technological affordances:** The advantages and disadvantages which emerge from the uses and misuses of a particular technology. The affordances, or the properties a technology offers, are politically and socially biased.

## QUESTIONS FOR REVIEW AND REFLECTION

1. Distance education is materials and teacher-centered. How does this 'center' change in the move to online learning?
2. Describe what contributed to the development of online learning that gave it a distinctly social constructivist character.
3. Discuss the potential educational constraints of each of the three broad areas of technological innovation described in the first section of this chapter: access to information, multimedia integration, and collaboration. What ways of knowing do they marginalize, which learners might be hurt by their adoption, what pedagogical strategies or techniques do they not support?
4. Identify one way an online course or program could be designed to make it more learner-centered, knowledge-centered, assessment-centered, community-centered. Are the changes you have identified compatible?
5. Marshall McLuhan wrote, "we shape our tools and then our tools shape us." What do you think he meant by that and how does it relate to emerging technologies and constructivist pedagogy?
6. List as many strategies as you can think of to increase social presence, cognitive presence, and teaching presence in a hypothesized online discussion. Which of these do you think are most important for the development of a community of inquiry?

**Significant Contributor**

**Robbie McClintock** is the John L. and Sue Ann Weinberg Professor in the Historical and Philosophical Foundations of Education at Teachers College, Columbia University, where he has taught since 1967. He earned his BA degree from Princeton University in

1961 and his Ph.D. from Columbia University in 1968. From 1965 to 1967, he was Assistant Professor at Johns Hopkins University and since 1967 he has been a member of the faculty at Teachers College. As an undergraduate, Professor McClintock became interested in formative education as an agent of cultural change. In light of this interest, he has published primarily on the history of political and educational theory and on the cultural significance of information and communications technologies. During the 1970s, his interest in 'the place for study in a world of instruction' sensitized him to the possibility that digital technologies were becoming disruptive historical forces, providing important challenges and opportunities in the intellectual sphere. Since then he has been acting on these contingencies as an accidental technologist and advancing reflective ideas about the historical interaction between technological and cultural change in diverse essays and proposals, mostly online, the fullest of which were *Power and Pedagogy* (1992) and *The Educators Manifesto* (1999). To further these goals, McClintock founded the Institute for Learning Technologies (ILT) in 1985 and directed it through 2002, prototyping advanced curricular resources over the Internet. Through ILT he tried to act on his ideas about historical change by proposing and implementing activities like the Cumulative Curriculum Project, which became the Dalton Technology Plan (1991–1996), and the Eiffel Project (1996–2001). In all, he helped to mobilize well over $20 million in gifts and grants to support prototypical places for study that he designed and managed during the 1990s. The effort has had enduring effects through the Columbia Center for New Media Teaching and Learning (ccnmtl.columbia.edu) and in several schools. Currently, he collaborates on www.StudyPlace.org, an open-source, peer-produced, wiki-based digital commons for explorations in education, communications and culture, responding to the basic question: What educates?

References

Akyol, Z., Arbaugh, B., Cleveland-Innes, M.F., Garrison, D.R., Ice, P., Richardson, J. & Swan, K. (2009). A response to the review of the community of inquiry framework. *Canadian Journal of Distance Education*, 23(2), 123–136.

Akyol, Z. & Garrison, D.R. (2008). The development of a community of inquiry over time in an online course: Understanding the progression and integration of social, cognitive and teaching presence. *Journal of Asynchronous Learning Networks*, 12(3), 3–22.

Anderson, T., Rourke, L., Garrison, D.R., & Archer, W. (2001). Assessing teaching presence in a computer conferencing context. *Journal of Asynchronous Learning Networks*, 5(2), 1–17.

Arbaugh, J.B., Cleveland-Innes, M.F., Diaz, S., Garrison, D.R., Ice, P., Richardson, J.C., Shea, P., & Swan, K. (2008). Developing a community of inquiry instrument: Testing a measure of the Community of Inquiry framework using a multi-institutional sample. *The Internet and Higher Education*, 11(3–4), 133–136.

Boutell, T. (February 15, 2007) WWW FAQS: How many web sites are there? Retrieved December 10, 2008 from: http://www.boutell.com/newfaq/misc/sizeofweb.html.

Bransford, J.D, Brown, A.L., & Cocking, R.R. (2000). *How people learn: Brain, mind, experience, and school*. Washington, DC: National Academy Press.

Brown, J.S., Collins, A., & Duguid, S. (1989). Situated cognition and the culture of learning. *Educational Researcher*, 18(1), 32–42.

Dewey, J. (1933). *How we think*. Boston: D.C. Heath.

Dewey, J. (1938). *Experience and education*. New York: Macmillan.

Duffy, T.M. & Jonassen, D.H. (1992). *Constructivism and the technology of instruction: A conversation*. Hillsdale, NJ: Erlbaum.

Eastmond, D.V. (1995). *Alone but together: Adult distance study through computer conferencing*. Cresskill, NJ: Hampton Press.

eBizMBA (2008). Top 25 Web 2.0 Sites. Retrieved December 10, 2008 from: http://www.ebizmba.com/articles/user-generated-content.

Eisenstein, E. (1980). *The printing press as an agent of change: Communications and cultural transformations in early-modern Europe*. Cambridge: Cambridge University Press.

Garrison, D.R. (2003). Cognitive presence for effective asynchronous online learning: The role of reflective inquiry, self-direction and metacognition. In J. Bourne & J. C. Moore (Eds.), *Elements of quality online education: Practice and direction*. Needham, MA: Sloan Center for Online Education.

Garrison, D.R. & Anderson, T. (2003). *E-learning in the 21st century: A framework for research and practice*. London: Routledge/Falmer.

Garrison, D.R., Anderson, T., & Archer, W. (2000). Critical inquiry in a text-based environment: Computer conferencing in higher education. *The Internet and Higher Education*, 2: 87–105.

Garrison, D.R. & Arbaugh, J.B. (2007). Researching the community of inquiry framework: Review, issues, and future directions. *The Internet and Higher Education*, 10(3), 157–172.

Garrison, D.R. & Cleveland-Innes, M.F. (2005). Facilitating cognitive presence in online learning: Interaction is not enough. *American Journal of Distance Education*, 19(3), 133–148.

Gibson, J.J. (1979). *The ecological approach to visual perception.* Boston: Houghton Mifflin.

Gunawardena, C. & Zittle, F. (1997). Social presence as a predictor of satisfaction within a computer mediated conferencing environment. *American Journal of Distance Education*, 11(3), 8–26.

Harasim, L. (1990). *On-line education: Perspectives on a new environment.* New York: Praeger.

Hiltz, S.R. (1994). *The virtual classroom: Learning without limits via computer networks.* Norwood, NJ: Ablex.

Jenkins, H. (2006). *Convergence culture: Where old and new media collide.* New York: New York University Press.

Jenkins, H. (2008). Confronting the challenges of participatory culture: Media education for the 21st century. Retrieved April 11, 2009 from: http://digitallearning.macfound.org/atf/cf/%7B7E45C7E0-A3E0-4B89-AC9C-E807E1B0AE4E%7D/JENKINS_WHITE_PAPER.PDF

Jiang, M. & Ting, E. (2000). A study of factors influencing students' perceived learning in a Web-based course environment. *International Journal of Educational Telecommunications*, 6(4), 317–338.

Kanuka, H. & Anderson, T. (1998). Online social interchange, discord, and knowledge construction. *Journal of Distance Education*, 13(1), 57–75.

Kashy, D.A., Abertelli, G., Bauer, W., Kashy, E., & Thoennessen, M. (2003). Influence of non-moderated and moderated discussion sites on student success. *Journal of Asynchronous Learning Networks*, 7(1), 31–36.

Keen, A. (2007). *The cult of the amateur: How today's Internet is killing our culture.* New York: Doubleday/Currency.

Luebeck, J.L. & Bice, L.R. (2005). Online discussion as a mechanism of conceptual change among mathematics and science teachers. *Journal of Distance Education*, 20(2), 21–39.

Massachusetts Institute of Technology. (2004). MITOpenCourseware. Retrieved December 10, 2008 from: http://ocw.mit.edu/OcwWeb/How To/index.htm.

McClintock, R.O. (1999). The educators' manifesto: Renewing the progressive bond with posterity through the social construction of digital learning communities. Retrieved March 31, 2009 from: http://www.ilt.columbia.edu/publications/manifesto/contents.html.

McLuhan, M. (1964). *Understanding media: The extensions of man.* New York: New American Library.

Meyer, K.A. (2003). Face-to-face versus threaded discussions: The role of time and higher-order thinking. *Journal of Asynchronous Learning Networks*, 7(3), 55–65.

Murphy, E. (2004). Identifying and measuring ill-structured problem formulation and resolution in online asynchronous discussions. *Canadian Journal of Learning and Technology*, 30(1), 5–20.

Papert, S. (1993). *The children's machine: Rethinking school in the age of the computer.* New York: Basic Books.

Pelz, B. (2004). (My) three principles of effective online pedagogy. *Journal of Asynchronous Learning Networks*, 8(3), 33–46.

Piaget, J. (1957). *Construction of reality in the child*. London: Routledge.

Picard, R.W. (1997). *Affective computing*. Cambridge, MA: MIT Press.

Picciano, A. (2002). Beyond student perceptions: Issues of interaction, presence, and performance in an online course. *Journal of Asynchronous Learning Networks*, 6(1), 21–40. Retrieved May, 2009 from: http://www.aln.org/publications/jaln/v6n1/v6n1_picciano.asp.

Poole, D.M. (2000). Student participation in a discussion-oriented online course: A case study. *Journal of Research on Computing in Education*, 33(2), 162–177.

Postman, N. (1994). *Technopoly: The surrender of culture to technology*. New York: Viking.

Riccomini, P. (2002). The comparative effectiveness of two forms of feedback: Web-based model comparison and instructor delivered feedback. *Journal of Educational Computing Research*, 27(3), 213–228

Rice, R.E. (1992). Contexts of research in organizational computer-mediated communication. In M. Lea (Ed.), *Contexts of computer-mediated communication*. New York: Harvester Wheatsheaf.

Richardson, J.C. & Swan, K. (2003). Examining social presence in online courses in relation to students' perceived learning and satisfaction. *Journal of Asynchronous Learning Networks*, 7(1), 68–88.

Rothkopf, E.A. (2008). An immodest proposal: Pedagogic information supports for teachers. *Teachers College Record*, 111(1). Retrieved December 12, 2008 from: http://www.tcrecord.org/content.asp?contentid=15218.

Rourke, L., Anderson, T., Garrison, D.R., & Archer, W. (2001). Assessing social presence in asynchronous text-based computer conferencing. *Journal of Distance Education*, 14(2), 50–71.

Rovai, A.P. (2002). A preliminary look at structural differences in sense of classroom community between higher education traditional and ALN courses. *Journal of Asynchronous Learning Networks*, 6(1). Retrieved May 1, 2008 from: http://www.sloan-c.org/publications/jaln/v6n1/pdf/v6n1_rovai.pdf.

Salomon, G. (1981). *The interaction of media, cognition, and learning*. San Francisco: Jossey-Bass.

Shank, R. (1998). Horses for courses. *Communication of the ACM*, 41(7), 23–25.

Shea, P. (2006). A study of students' sense of learning community in online environments. *Journal of Asynchronous Learning Networks*, 10(1), 35–44.

Shea, P. & Bidjeramo, T. (2008). Community of Inquiry as a theoretical framework to foster 'epistemic engagement' and 'cognitive presence' in online education. Paper presented at the Annual Meeting of the American Educational Research Association, New York, March.

Shea, P., Li, C., Swan K., & Pickett, A. (2005) Developing learning community in online asynchronous college courses: The role of teaching presence. *Journal of Asynchronous Learning Networks*, 9(4). Retrieved May 1, 2008 from: http://www.sloan-c.org/publications/jaln/v9n4/v9n4_shea.asp.

Short, J., Williams, E., & Christie, B. (1976). *The social psychology of telecommunications.* Toronto: Wiley.

Snyder, I. (Ed.) (1998). *Page to screen: Taking literacy into the electronic age.* London: Routledge.

Spiro, R.J. & Jheng, J.C. (1990) Cognitive flexibility and hypertext: Theory and technology for the nonlinear and multidimensional traversal of complex subject matter. In D. Nix & R.J. Spiro (Eds.), *Cognition, education, and multimedia: Explorations in high technology.* Hillsdale, NJ: Erlbaum.

Stephens, M. (1998). *The rise of the image; the fall of the word.* Oxford: Oxford University Press.

Surowiecki, J. (2005). *The wisdom of crowds.* New York: Anchor Books.

Swan, K. (2002a). Building communities in online courses: The importance of interaction. *Education, Communication and Information,* 2(1), 23–49.

Swan, K. (2002b). Immediacy, social presence, and asynchronous discussion. In J. Bourne & J.C. Moore (Eds.), *Elements of quality online education, Volume 3.* Needham, MA: Sloan Center for Online Education.

Swan, K. (2003). Developing social presence in online discussions. In S. Naidu (Ed.), *Learning and teaching with technology: Principles and practices.* London: Kogan Page.

Swan, K., Garrison, D.R., & Richardson, J.C. (in press). A constructivist approach to online learning: The Community of Inquiry framework. In C.R. Payne (Ed.), *Information technology and constructivism in higher education: Progressive learning frameworks.* Hershey, PA: IGI Global.

Swan, K., Shea, P., Fredericksen, E., Pickett, A., Pelz, W., & Maher, G. (2000). Building knowledge building communities: Consistency, contact and communication in the virtual classroom. *Journal of Educational Computing Research,* 23(4), 389–413.

Swan, K. & Shih, L.-F. (2005). On the nature and development of social presence in online course discussions. *Journal of Asynchronous Learning Networks,* 9(3), 115–136.

Tapscott, D. & Williams, A.D. (2006). *Wikinomics: How mass collaboration changes everything.* London: Portfolio.

Tu, C.-H. (2000). On-line learning migration: From social learning theory to social presence theory in CMC environment. *Journal of Network and Computer Applications,* 23(1), 27–37.

Tu, C.-H. & McIsaac, M. (2002). The relationship of social presence and interaction in online classes. *The American Journal of Distance Education,* 16(3), 131–150.

Twigg, C. (2001). *Innovations in online learning: Moving beyond no significant difference.* Troy, NY: Center for Academic Transformation, Rensselaer Polytechnic Institute. Retrieved December 12, 2008 from: http://www.center.rpi.edu/Monographs/Innovations.html.

Tyner, K. (1998). *Literacy in a digital world: Teaching and learning in the age of information.* Mahwah, NJ: Lawrence Erlbaum Associates.

Vandergrift, K.E. (2002). The anatomy of a distance education course: A case study analysis. *Journal of Asynchronous Learning Networks,* 6(1), 76–90.

Vaughan, N. & Garrison, D.R. (2006). How blended learning can support a faculty development community of inquiry. *Journal of Asynchronous Learning Networks*, 10(4), 139–152.

Vygotsky, L.S. (1978). *Mind in society*. Cambridge, MA: Harvard University Press.

Walther, J. (1994). Interpersonal effects in computer mediated interaction. *Communication Research*, 21(4), 460–487.

Wang, Y.-M. & Chang, V.D.-T. (2008). Essential elements in designing online discussions to promote cognitive presence—a practical experience. *Journal of Asynchronous Learning Networks*, 12(3–4), 157–177.

Wikipedia (2008). Wikipedia:About. Retrieved December 10, 2008 from: http://en.wikipedia.org/wiki/Wikipedia:About.

Wu, D. & Hiltz, S.R. (2004). Predicting learning from asynchronous online discussions. *Journal of Asynchronous Learning Networks*, 8(2), 139–152.

YouTube (2008). YouTube fact sheet. Retrieved December 10, 2008 from: http://www.youtube.com/t/fact_sheet.

# PART III
# A UNIFIED APPROACH

# 8

# THE FUTURE OF LEARNING TECHNOLOGIES

## Transformational Developments

### DR. PHIL ICE

Director of Course Design, Research and Development
American Public University System

> I have been having these two parallel dreams about eLearning. One is rosy and rich with possibilities. The other isn't quite a nightmare, but it has people running down corridors and bumping into walls.
>
> (Rossett, 2002, p. 1)

## Introduction

While it was made in 2002, the above statement is as true today as it was then—even though that span of time equates to an age in Internet time. In understanding Rossett's nightmare scenario, the word 'corridor' may be the most informative. Grounded in an industrial model, described in Chapter 2, distance learning has had great difficulty freeing itself from the governing, linear paradigm that fails to differentiate between quantifiable training outcomes and the construction of knowledge. Complicating the evolution of eLearning is the rapid proliferation of new applications, communication modalities and competing visions of what the future of technological convergence will look like. However, despite issues revolving around the rapid pace of transformation, contemporary and emerging technologies provide practitioners to select from an array of tools that allow for co-construction of knowledge as opposed to mere transmission of facts. The purpose of this chapter is thus twofold. Paralleling a review of where we have been and where we may be going is a discussion of the underlying pedagogical possibilities of technologies that increasingly tie together the physical and virtual worlds.

### Background and Contemporary Applications

*The Evolution of Web 2.0*

In 1993 the first iteration of what we think of as the modern World Wide Web took form as a result of the implementation of the Mosaic Web browser. For the first time in the history of computing, Mosaic made the presentation of text-wrapped graphics ubiquitous. As such the Web began to expand from news groups to a richer environment where materials could be presented using combinations of media. The key word in this last sentence is 'presented.' Though the ability to intertwine text and graphics had been made possible, it was still a relatively daunting process and control of the media was retained by the creator.

In the mid- to late 1990s the concept of online learning revolved around the realization that the World Wide Web had the potential to transform teaching and learning radically through both enhanced media availability and access. However, as was the case with virtually all areas impacted by the Tech Bubble, the vast majority of eLearning's proponents over-promised on what they believed could be delivered— at least in the near term. As a result promises of ubiquitous access to streaming content, simulations, and interactive environments were not realized quickly enough to stem the hemorrhage in supporting investment streams. Following the dot-com crash of 2001, eLearning practitioners, especially early adopters, began a critical assessment of what had worked in exemplar programs, as well as concepts that had failed to reach maturity. Much to the dismay of constructivist-oriented academics, what emerged from a business and administrative perspective was an appreciation for standardized, scalable courses that had achieved consistent results. While this initially resulted in a template-based approach to eLearning, as exemplified by the University of Phoenix and DeVry, the emergence of rapid eLearning software such as Captivate® and Camtasia® served as a catalyst for the subsequent proliferation of Web 2.0 technologies (Wagner, 2008).

Building upon the concept of rapid content development and delivery, around 2003 designers and instructors began aggregating text, graphics, audio, video, and animation files into unified works. By 2006 this practice had become so widespread that it was formalized in the term 'mashup' (Hill & Dudley, 2006). Though questions persist about intellectual property rights, the mashup has become a common means of representing a conceptual framework using a combination of assets, in a process that is thematically similar to combining text-based works into a paper or book chapter.

Facilitating the emergence of mashups was the rise of Web 2.0 technologies. Perhaps one of the best and most concise descriptions of Web 2.0 comes from the most widely recognized Web 2.0 technology, Wikipedia (2009):

> Web 2.0 websites allow users to do more than just retrieve information. They can build on the interactive facilities of 'Web 1.0' to provide 'Network as platform' computing, allowing users to run software-applications entirely through a browser. Users can own the data on a Web 2.0 site and exercise control over that data. These sites may have an 'Architecture of participation' that encourages users to add value to the application as they use it. This stands in contrast to traditional websites, the sort that limited visitors to viewing and whose content only the site's owner could modify.

The highly interrelated and continually evolving technology infrastructure of Web 2.0 includes combinations of some or all of the following: server-side software, content syndication, messaging protocols, standards-oriented browsers with plugins and extensions, and various client applications. These diverse, yet complementary, approaches provide Web 2.0 sites with information storage, content creation, and dissemination capabilities that are finally starting to align with the Tech Bubble promises of what eLearning would eventually become. Ironically, these capabilities are also a direct result of the previously discussed move toward standardized, rapid eLearning tools that were produced by the bursting of the Tech Bubble.

Though diverse in terms of conceptual frameworks, all Web 2.0 tools deliver a set of functionalities that McAfee (2006) refers to as SLATES:

- *Search:* The ease of finding information through keyword search which makes the platform valuable.
- *Links:* Guide to important pieces of information. The best pages are the most frequently linked to.
- *Authoring:* The ability to create constantly updated content over a platform that is shifted from being the creation of a few to being constantly updated, interlinked work. In wikis, the content is iterative in the sense that the people undo and redo each other's work. In blogs, content is cumulative in that posts and comments of individuals are accumulated over time.
- *Tags:* Categorization of content by creating tags that are simple, one-word descriptions to facilitate searching and avoid rigid, pre-made categories.
- *Extensions:* Automation of some of the work and pattern matching by using algorithms (e.g. amazon.com recommendations).
- *Signals:* The use of RSS (Really Simple Syndication) technology to notify users of any changes of the content by sending them emails.

In his keynote address to the 14th Sloan-C International Conference on Online Learning, Terry Anderson (2008) noted that, as of November 2008, there were over 2500 Web 2.0 applications. Though certainly some degree of redundancy exists between many of these applications, it is important to note that each must have some particular relevance to its user base or it would cease to exist. As Tapscott and Williams (2006) point out, the success of any collaborative online medium is dependent upon the desire of free agents to come together and cooperate to improve a given operation or solve a problem. From an eLearning perspective, academic endeavors that involve activities of this nature are reflective of the paradigmatic shift from a highly linear, modernist view of learning to a problem-posing model that is methodologically reflective of Freire's (1970) foundational work in critical pedagogy.

In terms of application, the value of Web 2.0 technologies to eLearning can be directly tied to the Community of Inquiry (CoI) framework. Discussed in earlier chapters, the CoI is predicated on the Deweyan ideal of constructivist learning (Swan, Garrison, &

Richardson, 2009). In this model, guided exploration and conceptual integration by a group of learners, in a socially rich atmosphere, are catalysts and prerequisites for individual construction of meaningful knowledge. Thus, a Web 2.0 tool such as a wiki or blog can be viewed as a means for facilitating deep and meaningful aggregation of information into a knowledge base. Significantly, when considering the optimal technology for facilitation of learning, the ability to expose rich media should be considered. Utilizing a relatively simple Web 2.0 technology, I found that increased instances of higher-level thought could be directly attributed to the utilization of an online document editor (Buzzword) that allowed for rapid incorporation and manipulation of Flash-based media than when similar projects were completed using traditional word-processing programs (Ice, 2008).

*While the potential of Web 2.0 technologies is promising, it is important for practitioners to remember that Web 1.0 technologies are still useful and can serve as a launching point for collaborative activities.*

While the potential of Web 2.0 technologies is promising, it is important for practitioners to remember that Web 1.0 technologies are still useful and can serve as a launching point for collaborative activities. As an example, the Smithsonian and Louvre both have exceptional online tours of their collections, which can easily serve as the cornerstone for school-pupil explorations. Though rich and beneficial on a stand-alone basis, such activities can be enriched by asking students to blog about their impressions of the collections, form wikis that relate the information on these sites to materials from other sources, or collaborate with peers.

With respect to peer collaboration, one exciting example of Web 2.0 usage can be found in the Global Nomads Group (GNC) initiative. Founded in 1998, the GNC is a project that facilitates communication between school pupils across the globe (Morrison & Macquart, 2006). Initially the project relied upon simple discussion boards and email; however, with technological advancements streaming video, wikis, blogs, Facebook postings, Twitter and other media have become staples in helping students worldwide connect and share perspectives. In the previous paragraph the concept of having students explore the Louvre website and develop wikis or blogs was discussed. Imagine the power of supplementing those artifacts with contributions by students living in Paris or Twitter streams, Flickr postings, etc. coming from individuals actually touring the Louvre. That is the power of Web 2.0 and the emerging realization of the last decades eLearning visionaries.

*Software as a Service*

Powering Web 2.0 applications is the emergence of Software as a Service (Saas), also known as 'Cloud Computing.' Instead of relying only on expensive desktop-based software, SaaS enables students and educators to work together online using hosted productivity software solutions and the Web for real-time collaboration. With Web 2.0 technology, students and instructors can collaborate in small or large groups to comment on research papers and other documents at their convenience. Through four core propositions, SaaS has the ability to transform software into a utility, creating ubiquitous interactivity and collaboration:

1. The illusion of infinite computing resources available on demand, thereby eliminating the need for Cloud Computing users to plan far ahead for provisioning.
2. The elimination of an up-front commitment by Cloud users, thereby allowing companies to start small and increase hardware resources only when there is an increase in their needs.
3. The ability to pay for use of computing resources on a short-term basis as needed (e.g., processors by the hour and storage by the day) and release them as needed, thereby rewarding conservation by letting machines and storage go when they are no longer useful.
4. The ability of users to access information, software, and collaborative environments on a variety of devices and platforms without reliance on installed software (Armbrust et al., 2009; Johnson, Levine, & Smith, 2009).

A relatively simple SaaS application is the online document editor. Several variations exist, including Adobe Buzzword, Google Docs, and Zoho Writer, and they all provide the same core functionality: offering word-processor functionality within a Web browser. Because the application and associated documents reside online, local software maintenance is eliminated. Utilizing this type of application also drastically changes workflow models by allowing for email independent access and collaboration with any number of peers writing, editing, and commenting on documents while controlling access and tracking the edits of each contributor. As some of these applications are based on media-rich languages, such as Flash in the case of Buzzword, the ability to insert, manipulate, and edit associated elements like images and tables becomes far more intuitive and user-friendly.

At first glance this type of application may not appear to be revolutionary; however, it does represent a significant paradigmatic shift in that it allows students and educators to work on master documents without having to manage numerous copies and versions. From a pedagogical perspective there is also evidence that the ability to add and manipulate rich media easily is associated with significant cognitive gains when using these types of document creation tool as opposed to more cumbersome, traditional desktop editors (Ice, 2008).

*From a pedagogical perspective there is also evidence that the ability to add and manipulate rich media easily is associated with significant cognitive gains.*

Moving beyond the relatively simple document creation application described above allows us to envision the full potential of Cloud Computing. The Open Science Grid (http://www.opensciencegrid.org/) is a multi-institutional initiative, funded by the National Science Foundation and Department of Energy, that provides scientists with interconnected computing infrastructure to carry out complex computations. Previously this type of initiative would have required either supercomputers or large network arrays at a single institution. Now, through placing dispersed computing functions across a grid, 30 participating institutions are able to access unprecedented computational capabilities for a fraction of the cost associated with a locally hosted solution.

A more pragmatic application of SaaS can be seen in initiatives such as North Carolina State University's Virtual Computing Lab (http://vcl.ncsu.edu/)—a service that allows faculty and students to access relatively high-cost implementations such as Solidworks, Matlab, and a variety of other programs on a grid-oriented basis, thus reducing the need for physically located services. The benefit of grid implementations can also be seen in Mathematica's new software release that allows user groups to create parallel computing solutions on demand. Previously this type of architecture would have been intensive in terms of requisite IT labor costs, thus making collaboration for all but highly funded projects cost prohibitive (Wolfram Research, 2008).

Though typically thought of in terms of a product creation, SaaS is also being leveraged for administrative functions in higher education. As an example, student information systems, enrollment portals and campus-wide notification systems have traditionally been silo-type functions with little or no cross-platform compatibility. As Merante (2009) points out, these systems are typically internally focused and based on the one-way communication strategies of the 1990s. However, through API integration, many institutions are now starting to tie their student enrollment management systems to social networking applications such as Facebook, MySpace, and Twitter.

A more comprehensive model can also be seen in systems such as Blackboard Connect (http://www.blackboardconnect.com/), which aggregates existing data across systems and builds a relational model that allows for a unified delivery system. From there, institutions can automate enrollment follow-ups, monitor customer care-oriented functions, propagate emergency messaging, and promote social networking on a selective basis. As with all SaaS implementations, this type of product is infinitely scalable and provides for robust backend analytics at a significantly reduced cost over comparable locally hosted solutions.

## Future Issues and Emerging Technologies

### Ubiquitous Access

While Cloud applications can provide powerful, on-demand capabilities, they are limited by the end-users' access to adequate connectivity. In rural areas or restricted environments (e.g., airplanes, firewalled work facilities, etc.) this can be an impediment to adoption.

However, a new generation of applications such as Adobe AIR, JavaFX, and Microsoft Silverlight are providing a bridge by creating the means to deploy traditional Web-based browsing experiences in a desktop environment. By stripping away the browser chrome and exposing the runtime in a lightweight skin, these applications allow for a desktop version of an online application that is fully functional without the need for connectivity. The end product is what is known as a Rich Internet Application (RIA)—an application that integrates the best features of Web tools with the robustness of traditional desktop applications

The practical application of this technology is that it allows for anywhere, anytime usage of an application that can be stored locally while no connectivity is available, and synchronization with the online version at a later time. Another use case might be when a user wants to load significant local assets to an application without consuming current bandwidth. In this case the user could load a large asset onto the desktop version and then allow it to upload at a later time—a functionality that is currently available through the Share desktop utility (http://tinyurl.com/bgkztk).

Though promising, and currently being utilized in business and personal productivity applications (see http://tinyurl.com/csrkwt for numerous examples), there are still significant technical problems to be overcome. Earlier in this chapter, the Buzzword document editor was presented as an example of a SaaS application. On the Buzzword discussion board, there is significant talk about the benefits of creating a desktop version of this application, thus allowing collaboration by authors who may temporarily be without connectivity. Though the developers of Buzzword have publicly expressed their intent to move in this direction they note that issues with version matching will be problematic and require some significant technical hurdles to be overcome. However, it is expected that within the next one to two years, many of these problems will be resolved and an age of true ubiquity will have arrived—at least from an application perspective. Populations that will likely benefit from innovation in this area are diverse and include individuals who live in areas (mostly rural) that have poor connectivity, frequent travelers who may experience periods of time in which productivity is limited by their inability to access online applications, and deployed military who can share characteristics of both of the aforementioned groups.

From a hardware perspective the age of ubiquity is already upon us in the form of mobile access. Within the past few years, mobiles have became increasingly robust, offering the ability to record audio and video, increased storage, Web browsing, and email. Coupled with markedly increased speed, via 3G and 4G networks and wifi, the range of applications that can be deployed to mobile has equaled or surpassed desktop applications of a decade ago (Johnson, Levine & Smith, 2009).

Historically, one of the biggest problems confronting mobile learning has been the issue of cross-platform extensibility. Unlike the desktop/laptop market, which is dominated by three operating systems (Windows, Mac, and Linux), the mobile market is highly segmented with numerous idiosyncratic operating systems. However, recently device makers have been responding to calls to allow for the development of third-party applications and the uptake has been rapid. In mid-2008, Apple launched the App Store for the Apple iPhone, and less than six months later more than 10,000 such applications were offered. The Android platform developed by Google and the Open Handset Alliance was marketed in October 2008 and quickly attracted a developer community that is growing rapidly. At the 2009 Mobile World Conference, Adobe, Fox Mobile, Intel, and Nokia discussed collaborating through the Open Screen Project Fund to encourage developers to adopt common applications for distribution to the approximately 800 mobile devices that have been shipped with Flash.

Though segmentation still exists, the above efforts to allow for broader dissemination of applications across mobile platforms is indicative of an eventual convergence in the mobile market. From an educational perspective, the benefits of reaching this nexus would be ubiquity across mobile platforms, which, when combined with Cloud applications, will allow for consumption and creation of content in a seamless manner, regardless of where a student is located or the platform they choose to utilize. Notably, the ability to provide this type of tight integration will probably not be a choice for institutions in an increasingly market-driven landscape. In a 2008 survey of 280,000 school pupils, the ability to utilize Web 2.0 services across a variety of devices was viewed as being of the greatest value (Prabhu, 2009). Another survey by the Pew Internet & American Life Project predicts that by the year 2020, most of the world's population will be using mobile devices as their primary means of connecting to the Internet (Rainie & Anderson, 2008). Thus, if institutions are to attract and retain students in an increasingly competitive market, provisioning for mobile learning will be considered a strategic priority, not an amenity. In fact, in many parts of the world, such as Japan, young people have already adopted mobile devices as their primary means of connecting with the Internet, no longer seeing a need for cumbersome laptops.

Moving in the opposite direction, there are indications that media from traditionally online sources will become more common in the 'living-room' environment. At the 2009 National Association of Broadcasters trade show, Adobe, Intel, Broadcom, and NXP announced plans to produce chips for TVs and set-top boxes that include Flash technology. The new devices with Flash chips would be able to play Flash videos and games on TVs that are connected to the Internet (Martin, 2009). The result of this initiative would thus be an extension of the Open Screen Project in that it would allow the same content that was consumed, through Flash, on desktops, laptops, and mobile devices to be consumed through more graphically robust televisions.

> *If institutions are to attract and retain students in an increasingly competitive market, provisioning for mobile learning will be considered a strategic priority, not an amenity.*

## Personal Webs, Serious Games, Semantics, and 'Talking Things'

Until this point, we have discussed existing technologies or extensions thereof. Now, at the end of this chapter, some cutting-edge applications will be considered.

### Personal Webs

Earlier in this chapter the creation of mashups to aggregate Web 1.0 applications was discussed. With the proliferation of information and Web 2.0 applications a new form of mashup is starting to emerge in what is referred to as Personal Webs. As RSS feeds began to become more mundane the need to view relevant information in a coherent fashion became apparent. Early initiatives such as iGoogle allowed users to aggregate blogs, custom widgets, and feeds from their favorite media. More recently AIR-based applications such as TweetDeck and Skimmer have allowed for the aggregation of social media such as Facebook, Twitter, Blogger, Flickr, and YouTube. In the case of Nomee, this capability has also incorporated the blog reader and widget aggregation found in iGoogle.

Moving forward, the NMC/ELI *Horizon Report 2009* sees this as a technology that within two to three years will allow for the formation of individualized usage and learning spaces in which content can be saved, tagged, categorized, and multipurposed with ease for both social and professional purposes (Johnson, Levine, & Smith, 2009). From a learning perspective these types of environment will accelerate the pace of collaboration by allowing users to access and create materials through an invisible layer that is not dependent upon their understanding of the underlying technology. As an example, Delicious is a tool that allows for rapid bookmarking and categorization of online content, while Zotero adds the equivalent of a notecard to online resources. In the Personal Web the functions of these two tools would be combined to allow a newly created resource to reference the Delicious object automatically while also automatically adding the Zotero reference information. Upon subsequent use or review by the creators or other individuals, each of these layers would then be exposed as a resource for further exploration. In addition, a variety of widgets could be used to cross-post newly acquired resources to YouTube, numerous blogging platforms, Flickr, Facebook, etc.

*Serious Games*

Pong, Pac Man, Donkey Kong, Doom, Grand Theft Auto, and World of Warcraft: regardless of your feelings about the merits of each of the foregoing, they represent the evolution of gaming that has paralleled the evolution of the computer. By general consensus, these all fall into the category of casual games, or games that are pursued purely for their entertainment value. Though, as Steinkuehler (2008) points out, the level of organization and cognitive engagement in massively multi-player online role-playing games (MMORPGs) frequently exceeds similar levels of engagement in traditional online and face-to-face academic activities. However, when learning occurs in casual games it is a by-product rather than an outcome of design features.

To move beyond incidental learning there must be a focus on specific and intentional cognitive outcomes to achieve serious, measurable, sustained changes in performance and behavior. As such, learning design represents a new, complex area of design for the gaming, in which designers must do more than create a virtual classroom space to be inhabited by avatars. Though there is merit to providing virtual spaces that allow for presentations, streaming, and inclusion of rich media for collaboration, to provide truly enhanced cognitive outcomes designers must work with teams of instructional technologists, content area experts and cognitive psychologists to focus on changing, in a predefined way, the beliefs, skills, and/or behaviors of those who will play the game, while preserving the entertainment aspects to insure continued engagement (Dondlinger, 2007).

> *To move beyond incidental learning there must be a focus on specific and intentional cognitive outcomes to achieve serious, measurable, sustained changes in performance and behavior.*

Forterra's OLIVE (http://forterrainc.com/) is a virtual world training environment that allows for incorporation of Web 2.0 technologies to create a richer learning environment. Through importing social networking functions and information, users are able to create profiles that include information about personal areas of expertise and interest, allowing them to locate colleagues with similar or complementary talents and skills. When combined with presence technologies, which help users know who is in-world with them, these technologies can help accelerate the development of social presence through rich, immersive experiences. As the Forterra platform has been widely used for delivery of military, medical, emergency response, and retail training, the ability to develop rich personas has significantly impacted the ability of learners to interact with each other in a more fluid manner, given their deeper understanding of other participants whom they have never met in person (Derryberry, 2008).

Looking forward, we can expect educational gaming to follow the path of realism that has begun to emerge in entertainment-based gaming environments. This will include more advanced avatars, with the ability of owners to express emotions through elaborate gestures and subtle facial movements. While at first glance this may appear extraneous to learning, it is in fact a means of further enhancing the development of social presence and therefore the sense of community in general. However, avatar enhancement is not the only means of enriching virtual worlds and simulations. The ability to import even more personalized data will drastically impact the way in which participants interact with each other in the near future (Derryberry, 2008).

Though there is still no clear picture of what this type of enhancement will consist of, many visionaries believe it will certainly include a superimposition of the aforementioned Personal Web onto virtual worlds and potentially the ability of an avatar generated in the Personal Web space to enter and exit any virtual world or simulation. The significance of this later capability is that it would allow not only for the avatar to move highly detailed information into a given virtual environment, but also transfer information from other environments. Through this process, when avatars meet they will be able to learn about their owners *and* about previous experiences of the other avatar that may be of interest to them, thus perpetuating incidental learning outcomes through comparison of prior virtual experiences.

*Semantics*

Anyone who has ever Googled a term and received a reply that reads something to the effect of "Displaying results 1–10 of 2,347,892" knows the frustration of trying to find specific information on the Web. Though advanced filters and arcane methods for narrowing search results exist, the Web still remains a fairly hostile environment for the average user. In large part, this is due to search algorithms that rely largely on identification of key words. As an example, a search for "Big Bang Theory" would likely yield some combination of results from cosmology and the popular American television show.

Using latent semantic analysis, the next generation of search engines will be able to ingest complex sentences instead of key words. The by-product will be more precisely focused search results. Using the above example, a user might enter a phrase such as "Actors in the Big Bang Theory." The returned data would then produce sites where relevant data related to the series could be found and exclude cosmological data that would be of no value in this case.

Similar to contemporary object-oriented programming language, semantic analysis is reliant on defining data in terms of classes with attributes and instances. The vision of the semantic-aware applications builds upon this concept by refining these ontologies through comparisons of associated metadata. Currently there are two approaches for developing semantic applications. One, the bottom-up approach, is problematic in that it assumes metadata will be added to each piece of content to include information about its context; tagging at the concept level, if you will. The top-down approach appears to have a far greater likelihood of success, as it focuses on developing natural language search capability that can make those same determinations without any special metadata (Johnson, Levine, & Smith, 2009).

Though the NMC/ELI *Horizon Report 2009* indicates that semantically aware applications are not likely to become mainstream for four to five years, a few cutting-edge prototypes are currently being utilized. Though still undergoing refinement, these applications demonstrate the potential power of semantic applications for both formal and informal learning.

Developed from the ground up to address specific needs in education, Common Library (http://commonlibrary.org) is the first standards-based content management system to enable true collaborative potential through the integration of content development and social networking. The Common Library latent semantic search engine defines a unique and powerful aspect of the application. In the current 2.0 implementation of the system, the metadata and content of each learning object are compared against defined standards systems. This higher-order logic enables Common Library to suggest interconnections dynamically between content items and applicable state standards, providing immediate value for users in the school-pupil educational market. This functionality also defines the potential for constructing dynamic relationships between state standard systems that evolve over time. The implementation of search and aggregate technology generates references that feed new granularly addressable connections between content and curriculum structures as more is learned about a specific users' requirements.

The Calais Web Service (http://www.opencalais.com/) automatically creates rich semantic metadata submitted in under a second. Using natural language processing, machine learning and other methods, Calais analyzes documents and finds the entities within it. Moving beyond classic entity identification, Calais returns the facts and events hidden within text as well. This metadata gives users the ability to build maps, graphs or networks, linking documents to people to companies to places to products to events to geographies and a host of other criteria. These maps (or other products) can then be used to improve site navigation, provide contextual syndication, tag and organize content, create structured folksonomies, filter news feeds, or analyze content.

TripIt (http://www.tripit.com), a social semantic-aware application for travelers, organizes travel plans and makes useful connections. By forwarding as a confirmation email from any travel provider, TripIt automatically creates an itinerary by interpreting and organizing the information in the email according to its semantic context. Though backend tweaking may be required to suit individual preferences, the time savings provided by the initial return can be highly beneficial to the majority of users.

These types of applications will allow learners to refine searches and find relevant information among the virtual flood of media that is being generated on a daily basis, by automatically inferring intent from content and context. In addition, there are two greater implications to the evolution of semantic applications. First, these applications will provide users with the ability to see not only existing connections but connections that are invisible to current search algorithms and would otherwise take months or possibly years to uncover (Johnson, Levine, & Smith, 2009). Second, semantic analysis could analyze data sets to find similarities and suggest active collaboration on topics between creators who might previously have been unaware of each other's work (Jain, 2008).

*'Talking Things'*

Every human being is surrounded by 1000—5000 things (Dodson, 2008). The combinations are innumerable, and consist of everything from home/office furnishings to food to automobiles to pets to other people. However, humans are only partially aware of the things themselves let alone the relationships between them—a fact that is painfully apparent to anyone who has ever misplaced their car keys or experienced the painful process of moving house. How many times have we thought that it would be nice if a misplaced item could talk and identify its location?

The Internet of Things is a concept that seeks to give all objects abilities analogous to speech. The lowly barcode has been with us several decades and conveys some of this capability; it allows a cashier to ascertain price rapidly and luggage handlers (hopefully) to direct our bag to the correct flight. More recently barcodes have been paired with quick response technology and placed on static advertisements (e.g., posters, flyers, displays, etc.) to allow smartphone users to take a picture of the barcode and automatically receive more information about the product.

> The Internet of Things is a concept that seeks to give all objects abilities analogous to speech.

Moving beyond barcodes, radio frequency identification (RFID) tags, GPS chips, and smartcards have the ability to convey not only rudimentary information about an object but a history of where the object has been and other objects it has been in contact with. In turn, this interaction with other tagged objects will allow for the compilation of complex histories of relationships and the creation of predictive models that can be used to form a holistic portrait of places, events, and group dynamics (Johnson, Levine, & Smith, 2009; Jean-Baptiste, 2008). At a more mundane level, an Internet of Things would allow an individual with a GPS tracking program such as Lattitude (http://www.google.com/latitude/intro.html) installed on a mobile device to ascertain information about their surroundings that had been obtained from tagged objects that currently exist in that environment or had previously passed through it.

Conclusion

*A Vision of the Future*

In this chapter several new and emerging technologies have been explored in a cursory fashion. One question remains: how will they all be applied to future learning environments? Let us assume that we are in the year 2015 (by which time the sources cited in this review believe that all of the covered technologies will have become part of our everyday lives) and worldwide groups of schoolteachers are working on a global warming project in conjunction with institutions of higher education. Elementary and high school students, in each of the participating classrooms, take temperature, precipitation, carbon dioxide, methane, and other readings in their local environments on mobile devices. If these students are in rural areas where access is not available, the readings are stored in local applications. Smart tags at the data collection sites will record the interactions and provide locating and geographically relevant historical data to the same mobile devices. The data is then transferred to a central repository where it is tagged, compiled, and related to similar data sets provided by other groups of students. Additionally, the data collected will be refined by GPS markers to contextualize it geographically and compare it to normative historical values.

Students will then be able to create personalized presentations of their findings and aggregate relevant resources in their personal spaces. Semantic scans of the media produced will help suggest pathways for further exploration and suggest potential avenues for collaboration. Cooperating personnel at institutions of higher education will receive holistic maps of the data collected and produce on-demand drill-downs, which in turn they will supplement with expert insights or suggestions for further collaboration. In some instances this may include importation of data into virtual environments where simulations about future actions can be gamed out.

Findings will then be compiled into rich multimedia applications that can be disseminated across a full spectrum of devices for on-demand consumption by interested parties or as the foundation of a knowledge base. Geographically relevant information can also be linked to tagged objects for reference by individuals who may be interested in the relationship between a given location and associated data.

At first glance it may appear that in this environment the degree of automation will be such that there will be little room left for the instructor; a theme that has been proclaimed since the first automated training programs were developed. Just as those prophecies failed to come to fruition so it will be when the above scenario becomes mundane. However, the role of the instructor will need to change significantly.

In this text, the Community of Inquiry framework has been reviewed extensively (Garrison & Arbaugh, 2007) and it may provide the best guidance for how the role of the instructor will have to evolve into that of a facilitator. Specifically, the three roles defined in the teaching presence construct can serve as a guide. First, given the proliferation of technologies that are currently available and will become available in the near future, the ability to design and organize learning activities in a clear, concise manner will be essential. Second, even when adequate design elements are associated with an activity, keeping learners on task, identifying areas of agreement and disagreement, and encouraging continued exploration will become as much of an art as a prescription for learning. Finally, the ability to provide effective feedback about the methodologies utilized and conclusions reached will be imperative to insuring learner success and insuring cognitive resolution that results in highly applicable and portable knowledge.

### Adoption—Barriers and Necessity

From an institutional perspective SaaS and Web 2.0 applications in general can be viewed as both a blessing and a challenge. As discussed, these tools have the ability to provide a vast array of powerful and highly scalable applications at a fraction of the cost associated with locally hosted solutions. As such, they certainly meet the criteria for enhancing student satisfaction, faculty satisfaction, learning effectiveness, access, and cost effectiveness—the five pillars of quality effectiveness put forth by the Sloan Consortium (Moore, 2002). However, adoption of these technologies requires a significant paradigm shift on the part of institutions.

Moving applications and services into the Cloud will significantly change the role of many institutional stakeholders and force realignment of traditionally compartmentalized functions. Most directly impacted will be the role of IT personnel as progressive chief information officers transform their department's role in the institution. Over the last three decades IT departments have been transformed into an authoritarian structure that frequently has a governing voice over all other administrative layers in the institution through the tight control exerted on resource selection and allocation. With the ability to shift quickly from application to application, while avoiding extensive capitalized costs, the chief information officer's ability to justify high-level control over implementations will be significantly degraded. To be successful in a Cloud-based environment the role of IT will have to shift to one of resource monitoring, capacity analysis, utilization projections, and efficacy analysis (Wexler, 2009; Yanosky, 2008).

For faculty and instructional designers, one of the major obstacles to adoption may be overcoming the hype cycle. Originally conceived of by Gartner Research, Inc., the hype cycle is a construct that illustrates the phases a technology goes through before becoming mainstream. In the early phases a technology is created and its value is evangelized by innovators within an organization. However, because of problems typically related to technological complexity with implementation, a period of disillusionment tends to follow among the general population. After this a gradual enlightenment phase follows in which technological barriers are overcome and use cases are developed to illustrate practical applications of the technology. If successful, a productivity plateau will be reached in which adoption of the technology becomes relatively ubiquitous (Wagner & Davis, 2009).

Interestingly, the eventual successful implementation of a technology does not depend as much on an organization's innovators as with its early adopters. Though early adopters tend to look to innovators for ideas, they are more thoughtful and deliberate in their considerations, tending to avoid beta products, instead looking for applications that can be utilized with a moderate degree of effort and large effect size. Consisting of about 15 percent of the population in an organization (as compared to about 1 percent for innovators), it is the adoption by these individuals that will eventually influence the vast

VISIBILITY

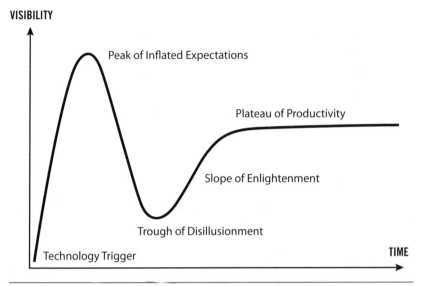

**Figure 8.1** The Hype Cycle

*Source:* Image created by Jeremy Kemp, licensed under Creative Commons Attribution-ShareAlike license versions 3.0, 2.5, 2.0, and 1.0

majority of other stakeholders to adopt a given technology. Thus, for instructional designers and innovators, it is imperative to focus energy and resources on helping early adopters develop lighthouse applications that can be showcased across the organization (Dublin, 2009).

Institutions that can quickly adapt to a Cloud/SaaS model will gain a financial advantage over their peers, as large data center operations can add node capability at a cost of less than half of that required for comparable onsite implementations (Hamilton, 2008). Though online programs are growing approximately five times faster than face-to-face programs (Allen & Seaman, 2008), the ability to control costs and thus tuition for the key adult learner demographic is vital to a program's ongoing success, especially in light of the overall decrease that is predicted in high school graduations over the next decade (Western Interstate Commission for Higher Education, 2008).

> *[S]uccessful institutions should not think in terms of a single technological paradigm shift, but rather adopting a culture of continual change.*

Significantly, adapting to the Cloud/SaaS implementations should not be considered an end point in the adoption process. The technologies covered in this chapter have been predicted to evolve over the next five years and assuredly many more advances will follow. As such, successful institutions should not think in terms of a single technological paradigm shift, but rather adopting a culture of continual change. Failure to do so will result in stagnation, lack of innovation, and, most importantly, an inability to meet the needs of learners.

*Final Thoughts*

When I was approached about writing this chapter, in the fall of 2008, I was both excited and apprehensive. The excitement was derived from the fact that about 50 percent of my time is consumed by beta testing, reading about emerging technologies for education and participating in professional forums related to the same. Thus, authoring a chapter on the future of technological innovation in education offered the perfect forum for elaborating on my thoughts. However, I was also quite anxious for a couple of reasons. First, when you are consumed with a topic as broad as this the thought of trying to condense your ideas to a few pages is overwhelming. Second, I clearly remember a doctoral seminar many years ago in which one of the major topics of discussion was how wrong an author was in her predictions about the future of technological innovation.

After much trepidation, I finally put metaphorical pen to paper and began outlining what I would put in this chapter. Though everyone who enjoys technology has the urge to engage in arm-waving of windmill proportions and start rambling on about augmented reality and neural implants, the truth is that if we are lucky we might be able to predict innovations within a two-year timeframe with a 50 percent degree of accuracy, with that number falling to 10 percent at five years. As Tancer (2008) points out, in his excellent work on human behavior and the Web, a new application can rise from obscurity to prominence in literally a matter of weeks. Attesting to the accuracy of this assertion is the fact that while writing this chapter I came very close to thoroughly exhausting the patience of the editors by insisting on changes and additions until eight days before I submitted a final draft.

So you are probably asking what business I had writing a chapter on emerging technologies when I thought from the outset that my predictions had only a modest to negligible chance of being right beyond a two-year time horizon. In response, I would refer back to that doctoral seminar in which we dissected the author's faulty predictions. Interestingly, the precise applications she predicted did indeed fail to gain traction; however, some of the conceptual frameworks she espoused have finally manifested, albeit in a different manner than she envisioned. Thus, my hope is that even if you do not see the specific technologies I have discussed rising to prominence, much of the theoretical basis will be visible and in some small way spur at least a few readers to continue imagining what the future may hold when this chapter has become irrelevant.

## TERMS AND DEFINITIONS

**Cloud Computing:** Hosted productivity applications that allow users to perform traditionally desktop-based tasks on lightweight devices such as netbooks or smart phones. *See also Web 2.0.*

**Hype cycle:** A construct that illustrates the phases a technology goes through before becoming mainstream. After an initial trigger, new technologies are hyped and a phase of inflated expectations is reached. As implementation issues become known, users become disillusioned, with a sustained productivity plateau reached after a gradual rebound via enlightenment and usage by early adopters.

**Internet of Things:** A vision of the future of the Web in which smart tags are embedded in virtually all objects in the physical world. Information gathered by these objects is then aggregated to form comprehensive data sets related to all interactions and physical locations. The Internet of Things is also referred to as Web 4.0.

**Personal Webs:** Individualized usage and learning spaces in which content can be saved, tagged, categorized, and multipurposed with ease for both social and professional purposes

**Rich Internet Application (RIA):** Web applications that have some of the robust characteristics of desktop applications, typically delivered by way of proprietary Web browser plug-ins or independently via sandboxes or virtual machines. Languages such as

Adobe AIR, JavaFX, and Microsoft Silverlight are frameworks commonly used for developing RIAs. RIAs can be developed for online deployment or desktop deployment with synchronization with SaaS counterparts.

**Semantic Web:** An evolving standard that seeks to relate not just key words and meta tags, but the relation between the same that will allow information to be contextualized. Also referred to as Web 3.0.

**Serious games:** Games or gaming environments that move beyond incidental learning and focus on specific and intentional cognitive outcomes to achieve serious, measurable, sustained changes in performance and behavior or serve as a catalyst for the achievement of higher-order thought.

**Software as a Service (SaaS):** Software deployed through data centers to end-user devices, as opposed to local hosting. Though some differences exist with respect to enterprise-level deployments (e.g., hosted email servers, client information systems, etc.), this term is often used interchangeably with Cloud Computing.

**Web 1.0:** The first iteration of the modern Web. Defined by a browser-based experience in which text wraps around graphics. Characterized by static webpages with users given little to no ability to modify content.

**Web 2.0:** A designation given to robust Web-based applications that allow users to create or modify original content. Social networking tools such as Twitter, Facebook, and Ning and productivity solutions such as Adobe Buzzword and Google Docs are representative of Web 2.0 platforms. Because the software is hosted, the perception of infinite scalability, elimination of upfront costs, and elimination of reliance on installed software are characteristics of Web 2.0 environments.

## QUESTIONS FOR REFLECTION AND REVIEW

1. What factors influenced technological adoption after the 2001 dot.com collapse?
2. How did rapid content creation influence the emergence of Web 2.0 technologies?

3. What are some of the benefits of SaaS/Cloud Computing?

4. What are some of the barriers to ubiquitous access? What new/emerging technologies offer solutions to these challenges?

5. What are some of the factors that lead to disillusionment with new technologies?

6. How will SaaS/Cloud Computing influence the way in which instructional designers think about learning environments? How are these types of changes managed from instructional design, faculty, and administrative perspectives?

7. Personal Webs have the potential significantly to influence the way in which information is utilized and knowledge constructed; however, it is possible that they could also have a negative impact on collaboration if not properly managed. Reflect on the discussion of Personal Webs and describe some considerations for faculty and/or instructional designers when these technologies become prevalent.

8. The special case of leveraging technologies such as Adobe AIR, JavaFX, and Microsoft Silverlight to build RIAs that have both desktop and online components was discussed in this chapter. Envision an application, of your own design, that utilizes this framework. Describe the application and, from a pedagogical perspective, why you believe it would be effective.

9. Describe an assignment that would leverage the capabilities of an Internet of Things.

10. The technologies described in this chapter have the potential dramatically to alter the way information is acquired, integrated, and utilized. Reflect upon how you see some of these changes manifesting. Will the new environments that evolve require us to rethink the frameworks that describe how technology-mediated learning occurs? If so, how? If not, why?

### Significant Contributor

**Terry Anderson** is Professor and Canada Research Chair in Distance Education at Athabasca University—Canada's Open University. He has published widely in the area of distance education and educational technology and has co-authored or edited six books and numerous

papers. He is active in provincial, national and international distance education associations and is a regular presenter at professional conferences. He teaches educational technology courses in Athabasca University Master's and Doctorate of Distance Education programs. His research has focused on interaction and its use and impact in distance education contexts. Beginning with audioconferencing, he has moved with the technology through studies on videoconferencing, immersive worlds and most recently application of social software and Web 2.0 technologies to distance contexts. He also maintains a keen interest in professional development and especially those forms accessible at a distance. He organized the first ever virtual conference, in conjunction with the ICDE Bangkok Conference in 1992. He is the Director of CIDER—the Canadian Institute for Distance Education Research (cider.athabascau.ca)—and Editor of *The International Review of Research on Distance and Open Learning* (*IRRODL*, www.irrodl.org). The complete text of his most recent edited book, *The Theory and Practice of Online Learning* (2nd edn), is available as an open access resource at: http://www.aupress.ca/books/Terry_Anderson.php. This text was the winner of the 2009 Charles E. Wedemeyer Award for the Outstanding Book of 2008, awarded by the Distance Learning Community of Practice of the University Continuing Education Association. His blog, Virtual Canuck, is accessible at: terrya.edublogs.org.

## References

Allen, E. & Seaman, J. (2008). Staying the course: Online education in the United States, 2008. *The Sloan Consortium: Babson Survey Research Group.* Retrieved December 12, 2008 from: http://www.sloan-c.org/publications/survey/pdf/staying_the_course.pdf.

Anderson, T. (2008). Open education resources & a good education system. Keynote address at the 14th Annual Sloan-C International Conference on Online Learning, Orlando, November.

Armbrust, M., Fox, A., Griffith, R., Joseph, A., Katz, R., Konwinski, A., Lee, G., Patterson, D., Rabkin, A., Stoica, I., & Zaharia, M. (2009). Above the clouds: A Berkeley view of Cloud computing. Retrieved February 16, 2009 from: http://d1smfj0g31qzek.cloudfront.net/abovetheclouds.pdf.

Derryberry, A. (2008). The power and benefit of using virtual worlds for real world collaboration, learning, productivity, and innovation. Retrieved April 15, 2009 from: http://imserious.typepad.com/imserious/files/white_paper_collab_072508.pdf.

Dodson, S. (2008). The Net shapes up to get physical. *Guardian*, October 16. Retrieved December 4, 2008 from: http://www.guardian.co.uk/technology/2008/oct/16/internet-of-things-ipv6.

Dondlinger, M. (2007). Educational video game design: A review of the literature. *Journal of Applied Educational Technology*, 4(1), 21–31.

Dublin, L. (2009). The learning management system research symposium. Presentation at the ELearning Guild Annual Gathering, Orlando, March.

Freire, P. (1970). *Pedagogy of the oppressed.* New York: Herder and Herder.

Garrison, D.R. & Arbaugh, J.B. (2007). Researching the community of inquiry framework: Review, issues, and future directions. *Internet and Higher Education*, 10(3), 157–172.

Hamilton, J. (2008). Cost of power in large-scale data centers. Retrieved January 27, 2009 from: http://perspectives.mvdirona.com/2008/11/28/CostOfPowerInLargeScaleDataCenters.aspx.

Hill, M. & Dudley, J. (2006). Do the mixed-up movie mash. *Courier Mail* [Australia], March 9, 17.

Ice, P. (2008). Using online collaborative document editors to enhance student satisfaction and cognitive presence outcomes. *Sloan-C Effective Practice.* Retrieved March 10, 2009 from: http://www.sloan-c.org/node/1243.

Jain, R. (2008). Multimedia semantic Web. Keynote address at the 7th International Semantic Web Conference, Karlsruhe, October.

Jean-Baptiste, W. (2008). *Nanocomputers and swarm intelligence.* London: ISTE.

Johnson, L., Levine, A., & Smith, R. (2009). *The 2009 Horizon Report.* Austin, TX: New Media Consortium.

McAfee, A. (2006). Enterprise 2.0: The dawn of emergent collaboration. *MIT Sloan Management Review*, 47(3), 21–28.

Martin, R. (2009). Adobe brings Flash to TV. Retrieved April 23, 2009, from: http://www.xchangemag.com/articles/509/adobe-brings-flash-to-tv.html.

Merante, J. (2009). Integrating enrollment management strategies and digital tactics during demographic changes and economic turbulence. Presentation at the Chronicle Technology Forum, Washington, DC, April.

Moore, J. (2002). *Elements of quality: The Sloan-C framework.* Needham, MA: SCOLE (Sloan Center for Online Education).

Morrison, J. & Macquart, D. (2006). World's youth connect through Global Nomads Group: An interview with GNG's David Macquart. *Innovate*, 2(4). Retrieved February 1, 2009 from: http://www.innovateonline.info/index.php?view=article&id=219.

Prabhu, M. (2009). Forum calls for better use of data in education. *eSchool News*, 12(4), 14.

Rainie, L. & Anderson, J. (2008). The future of the Internet III. Retrieved December 29, 2008 from: http://www.pewinternet.org/Reports/2008/The-Future-of-the-Internet-III.aspx?r=1

Rossett, A. (2002). *The ASTD e-learning handbook: Best practices, strategies, and case studies for an emerging field.* New York: McGraw-Hill.

Steinkuehler, C.A. (2008). Cognition and literacy in massively multiplayer online games. In J. Coiro, M. Knobel, C. Lankshear, & D. Leu (Eds.), *Handbook of research on new literacies.* Mahwah, NJ: Erlbaum.

Swan, K., Garrison, D.R., & Richardson, J. (2009). A constructivist approach to online learning: The community of inquiry framework. In C.R. Payne (Ed.), *Information technology and constructivism in higher education: Progressive learning frameworks.* Hershey, PA: IGI Global.

Tancer, B. (2008). *Click: What millions of people are doing online and why it matters.* New York: Hyperion.

Tapscott, D. & Williams, A. (2006). *Wikinomics: How mass collaboration changes everything.* New York: Portfolio.

Wagner, E. (2008). Delivering on the promise of elearning. Retrieved December 3, 2008 from: http://www.adobe.com/education/pdf/elearning/Promise_of_eLearning_wp_final.pdf.

Wagner, E. & Davis, B. (2009). Where eLearning is coming from. Presentation at the ELearning Guild Annual Gathering, Orlando, March.

Western Interstate Commission for Higher Education (2008). *Knocking at the college door: Projections of high school graduates by state and race/ethnicity 1992–2022.* Boulder, CO: WICHE.

Wexler, J. (2009). IT trembles over mobile management. Retrieved April 14, 2009 from: http://www.networkworld.com/newsletters/wireless/2009/041309wireless1.html?nlhtwless=ts_041309&nladname=041309wirelessal.

Wikipedia (2009). Web 2.0. Retrieved January 9, 2009 from: http://en.wikipedia.org/wiki/Web_2.0.

Wolfram Research (2008). Wolfram Research defines frontiers of high-performance computing with Mathematica 7. Retrieved December 19, 2008 from: http://www.wolfram.com/news/m7hpc.html.

Yanosky, R. (2008). From users to choosers: The Cloud and the changing shape of enterprise authority. In R. Katz (Ed.), *The tower and the Cloud: Higher education in the age of Cloud Computing.* Denver, CO: Educause.

# 9

# BLENDED LEARNING

## DR. NORMAN D. VAUGHAN
### Assistant Professor
### Mount Royal University

## Introduction

> Blended learning is the organic integration of thoughtfully selected and complementary face-to-face and online approaches and technologies.
>
> (Garrison & Vaughan, 2008, p. 148)

The idea of blending different learning experiences has been in existence ever since humans started thinking about teaching (Williams, 2003). What has recently brought this term into the limelight is the infusion of Web-based technologies into the learning and teaching process (Clark, 2003). These technologies have created new opportunities for students to interact with their peers, faculty, and content in online courses and programs. This chapter describes: blended learning environments in higher education, the opportunities and challenges associated with these environments from the student, faculty, and administrative perspectives, and how the Community of Inquiry (CoI) framework (Garrison, Anderson, & Archer, 2001) can be used to design online blended learning courses and programs.

## Background

Blended learning is often defined as the combination of face-to-face and online learning (Williams, 2002). Ron Bleed, the former Vice-Chancellor of Information Technologies at Maricopa College, argues that this is not a sufficient definition for blended learning as it simply implies 'bolting' technology onto a traditional course, using technology as an add-on to teach a difficult concept or adding supplemental information. He suggests that, instead, blended learning should be viewed as an opportunity to redesign the way that courses are developed, scheduled and delivered in higher education through a combination of physical and virtual instruction, "bricks and clicks" (Bleed, 2001). The goal of these redesigned courses should be to join the best features of in-class teaching with the best features of online learning to promote active, self-directed learning opportunities for students with added flexibility (Garnham & Kaleta, 2002). This sentiment is echoed by Garrison and Vaughan (2008), who state that "blended learning is the organic integration of thoughtfully selected and complementary face-to-face and online approaches and technologies" (p. 148). A survey of e-learning activity by Arabasz, Boggs, & Baker (2003) found that 80 percent of all higher education institutions and 93 percent of doctoral institutions offer hybrid or blended learning courses (p. 2).

With the development and growth of Web-based synchronous communication tools, Power (2008) argues that a campus-based definition of blended learning needs to be expanded. He has coined the term Blended Online Learning Design (BOLD) to describe the simultaneous and complementary integration and implementation of an asynchronous-mode learning environment (i.e., a course management system, or CMS) and a synchronous desktop conferencing environment (i.e., virtual classroom).

Campus-based environments have their roots in traditional higher education systems where classes have been delivered by faculty in synchronous lecture settings. Initially, blended learning has been used

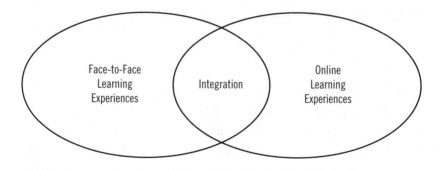

**Figure 9.1** Campus-Based Blended Learning Approach

to complement these synchronous lectures through the use of asynchronous discussion forums and learning management systems such as Blackboard and Web CT. With the advent of synchronous tools, such as Elluminate Live! and Horizon Wimba, opportunities have been created to provide students at a distance with both synchronous and asynchronous communication possibilities. In this chapter, these educational contexts are referred to as *online* blended learning environments in order to distinguish them from the campus-based versions.

## Opportunities and Challenges

The adoption of blended learning environments in higher education poses a series of opportunities and challenges for students, faculty and administration. This section provides an overview to the benefits and drawbacks of both campus-based (see Garrison & Vaughan, 2008) and online blended learning (see Power, 2008), from student, faculty, and administrative perspectives.

### *Student Perspective*

*Opportunities*
Students who have been involved in campus-based blended learning courses are generally very positive about their experiences. At the University of Wisconsin, Milwaukee campus, 80 percent of the students who took a blended learning course indicated they thought the experience was worthwhile and that they would recommend a course offered in a blended format to others (Aycock, Garnham, & Kaleta, 2002). The principal reason that students gave for their high level of satisfaction was the time flexibility provided by a blended format (see Table 9.1). Time flexibility was defined as the ability to control the pace of one's learning, the convenience of scheduling coursework, and a decrease in time spent commuting (Garnham & Kaleta, 2002). Table 9.1 summarizes the key findings from the University of Wisconsin student survey.

**Table 9.1** Survey Questions Administered to Students (n=282) in Blended Courses at the University of Wisconsin, Milwaukee, at the End of the Spring 2001 Semester

| STATEMENT | AGREE | DISAGREE | NO OPINION |
|---|---|---|---|
| I could control the pace of my own learning | 69% | 19% | 12% |
| I could organize my time better | 77% | 11% | 12% |
| The time I spent online would better have been spent in class | 16% | 67% | 17% |
| There should be more courses like this | 61% | 16% | 23% |

*Source*: Garnham & Kaleta, 2002; reproduced with permission

TIME FLEXIBILITY

The students surveyed indicated that they liked to be able to control the pacing and location of their learning. They appreciated the blended design because it provided them with the flexibility to work from home. Working from home was perceived much more positively than working from other locations, such as campus computer labs or workplaces (Garnham & Kaleta, 2002).

The blended design also provided students with a much greater range of course scheduling options because of the reduction in synchronous meeting sessions. This convenience of scheduling is increasingly important for the growing number of students who have multiple responsibilities such as work and family commitments.

In addition, a study by the National Clearinghouse for Commuter Programs in the United States (1999) found that 87 percent of all postsecondary students in the United States do not live in institution-owned housing on campus and thus commute to get to school. The costs of commuting are steadily increasing, as are the challenges of finding an available parking space at higher education institutions.

IMPROVED STUDENT LEARNING OUTCOMES

Several research studies have demonstrated that blended learning designs contribute to improved learning outcomes for students (Twigg, 2003a; Dziuban, Hartman, Juge, Moskal & Sorg, 2005; Garnham &

Kaleta, 2002). In the United States, the Pew Foundation sponsored a study to investigate how large enrollment, introductory courses can be effectively redesigned using a blended format. The program involved 30 institutions: 20 of these reported improved learning outcomes and 10 reported no significant difference (Twigg, 2003b). In addition, 18 of the study institutions demonstrated a decrease in student drop–failure–withdrawal (DFW) rates compared to the face-to-face-only sections (out of 24 institutions which measured DFW changes).

The University of Central Florida has been involved in an ongoing evaluation of Web and Web-enhanced courses since the inception of its Distributed Learning Initiative in the fall of 1996 (Dziuban, Hartman, Moskal, Sorg, & Truman, 2004). These evaluation studies indicate that, on average, blended learning courses have higher success rates (percentage of students obtaining an A, B, or C) and lower withdrawal rates than their comparable face-to-face courses. The studies also show that student retention in blended courses is better than in totally online courses and equivalent to that of face-to-face courses.

Qualitative research studies at the University of Wisconsin in Milwaukee (Garnham & Kaleta, 2002) also suggest that students learn more in blended courses than they do in comparable traditional class sections. Teachers responsible for the blended sections report that students write better papers, perform better on exams, produce higher-quality projects, and are capable of more meaningful discussions on course material. Sands (2002, p. 1) states that because of the text-based nature of Web-based discussion forums and email, blended courses become "de facto writing intensive courses when the teachers work carefully to integrate the online and classroom components." Spika (2002) adds that the increased opportunities for self-directed learning in the blended model help students develop project- and time-management skills.

### Student Challenges

Studies at the University of Central Florida (Dziuban & Moskal, 2001) and the University of Wisconsin, Milwaukee (Garnham & Kaleta, 2002), indicate that students encounter a number of challenges with blended courses. The four key challenges identified are: the expectation that fewer classes meant less work, inadequate time management skills, problems with accepting responsibility for personal learning, and difficulty with more sophisticated technologies.

EXPECTATIONS
Students new to blended learning initially equate fewer in-person classes to less coursework. In addition, a number of these students do not perceive time spent in lectures as 'work,' but they definitely see time spent online as work, even if it is time they would have spent in class in a traditional course (Aycock et al., 2002).

TIME MANAGEMENT
Time management is a struggle for many higher education students. This struggle can become particularly acute in a blended online course where there is a lack of physical presence.

RESPONSIBILITY FOR LEARNING
Many first-year undergraduate students, who are away from home for the first time, are in the early stages of 'learning how to learn.' The notion of taking responsibility for one's own learning can be very difficult for students accustomed to being passive learners within a traditional lecture format. Initially, students may be unprepared for the active learning role they must play in a blended course.

TECHNOLOGY
Most technology-related problems that students encounter in blended online courses usually occur within the first weeks of the semester. These problems are usually related to the procedure for accessing the online material and resources (i.e., website address and log-on information). Problems that persist throughout the semester sometimes involve either downloading large files or accessing more sophisticated Web-based applications such as video clips (Aycock et al., 2002).

*Faculty Perspective*

*Benefits*
Faculty who have taught blended courses indicate that their teaching experiences were very positive. At the University of Wisconsin,

Milwaukee, 100 percent of the faculty members involved in a blended learning pilot project recommended using this approach to others and planned to teach a blended course again (Aycock et al., 2002). Reasons for this high level of satisfaction included: enhanced interaction with students, increased student engagement in learning, flexibility of the teaching and learning environment, and opportunities for continuous improvement.

ENHANCED TEACHER AND STUDENT INTERACTION

Initially, one of the major concerns expressed by faculty teaching blended courses at the University of Wisconsin was that they would become less connected with their students because of the decrease in face-to-face sessions (Aycock et al., 2002). In contrast, after teaching a blended course, faculty almost universally reported feeling more connected with their students and knowing them better. Faculty teaching blended courses at the University of Central Florida echoed these comments (Dziuban & Moskal, 2001). They indicated not only that more interaction occurred in their blended courses but that this interaction was of a higher quality than what they typically see in the face-to-face classroom. Aycock et al. (2002) suggest that this increased interaction is often fostered by teachers developing new ways to engage their students online and through the creation of online communities. Bleed (2001, p. 18) stresses how important this interaction is for restoring the "human moment in the educational process."

INCREASED STUDENT ENGAGEMENT IN LEARNING

Faculty who have taught blended courses have observed that students do a better job of writing, learning course material, mastering concepts, and applying what they have learned compared to students in their traditional sections (Aycock et al., 2002). They suggest that this improvement is due to students being more engaged in their learning process. This sentiment is captured in a comment from a faculty member at the University of Wisconsin who teaches blended courses: "My students have done better than I have ever seen; they are motivated, enthused and doing their best work" (Garnham & Kaleta, 2002, p. 3).

MORE FLEXIBLE TEACHING AND LEARNING ENVIRONMENT
Faculty at the University of Wisconsin indicate that they can accomplish course learning objectives more successfully within a blended course than within a traditional course because of the flexibility of the blended model (Garnham & Kaleta, 2002). The flexibility of time and the ability to use Web-based multimedia allow faculty to "develop solutions to course problems and to incorporate new types of learning activities that were not possible in traditional courses" (Aycock et al., 2002, p. 1).

THE ENVIRONMENT FORCES CONTINUOUS IMPROVEMENT
The blended model also allows teachers an ongoing opportunity to experiment with new approaches to learning and new types of educational technology. At the University of Central Florida, learning to use technology was cited as one of the outcomes that faculty liked most about teaching on the Web (Dziuban & Moskal, 2001).

*Challenges*
From a faculty perspective, the key challenges of teaching in a blended format are: the time commitment, lack of support for course redesign, difficulty in acquiring new teaching and technology skills, and the risk factors associated with this type of course (Voos, 2003; Dziuban & Moskal, 2001; Garnham & Kaleta, 2002).

TIME COMMITMENT
The increased time commitment involved in a blended course is regarded as the number one challenge by faculty (Dziuban & Moskal, 2001). Johnson (2002) states that planning and developing a large-enrollment, blended course takes two to three times the amount of time required to develop a similar course in a traditional format. Faculty at the University of Central Florida, who are considered 'Web veterans,' overwhelmingly indicate that a course with online components requires more time in both the development and weekly administrative duties than a similar course delivered face-to-face (Dziuban & Moskal, 2001). Despite this increase in workload, all the faculty members involved in a blended learning pilot program at the University of Wisconsin, Milwaukee, stated that they will teach these types of

courses again, as they believe their time was wisely invested in improving the learning environment for both students and themselves (Garnham & Kaleta, 2002).

PROFESSIONAL DEVELOPMENT SUPPORT

These faculty members also indicated that blended learning is not a 'solo' activity. In order to ensure a successful blended learning experience for students there must be faculty support for course redesign and learning new teaching and technology skills. The course redesign support involves assistance in deciding what course objectives can best be achieved through asynchronous online learning activities, what can best be accomplished in synchronous events and how to integrate these two learning environments (Dziuban et al., 2004). Faculty indicated that they needed to acquire new teaching skills such as how to foster online learning communities, facilitate online discussion forums, and address and manage students' online learning problems (Aycock et al., 2002).

In terms of technology, many faculty initially needed to overcome their own fears and resistance through 'hands-on' experience with various tools and applications. In addition, faculty are also challenged to provide 'frontline' technical support for their students. Faculty at both the University of Central Florida (Dziuban & Moskal, 2001) and the University of Wisconsin, Milwaukee (Aycock et al., 2002), are adamant that in order to overcome these support issues there must be an institutional professional development program for the development phase of a blended learning course and ongoing institutional support during the initial delivery phase (Voos, 2003).

RISK FACTORS

The major risk factors identified by faculty who have taught blended courses include: fear of losing control over the course, lower student evaluations, and an uneasiness about how this type of learning model fits into the university culture of teaching, research, and service (Dziuban & Moskal, 2001; Voos, 2003).

*Administrative Perspective*

*Benefits*

From an administrative perspective, blended learning presents opportunities to: enhance an institution's reputation, expand access to an
institution's educational offerings, and reduce operating costs.

ENHANCED INSTITUTIONAL REPUTATION

The opportunity to enhance an institution's reputation is often linked
to improving the quality of the institutional learning environment
for students and increasing student and
faculty satisfaction (Twigg, 2003b;
Garrison & Anderson, 2003). Heterick
and Twigg (2002) have found that
blended learning designs can positively
impact student learning when thoughtfully applied to support 'active learning pedagogies' and increased student
'time on task.' Voos (2003) suggests that

> [T]he ability of blended
> learning to support the
> convergence of online and
> residential instruction is
> "the single greatest
> unrecognized trend in
> higher education today."

blended designs can enhance student and faculty satisfaction with
learning when the design, the training and development, and the
systems and support are well organized. Graham Spanier, President of
Pennsylvania State University, boldly states that the ability of blended
learning to support the convergence of online and residential instruction is "the single greatest unrecognized trend in higher education
today" (cited in Young, 2002, p. 4). Bleed (2001) is also actively exploring how these types of courses can be used to recombine learning and
social experiences within the Maricopa Community College District
of Arizona.

EXPAND ACCESS TO THE INSTITUTION'S EDUCATIONAL OFFERINGS
AND INCREASE ENROLLMENTS

As previously mentioned, blended learning provides increased choice
and flexibility for students in the way that courses and entire programs
are delivered. Many students are now able to balance family and work
commitments with their academic studies as a result of this blended
model. Numerous higher educational institutions also hope that this

expanded access will translate into increased revenue streams but the results to date have been mixed (Carr, 2001).

COST-REDUCTION STRATEGIES

Many in higher education are currently asking the question: "How can we best serve our students in today's society in light of increased enrollments and decreased government funding?" (Bates & Poole, 2003, p. 24). Twigg (2003b) suggests that blended learning provides institutions with two principal cost-reduction strategies: either to increase student enrollments in courses with little or no change in course expenditures or to keep student enrollments the same while reducing the instructional resource costs for the course.

In the Pew course redesign study, coordinated by Twigg (2003b), the majority of the 30 institutions involved in the study selected the second option. They attempted to keep the same student enrollment numbers and reduce costs while maintaining quality. The predominant technique used to accomplish this objective was to reduce the time faculty and other instructional personnel spent on large enrollment courses by transferring a number of tasks to technology. This was achieved through the use of online course management systems, online automated assessments, online tutorials, shared resources, and staffing substitutions. These strategies are outlined in Table 9.2 and they allowed the study institutions to reduce course costs by about 40 percent on average, within a range of 20 to 84 percent (Twigg, 2003a).

One of the greatest cost savings currently attributed to blended learning is the reduction in space requirements. Prior to the deployment of blended course sections, the shortage of classroom space was so acute at the University of Central Florida that the university had to rent space at a nearby multiplex theater for classrooms during the day (Young, 2002). Through the deployment of blended courses, with a significant or total reduction in class time, the university was able to schedule two or three course sections in the same classroom where only one could be scheduled before. This then allowed the university to reduce the amount of rented space through the more efficient utilization of existing classrooms. Bleed (2001) states that reducing space costs may be the only way colleges and universities in the United States can keep up with the continuing population growth and the demands for lifelong learning.

**Table 9.2** Strategies for Using Technology to Reduce Costs in Blended Courses

| TECHNIQUE | DESCRIPTION |
| --- | --- |
| Course management systems | The course management systems played a central role in the majority of redesign projects. These systems reduced (and in some cases eliminated) the amount of time that faculty spent on non-academic tasks such as grade calculations, photocopying handouts, posting changes to the course schedule, sending out special announcements and updating course material for subsequent semesters. |
| Automated assessments | Over half of the projects used automated grading of exercises, quizzes, and tests. This dramatically reduced the amount of time faculty and/or teaching assistants spent on preparing quizzes as well as grading, recording, and posting results. |
| Tutorials | Online tutorials were used in a number of the course redesign projects. Faculty involved with these projects reported that students came to the lectures and the face-to-face tutorials more prepared to ask good questions. In addition, faculty and teaching assistants no longer had to present content in class which was already available online. This created more time for discussion and questions within the face-to-face sessions. |
| Shared resources | The use of shared resources across multiple sections of the same course allowed for significant savings of faculty time. This was usually achieved by having one common general resource website for all sections of a particular course. |
| Staffing substitutions | The substitution of graduate teaching assistants with lower-cost undergraduate learning assistants in these blended courses resulted in substantial cost savings (non-technology). |

*Source*: Twigg, 2003b

*Challenges*

There is an abundance of literature describing the challenges that higher education institutions face when attempting to incorporate technology into the teaching and learning environment (Cho & Berge, 2002; Twigg, 1999; Barone, 2001). The following issues can be particularly daunting when institutions attempt to adopt blended learning.

ALIGNMENT WITH INSTITUTIONAL GOALS AND PRIORITIES

Twigg (1999) suggests that blended learning can be effectively implemented only if an institution is committed to improving the quality of the student learning experience in a cost-effective manner. This implies that technology is viewed as a means of achieving this strategic goal and the institution is committed to integrating computing fully into the campus culture. Barone (2001) adds that this goal can be realized only if an institution's leaders demonstrate affirmative action through proper resource allocation and necessary policy revision. The course redesign study coordinated by Twigg (2003b) demonstrates that this strategic alignment can be a formidable challenge. Senior administrators in many of the study institutions were unable to create policy changes to increase enrollments in the blended sections and department chairs were unable to reduce seat time in these sections to the projected percentages. Resistance to organizational change was given as one of the main obstacles.

RESISTANCE TO ORGANIZATIONAL CHANGE

Resistance to organizational change in higher education is a well-documented phenomenon (Twigg, 1999; Barone, 2001). Change in post-secondary education is often compared to the 'turning of the *Titanic*.' Institutional bureaucracy and inertia can prevent changes in the curriculum, course structures and timetables, which are critical to the success of blended learning.

ORGANIZATIONAL STRUCTURE AND EXPERIENCE WITH
COLLABORATION AND PARTNERSHIPS

Lack of a collaborative organizational structure and internal partnerships can pose a formidable barrier to a blended learning initiative (Dziuban et al., 2005). Decisions must be made in a consultative fashion and communicated widely in order for a blended learning model to be successful (Barone, 2001). There must be significant cooperation through partnerships with students, faculty, instructional technology staff, faculty developers, and administrators in order to succeed (Twigg, 1999). In addition, there needs to be a commitment to assessing and communicating the impact of blended learning on student achievement, success, and satisfaction (Barone, 2001).

The next section of this chapter describes the Community of Inquiry (CoI) framework and how it can be used to design effective and efficient online blended learning environments.

*The Community of Inquiry (CoI) framework (Garrison & Anderson, 2003) has been instrumental in helping researchers and practitioners appreciate the core elements of online learning and what it takes to create and sustain collaborative communities.*

## Community of Inquiry

The Community of Inquiry (CoI) framework (Garrison & Anderson, 2003) has been instrumental in helping researchers and practitioners appreciate the core elements of online learning and what it takes to create and sustain collaborative communities. The CoI is a generic framework that directs attention to the process of constructing and confirming deep understanding. The three main elements of the CoI framework are social presence, cognitive presence, and teaching presence. Each of these elements and their overlap must be considered in the design and delivery of blended online learning activities and outcomes. Social presence is defined as the ability of participants to identify with the interests of the community (e.g., the course of study), communicate purposefully in a trusting environment, and develop interpersonal relationships by way of participants projecting their individual personalities. The CoI framework is about deep and meaningful learning experiences operationalized through cognitive presence. Cognitive presence is defined in terms of the practical inquiry model. Practical inquiry represents phases (problem, exploration, integration, and resolution) of a collaborative-constructive educational experience. The final element, teaching presence, provides the leadership that focuses and sustains a productive collaborative community. Teaching presence is responsible for the design, facilitation, and direction of the educational experience (Figure 9.2).

## Educational Design Considerations for Online Blended Learning Environments

This final section of the chapter focuses on educational design considerations for online blended learning courses and programs. These are learning environments where a combination of synchronous and

## Community of Inquiry

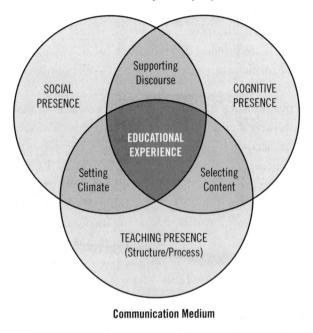

**Figure 9.2** Community of Inquiry Framework

*Source:* Garrison, Anderson, & Archer, 2000

asynchronous communication and information technologies (i.e., Web 2.0 tools) can be used to create communities of inquiry where participants are independent of campus and actively engaged in deep and meaningful learning. For example, social bookmarking applications can be used to share personal collections of Web-based resources to complete group projects. Blogs can facilitate student self-reflection and peer review of course assignments. Students can use wikis to summarize course discussions collaboratively, refine research papers, or even co-create online books. Social networking applications, such as Facebook and MySpace, can be used to extend the boundaries of the classroom to create online communities and discussions/debates that include past students, potential employers, and subject matter experts. Audio, graphic, and video files can now be created and shared through social media applications such as Podomatic, Flikr, and YouTube. These files and other data sources can then be recombined to create new meaning and interpretations by using mashup applications such as Intel's Mash

Maker and MIT's Piggy Bank. Synchronous technologies such as Skype and Elluminate Live! allow students to communicate and collaborate outside of the classroom. Moreover, virtual world applications such as Second Life provide opportunities for rich synchronous interaction in 3-D immersive worlds to support collaborative and creative project-based work.

Online communities of inquiry are places where all voices can be heard while testing and rejecting unproductive contributions. Historically, this has been the ideal of all learning environments in higher education. In order to help achieve this ideal, the CoI framework can be used to design an online blended learning course or program. This framework is based on an inquiry approach to learning. Inquiry learning is problem- or question-driven learning involving critical discourse, self-direction, research methods, and reflection throughout the learning experience. This process is outlined in the four phases of the Practical Inquiry model (see Table 9.3).

An online blended learning environment can be intentionally designed to use Web 2.0 tools to support the progression of inquiry through to resolution and/or application. This educational design consists of four interconnected phases:

**Table 9.3** Practical Inquiry Phases

| DESCRIPTION | CATEGORY/PHASE | INDICATORS |
|---|---|---|
| The extent to which learners are able to construct and confirm meaning through sustained reflection, discourse, and application within a critical community of inquiry. | 1 Triggering event | 1 Inciting curiosity and defining key questions or issues for investigation |
| | 2 Exploration | 2 Exchanging and exploring perspectives and information resources with other learners |
| | 3 Integration | 3 Connecting ideas through reflection |
| | 4 Resolution/application | 4 Applying new ideas and/or defending solutions |

1. Before a synchronous session
2. Synchronous session
3. After a synchronous session
4. Preparation for the next synchronous session.

*Before a Synchronous Session*

The first phase involves the use of communication and information technologies in advance of a synchronous session to 'plant the seeds' for triggering events that will then be more thoroughly defined within the actual synchronous session. Ausubel (1968) refers to these as "advance organizers" or anchoring events that provide entry points for connecting new information with the recall of prior related learning experiences. There are a variety of learning activities and related online tools that can be used to support this phase. They include the use of Web-based readings with an accompanying online survey, quiz, or discussion forum. This activity and several other examples are provided in Table 9.4.

The first priority is to establish online communication with the learners so that they are clear about the rationale and expectations for the pre-session assignments. This communication can be facilitated through a weekly course announcement, which can be transmitted through a learning management system (e.g., Blackboard) or via an RSS feed to a social network such as Facebook or a news aggregator application like Bloglines.

Teachers often require students to participate in a reading activity before a synchronous session. Traditionally, this activity involved reading from the course textbook. Online library resources and social bookmarking systems such as Del.icio.us and Edtags can now be used to provide students with access to relevant and engaging Web-based articles and resources. Some instructors also require students to find their own course-related articles and then post these resources to a social bookmarking network so that all members of the class can access and comment on these websites.

In addition, digital audio and video tools can be used to communicate with students before a synchronous event. For example, faculty can use podcasts (e.g., Podomatic), narrated PowerPoint presentations

**Table 9.4** Design Considerations before a Synchronous Session

| NATURE OF INQUIRY | LEARNING ACTIVITIES | WEB 2.0 TOOLS |
|---|---|---|
| **Learner** | **a) Reading/writing** | **i) Communication** |
| • Create a *triggering event* <br> • Advanced organizer <br> • Stimulate connections | • Pre-reading assignment or activity on a specified topic or issue <br> • Followed by a self-assessment quiz, survey, or discussion forum | • Announcement sent to students via a learning management system (e.g., Blackboard) or an RSS feed through a Social Networking Tool (e.g., Facebook) or News Aggregator Application (e.g., Bloglines) |
| **Teacher** | **b) Listening/Writing** | **ii) Posting or linking to pre-reading assignments** |
| • Determine learner's prior knowledge or experience with the topic or issue | • Auditory/visual presentation of information <br> • Followed by a self-assessment quiz, survey, or discussion forum activity | • Social bookmarking tools (e.g., Del.icio.us, Edtags) |
| | | **iii) Digital learning objects** |
| | | • Podcasts (e.g., Podomatic) <br> • PowerPoints (e.g., Slideshare) <br> • Videos (i.e. YouTube) |
| | | **iv) Self-assessment quizzes** |
| | | • Assessment tools (e.g., Moodle) |
| | | **v) Anonymous surveys** |
| | | • Survey tools (e.g., getfast.ca) |
| | | **vi) Discussion forum** |
| | | • Pre-class online discussion regarding questions and issue related to the required reading (e.g., Facebook, Ning) |

(e.g., Slideshare, Adobe Presenter), or video (e.g., YouTube) to communicate course concepts, scenarios, and case studies with students. The advantage of using these learning objects is that they allow students to listen and view course-related material at their own pace and as often as required to gain understanding.

Despite the ability to access learning material in a variety of formats there still exists the challenge of getting online students to engage in these pre-session activities meaningfully. Novak, Patterson, Gavrin, & Christian (1999) have used a survey or quiz tool to create triggering events for students in advance of a synchronous session. They have coined the term Just-in-Time Teaching (JiTT) to describe the process of getting students to read a textbook chapter or Web-based article and then respond to an online survey or quiz, shortly before a class. The instructor then reviews the student submissions 'just in time' to adjust the synchronous session in order to address the students' needs, identified by the survey or quiz results. A typical survey or quiz consists of four concept-based questions with the final question asking students: "What did you not understand about the required reading and what would you like me [the instructor] to focus on within the next synchronous session?" An alternative to this activity would be to construct an online discussion forum in a learning management system or social networking application like Facebook to allow students to post questions or issues related to the pre-session reading. This can be a powerful learning forum as students are able to read and respond to each other's questions in advance of the synchronous session.

*During a Synchronous Session*

The second phase of a blended online inquiry cycle involves a synchronous session where communication and information technologies can be used to define the triggering event(s), provide opportunities for exploration and create a first step towards the integration phase. These sessions can be facilitated through the use of Web-based synchronous communication systems such as Elluminate Live! and Horizon Wimba. The focus of these sessions should not be on information transmission such as lecturing, but instead be used to diagnose student misconceptions, foster critical dialogue, and support peer instruction.

Table 9.5 outlines several synchronous learning activities that can be supported with various online tools. These activities are further described in the subsequent paragraphs.

If a survey, quiz, or online discussion forum has been used to support assigned reading, then the synchronous session will often begin with a debriefing of this activity. Anonymous survey or quiz results can be

**Table 9.5** Design Considerations during a Synchronous Session

| NATURE OF INQUIRY | LEARNING ACTIVITIES | WEB 2.0 TOOLS |
| --- | --- | --- |
| • Defining the *triggering events* (key questions)<br>• Beginning to *explore* the questions | a) Talking/listening<br><br>• Dialogue with teacher and fellow learners about the specified issue or topic<br>• Mini-lecture and/or tutorial to address the results of the pre-class quiz or survey<br>• Large or small group discussion or activity<br>• Case study<br>• Initiation of an individual or group project | i) Displaying quiz or survey results<br><br>• In a synchronous communication system (e.g., Elluminate Live! or Horizon Wimba)<br><br>ii) Conducting synchronous quizzes and surveys to promote dialogue and small group work<br><br>• Survey tool and break-out room features (e.g., Elluminate Live! or Horizon Wimba)<br><br>iii) Displaying digital learning objects and resources<br><br>• Using social media sharing sites (e.g., Flikr, Slideshare, YouTube) and repositories such as merlot.org<br><br>iv) Displaying assignments<br><br>• Course blogs or wikis can be used to post assignment handouts, tutorials, resources, and links to examples of previous student work |

uploaded to synchronous communication application such as Elluminate Live! The ensuing debate helps to define the triggering event clearly and allows members of the class to begin sharing and comparing their perspectives and experiences related to the question or issue.

Digital learning objects, such as interactive demand and supply curves for economic principles, can also be accessed and discussed during the synchronous session to help students visualize and understand the relationships between key course concepts. These learning objects can be retrieved from social media sharing applications (e.g., Flikr, Slideshare, YouTube) or from repositories such as MERLOT (Multimedia Educational Repository for Learning Online Teaching: http://www.merlot.org/). Links to these objects can be made from a course website, blog, or wiki in order to allow students to manipulate and review these learning resources after the synchronous session.

Discussion and debate can be facilitated synchronously online through the use of the quiz and break-out room features in many synchronous communication applications. Crouch and Mazur (2001) describe how synchronous quizzes can be used to support a form of peer instruction. The process begins with the teacher posing a question or problem. The students initially work individually toward a solution and 'vote' on what they believe is the correct answer by selecting the desired response in an online poll. The results are then projected for the entire class to view. For a good question, there is usually a broad range of responses. Students are then required to compare and discuss their solutions online in a break-out room in order to come to a consensus. Another 'vote' is taken but this time only one response per group can be utilized. In most circumstances, the range of responses decreases and usually centers on the correct answer. An alternative to this process is to have groups of students generate the quiz questions in advance of the synchronous event.

Synchronous sessions also provide a good opportunity to initiate and clarify individual or group projects. To help students understand the expectations for these assignments, previous student work can be displayed and critiqued. Students can then either develop or use a pre-existing assessment rubric to review examples of past coursework. Similar to digital learning objects, these previous assignments can be linked to the course website, blog, or wiki so that students have access to this material after the synchronous session.

The synchronous session should conclude with a discussion that establishes student responsibilities and action items. This discussion can also be combined with a Web-based anonymous exit survey, which asks students to state what they learned during the session and what they are still unclear about. This closing discussion and survey helps students begin to integrate the new information received during the session with their prior learning experience. The survey data collected also provides valuable feedback for the teacher in terms of planning future synchronous sessions and activities.

*Between Synchronous Sessions*

The use of communication and information technologies between the synchronous sessions provides opportunities for the students to explore and reflect on course-related activities further. This phase begins with the use of a course website, blog, or wiki, to post a summary and a list of follow-up items from the synchronous session. An RSS feed can be used to 'push' this announcement out to students through a social networking system but it is also recommended that this summary be composed in a word-processing document so that it can be copied and pasted as a group email message to the students. Sreebny (2007, p. 3) states that "Email is still the most widely used collaboration tool in the world." An overview of how online learning technologies can be used to support a series of reflective learning activities is provided within Table 9.6. Each of these activities is then discussed in the accompanying paragraphs.

**Table 9.6** Design Considerations after a Synchronous Session (Garnham & Kaleta, 2002; reprinted with permission)

| NATURE OF INQUIRY | LEARNING ACTIVITIES | WEB 2.0 TOOLS |
| --- | --- | --- |
| • Further *exploration* towards *tentative integration* with the ability to connect theory to practice application | a) Reading/writing<br><br>• Anonymous class exit survey<br>• What did you learn from the class session?<br>• What are you still unclear about? | i) Anonymous surveys<br><br>• Survey tools (e.g., getfast.ca)<br><br>ii) Communication<br><br>• Announcement section of a course website, blog, or wiki for student 'to do' list |

**Table 9.6** Continued

| NATURE OF INQUIRY | LEARNING ACTIVITIES | WEB 2.0 TOOLS |
|---|---|---|
| | • Online discussion with student moderation<br><br>b) Talking/listening + Reading/writing<br><br>• Individual or group project work, case studies<br><br>**Preparation for next class**<br><br>a) Reading/writing<br><br>• Pre-class reading assignment or activity on a specified topic or issue<br>• Followed by a self assessment quiz, survey or discussion forum | • Email for individual student questions or clarification (try to put common questions into a Frequently Asked Questions discussion forum)<br>• Online discussion forums in social networking systems (e.g., Facebook) to facilitate student-moderated discussions<br>• Synchronous communication tools (e.g., Elluminate Live!, Second Life) for working sessions among student groups<br><br>iii) Individual and group project work<br><br>• Study groups within learning management systems (e.g., Blackboard) and social networking systems (e.g., MySpace, Ning)<br>• Blogs for reflective journaling e.g., Blogger)<br>• Wikis for collaborative writing projects (e.g., Seedwiki)<br>• Mashup tools for data analysis and representation of collaborative projects (e.g., Intel's Mash Maker) |

In terms of communication, students can email the instructor for individual questions or clarification of assignments but it is recommended that a Frequently Asked Questions online discussion forum be created within a learning management system (e.g., Blackboard) or social networking system (e.g., Facebook). Students can then share in the responsibility of answering questions and problem-solving course-related issues. Online discussion forums can be used to promote individual reflection and critical dialogue between the synchronous sessions. For example, a series of online discussion forums can be created by the instructor related to the key modules/topics for the course. Groups of students (three to five) then select a module based on course readings, previous experience, and/or interest in the topic. Each group is responsible for moderating and summarizing their selected online discussion for a set period of time (often one or two weeks). Garrison, Anderson, and Archer's (2001) practical inquiry model can be used to help frame these summaries. For example:

- Triggering event: What were the key questions discussed this week?
- Exploration: What opportunities and challenges (i.e., pros and cons) related to the discussion topic were identified?
- Integration: What were the connections between the discussion and the core concepts/learning outcomes for our course?
- Resolution/Application: What are the 'take-aways' from this discussion (i.e., recommendations, application to future practice, lessons learned)?
- Key resources (e.g., websites, articles, books) that we could use to find further information/ideas about this topic?

An online collaborative writing tool such as a wiki can then be used to make draft notes and a final summary (synthesis and analysis) of the online discussion based on these questions or additional guidelines that are co-created by the students and the teacher.

Online journals such as blogs can be used to support self-reflection and peer review of course assignments, allowing students to take a deeper approach to their learning by going 'public' with their work (Vaughan, 2008). At the beginning of the semester, the teacher can require each student to create their own blog. Once an assignment has been completed and the student has received assessment feedback they then post responses to questions such as the following on their blogs:

1. What did you learn in the process of completing this assignment?
2. How will you apply what you learned from this assignment to the next class assignment, other courses and/or your career?

A peer review process can also be supported through the use of blogs. Students can post drafts of course assignments to their blogs and then their peers can review these documents and post comments to the author's blog. Guiding questions for this peer review process could include:

1. What did you learn from reviewing this document?
2. What were the strengths (e.g., content, writing style, format and structure) of the document?
3. What constructive advice and/or recommendations could you provide for improving the quality of this document?

A common complaint from students about group work is the lack of time and the difficulty in arranging meetings between the synchronous sessions. Synchronous communication systems and virtual world applications (e.g., Second Life) can be utilized to overcome this challenge. These tools allow students to participate in 'real-time' online group meetings over the Internet. For example, Elluminate Live! allows students to use a whiteboard to brainstorm ideas; a common Web browser to explore and review websites; and shared desktop applications such as word processors, spreadsheets, and graphics software to create and revise documents together. Students can also use these applications to access mashup tools such as Intel's Mash Maker and MIT's Piggy Bank synchronously in order to analyze and visually represent project data. In addition, virtual worlds such as Second Life allow learners to collaborate on project work in rich 3-D immersive environments.

Toward the end of this phase a new, related, inquiry-based learning assignment can be introduced via the posting of another Web-based reading and survey/quiz. This pre-session assignment should be designed to help students synthesize their learning from the current activity and prepare for the subsequent synchronous session.

*Next Synchronous Session*

In the next synchronous session, communication and information technologies continue to play a key role in helping students 'close the loop' between the asynchronous and synchronous components of a blended online learning course. Table 9.7 describes the type of learning activities that can be used to help students achieve a sense of resolution and/or application to a course-related inquiry cycle.

This process can be facilitated with a class discussion at the beginning of the synchronous session. The inquiry phases of integration and tentative resolution are addressed by first reviewing the results of the anonymous exit survey from the last synchronous session and then discussing any student questions or concerns raised from this survey. If there was an online discussion between the synchronous sessions, the student moderators or the teacher can provide an oral summary or some reflections about the discussion. Students can also be invited to

**Table 9.7** Design Considerations for the Next Synchronous Session

| NATURE OF INQUIRY | LEARNING ACTIVITIES | WEB 2.0 TOOLS |
|---|---|---|
| • Resolution/ application | a) Talking/listening/ writing | i) Display quiz or survey results |
| | • Review of online discussion activities<br>• Individual or group presentations<br>• Final group thoughts on the topic or issue<br>• Initiation of dialogue on the next topic or issue | • In a synchronous communication system (e.g., Elluminate Live! or Horizon Wimba)<br><br>ii) Display of online discussion forum<br><br>• Online discussion forums within learning management system (e.g., Blackboard) or social networking systems (e.g., Facebook)<br><br>iii) Display assignments and student work<br><br>• Links to student blogs and wikis |

demonstrate assignments 'in-progress.' These types of activity help to clarify assignment expectations and consolidate student learning within the course. The inquiry cycle concludes with a brief 'wrap-up' discussion, including final thoughts or comments, and then moves on to the next related question or topic that in turn triggers the next related inquiry-based learning activity.

## Future Issues

Although blended learning environments have been associated with improved student learning outcomes and cost savings, realizing these educational designs across the institution have come with significant challenges. An institution must create the necessary policy, planning, resources, scheduling, and support systems to ensure that blended learning initiatives are successful (Garrison & Kanuka, 2004). A policy framework should be developed, which explicitly states how blended learning supports the vision, values, and principles of the institution. Related to this document should be a set of strategic and operational plans. The strategic planning involves the identification of needs, goals, and objectives; potential costs; and available resources. With respect to blended learning, operational planning entails "attending to the non-instructional components including the following: promotional and advertising strategies; creating relationships for shared resources (e.g., registration, fees); managing technology; and creating an effective assessment process" (Garrison & Kanuka, 2004, p. 101).

The scheduling of courses in higher education institutions is already a challenge and considerable thought must be given to the development of a scheduling format for campus-based and online blended courses, which allows for meaningful and flexible reduction of synchronous meeting time. As previously indicated, support for students and faculty is a key component of blended learning. Technology training and support should be available for students and professional development support for the faculty. Voos (2003) strongly emphasizes that a faculty development program is central to the success of an institution's blended learning initiative. The program should include opportunities for faculty to learn how to redesign their courses, teach well online, and effectively use technology (Garnham & Kaleta, 2002).

Without adequate preparation, most faculty will simply replicate their traditional class sections and the benefits resulting from a blended course will not be achieved. Hartman & Truman-Davis (2001, p. 55) note that to "achieve consistency, quality and scalability, it is necessary to establish a central service coordination unit with sufficient resources to develop and apply standards and support the expanding volume of work that will result from increased faculty demand."

> *The vision for blended learning must be in the best interests of the institution and truly shared among the constituent members.*

Conclusion

In closing, transformational leadership needs to be exhibited by senior administration fully to realize the benefits and overcome the challenges associated with blended learning in higher education institutions (Garrison, 2004). This leadership consists of three interrelated core elements: vision, interpersonal skills, and courage. The vision for blended learning must be in the best interests of the institution and truly shared among the constituent members. The senior administration team must possess the interpersonal skills to work collaboratively with others. This involves the ability to share ideas but also the willingness to listen to contrary views. Finally, these leaders must have the courage to stay the course and make the necessary hard decisions (e.g., creating new policies and procedures while discontinuing existing ones) required for the development and growth of blended learning opportunities in higher education institutions.

## TERMS AND DEFINITIONS

**Blended learning:** The organic integration of thoughtfully selected and complementary face-to-face and online approaches and technologies (Garrison & Vaughan, 2008, p. 148).

**Blended online learning environments:** The simultaneous and complementary integration and implementation of an asynchronous-mode learning environment (e.g., a course management system or CMS) and a synchronous desktop conferencing environment (e.g., virtual classroom) (Power, 2008).

**Community of Inquiry framework:** A generic framework that directs attention to the process of constructing and confirming deep understanding. The three main elements of the CoI framework are social presence, cognitive presence, and teaching presence (Garrison & Anderson, 2003).

**Just-in-time teaching (JiTT):** A teaching and learning strategy based on the interaction between Web-based study assignments and an active learner classroom. Students respond electronically to carefully constructed Web-based assignments which are due shortly before class, and the instructor reads the student submissions 'just-in-time' to adjust the classroom lesson to suit the students' needs. Thus, the heart of JiTT is the 'feedback loop' formed by the students' outside-of-class preparation that fundamentally affects what happens during the subsequent in-class time together (Novak, Patterson, Gavrin, & Christian, 1999).

**Peer instruction:** Involves students in their own learning during lecture and focuses their attention on underlying concepts. Lectures are interspersed with conceptual questions designed to expose common difficulties in understanding the material. The students are given one to two minutes to think about the question and formulate their own answers; they then spend two to three minutes discussing their answers in groups of three to four, attempting to reach consensus on the correct answer. This process forces the students to think through the arguments being developed, and enables them (as well as the instructor) to assess their understanding of the concepts even before they leave the classroom (Crouch & Mazur, 2001).

**Practical inquiry model:** Reflects four phases of critical thinking and cognitive presence: (a) the initiation phase with a triggering event that begins the dialogue about a particular issue; (b) the exploration phase in which learners move between private reflection and social exploration, exchanging information about the issue at hand; (c) the integration phase in which participants begin to 'construct meanings' or solutions to the issue from the ideas explored in the previous phase; and (d) the resolution phase in which the proposed solution is 'vicariously tested' (Garrison, Anderson, & Archer, 2001, p. 11).

**Web 2.0:** A term used to describe the trend in the use of World Wide Web technology and Web design that aims to enhance creativity, information sharing, and, most notably, collaboration among users.

## QUESTIONS FOR REVIEW AND REFLECTION

1. What are the three presences of the Community of Inquiry (CoI) framework? What is the relationship between these presences?
2. What are the four phases of the Practical Inquiry model and how are they progressively connected?
3. In an online blended learning course or program, what kind of instructional strategies could you use to help students prepare to engage actively in a synchronous session (triggering event ideas)?
4. What issues must a higher education institution address in order to ensure that a blended learning initiative is successful?
5. What is your definition of blended learning?
6. What are the opportunities and challenges that you would encounter implementing a blended learning initiative in your institution or workplace?
7. How would you design an online blended learning environment using the Community of Inquiry framework?
8. What role would Web 2.0 applications play in your education design?

**Significant Contributor**

**D.R. Garrison** is the Director of the Teaching & Learning Centre and a professor in the Faculty of Education at the University of Calgary. He has published extensively on teaching and learning in higher, adult, and distance education contexts. His most recent books are *E-Learning in the 21st Century* (2003) and *Blended Learning in Higher Education* (2008). Both books are shaped by the Community of Inquiry Framework.

# References

Arabasz, P., Boggs, R., & Baker, M.B. (2003). Highlights of e-learning support practices. *Educause Center for Applied Research Bulletin*, 9.

Ausubel, D.P. (1968). *Educational psychology: A cognitive view*. New York: Holt, Rinehart, and Winston.

Aycock, A., Garnham, C., & Kaleta, R. (2002). Lessons learned from the hybrid course project. *Teaching with Technology Today*, 8(6). Retreived from: http://www.uwsa.edu/ttt/articles/garnham2.htm.

Barone, C. (2001). Conditions for transformation: Infrastructure is not the issue. *Educause Review*, 36(3), 41–47.

Bates, T. & Poole, G. (2003). *Effective teaching with technology in higher education: Foundations for success*. San Francisco: Jossey-Bass.

Bleed, R. (2001). A hybrid campus for a new millennium. *Educause Review*, 36 (1), 16–24.

Carr, S. (2001). Is anyone making money on distance education? *Chronicle of Higher Education*, A41. Retrieved from: http://chronicle.com/free/v47/i23/23a04101.htm.

Cho, K. & Berge, Z.L. (2002). Overcoming barriers to distance training and education. *USDLA Journal*, 16(1). Retrieved from: http://www.usdla.org/html/journal/JAN02_Issue/article01.html.

Clark, D. (2003). Blend it like Beckham. *Epic Group PLC*. Retrieved from: http://www.epic.co.uk/content/resources/white_papers/blended.htm.

Crouch, C.H. & Mazur, E. (2001). Peer instruction: Ten years of experience and results. *American Journal of Physics*, 69, 970–977.

Dziuban, C.D., Hartman, J., Juge, F., Moskal, P.D., & Sorg, S. (2005). Blended learning: Online learning enters the mainstream. In C.J. Bonk & C. Graham (Eds.), *Handbook of blended learning environment*. Indianapolis, IN: Pfeiffer.

Dziuban, C., Hartman, J., Moskal, P., Sorg, S., & Truman, B. (2004). Three ALN modalities: An institutional perspective. In J. Bourne & J.C. Moore (Eds.), *Elements of quality online education: Into the mainstream*. Needham, MA: Sloan Center for Online Education.

Dziuban, C. & Moskal, P. (2001). Distributed learning impact evaluation. *Research Initiative for Teaching Effectiveness*. Retrieved from: http://pegasus.cc.ucf.edu/~rite/impactevaluation.htm.

Garnham, C. & Kaleta, R. (2002). Introduction to hybrid courses. *Teaching with Technology Today*, 8(6). Retrieved from: http://www.uwsa.edu/ttt/articles/garnham.htm.

Garrison, D.R. (2004). Transformative leadership and e-learning. In K. Matheos & T.Carey (Eds.), *Advances and challenges in eLearning at Canadian research universities*. University of Manitoba: Centre for Higher Education Research and Development.

Garrison, D.R. & Anderson, T. (2003). *E-learning in the 21st century: A framework for research and practice*. London: Routledge/Falmer.

Garrison, D.R., Anderson, T., & Archer, W. (2001). Critical thinking, cognitive presence, and computer conferencing in distance education. *American Journal of Distance Education*, 15(1), 17–23.

Garrison, D.R. & Kanuka, H. (2004). Blended learning: Uncovering its transformative potential in higher education. *The Internet and Higher Education*, 7(2), 95–105.

Garrison, D.R. & Vaughan, N. (2008). *Blended learning in higher education*. San Francisco: Jossey-Bass.

Hartman, J.L. & Truman-Davis, B. (2001). Institutionalizing support for faculty use of technology at the University of Central Florida. In R.M. Epper & A.W. Bates (Eds.), *Teaching faculty how to use technology: Best practices from leading institutions*. Phoenix, AZ: Oryx Press.

Heterick, B. & Twigg, C. (2002). Explaining college costs—It's not how fast you run. *The Learning MarketSpace*. Retrieved from: http://thencat.org/Newsletters/Mar02.html.

Johnson, J. (2002). Reflections on teaching a large enrollment course using a hybrid format. *Teaching with Technology Today*, 8(6). Retrieved from: http://www.uwsa.edu/ttt/articles/jjohnson.htm.

National Clearinghouse for Commuter Programs (1999). *The role of commuter programs and services— CAS standards contextual statement*. Retrieved from: http://www.nccp.umd.edu/.

Novak, G.M., Patterson, E.T., Gavrin, A.D., & Christian, W. (1999). *Just-in-time teaching: Blending active learning with Web technology*. New Jersey: Prentice Hall.

Power, M. (2008). The emergence of a blended online learning environment. *MERLOT Journal of Online Learning and Teaching*, 4(4), 503–514. Retrieved from: http://jolt.merlot.org/vol4no4/power_1208.pdf.

Sands, P. (2002). Inside outside, upside downside: Strategies for connecting online and face-to-face instruction in hybrid courses. *Teaching with Technology Today*, 8(6). Retrieved from: http://www.uwsa.edu/ttt/articles/sands2.htm.

Spika, P. (2002). Approximately 'real world' learning with the hybrid model. *Teaching with Technology Today*, 8(6). Retrieved from: http://www.uwsa.edu/ttt/articles/spilka.htm.

Sreebny, O. (2007). Digital rendezvous: Social software in higher education. *EDUCAUSE Centre for Applied Research Bulletin*, 2.

Twigg, C.A. (1999). Improving learning & reducing costs: Redesigning large-enrollment courses. *National Centre for Academic Transformation*. Retrieved from: http://www.thencat.org/Monographs/mono1.pdf.

Twigg, C.A. (2003a). Improving learning and reducing costs: New models for online learning. *EDUCAUSE Review*, 38(5), 29–38.

Twigg, C.A. (2003b). Program in course redesign. *National Centre for Academic Transformation*. Retrieved from: http://thencat.org/PCR.htm.

Vaughan, N.D. (2008). The use of wikis and weblogs to support deep approaches to learning. *The University College of Fraser Valley Research Review*, 1(3), 47–60.

Voos, R. (2003). Blended learning—What is it and where might it take us? *Sloan-C View*, 2(1). Retrieved from: http://www.sloan-c.org/publications/view/v2n1/blended1.htm.

Williams, C. (2002). Learning on-line: A review of recent literature in a rapidly expanding field. *Journal of Further and Higher Education*, 26(3), 263–272.

Williams, J. (2003). Blending into the background. *E-Learning Age Magazine*, 1(6), 35–38.

Young, J.R. (2002). Hybrid teaching seeks to end the divide between traditional and online instruction. *Chronicle of Higher Education*, 48(28), A33. Retrieved from: http://chronicle.com/free/v48/i28/28a03301.htm.

# 10

## THE FUTURE OF DISTANCE EDUCATION

Reformed, Scrapped or Recycled

DR. TERRY EVANS
Professor, School of Education
Deakin University

DR. BRIAN PAULING
Head (retired) and Principal Lecturer
New Zealand Broadcasting School

### Introduction

In an era in which diversity, fluidity and flexibility are its main characteristics (Greenslade, 2007, 2; Kristof, 2006), a discussion of the future of distance education needs to be about possibilities rather than predictions. What we can predict is that the demand for education will not disappear: it is structured into our future existence. A mass of under-educated people, an expanding population, major global crises and an expanding knowledge economy all combine to sustain a massive demand for basic, further, higher, continuing and lifelong education. This demand cannot be met solely in the world's classrooms; even if there were enough classrooms, many people will be unwilling or unable to attend them to learn. In this sense, distance education is essential for the future, but the fluidity around educational terms and practices means that it is also quite possible that 'distance education'—the term and its history—will be towed to the scrap yard. If so, we hope and expect that many of its useful parts will be recycled!

We consider three key elements of distance education—technology, students and educational institutions—and the educational possibilities that surround them by reflection on past and present changes. The future of distance education is intimately connected to broader social, economic and cultural changes. These changes are strongly influenced by the 'disruptive' technologies, demographic transformations in the nature of distance learners and the pressures of global techno-capitalism on educational institutions (Hughes & Hillebrand, 2006).

## Technology

As many distance education writers have noted over the decades, distance education is deeply connected to communications technologies: from writing and correspondence, radio and other audio media, to television and other video media (see, for example, Bates, 1995; Evans & Nation, 1993, 2007; Garrison, 1985; Hawkridge, 1976, 1995; Walker, 1993). *Correspondence* schooling and education changed its name in the 1970s to *distance education* to reflect its longstanding use of audio, and newer use of video media, to span the *distance* between teacher and learner. In a sense, nothing has changed: distance education still uses correspondence, audio and video. What have changed are the ways in which these media are mediated, in particular through digitally converged technologies. These technologies enable effectively continuous and instantaneous 'multi' media transmission and interaction, not just in education, but to most aspects of human and social activity *in the developed world* (Pearson, 2000). Digital technology is the enabling mechanism that drives the social, cultural and economic features of globalization (Bauman, 1997; Beck, 2000; Friedman, 2005) and it is reinforcing tendencies toward 'boundary-less' communications media (Bonnett, 1999, p. 2).

The 'traditional' broadcasters, telecommunications providers and publishers that had exclusive control over the creation, aggregation and distribution of their own 'product,' are reshaping to play multiple roles as 'content' providers who are creating content for multiple platforms; content aggregators who are supplying content for distribution; and content distributors who are providing access to content on discrete or multiple platforms. For example, telecommunications companies are taking multimedia content from a range of providers, broadcasters, newspapers and libraries, and behaving as aggregators (e.g., SBC). Broadcasters are using telecommunications networks to distribute content on Web pages that contain print material from newspaper sources as well as audio and video (e.g., BBC Online). Publishers are using the Internet to provide digital copies of their print-based product, including audio and video product as accompaniments to their books (e.g., Taylor & Francis, Prentice Hall). Newspapers are producing online versions of their papers that contain not just print, photographs and graphs, but embedded video and audio enhancements taken from broadcast sources (e.g., NewsStand, www.stuff.co.nz). All services are developing digital archives for the storage and retrieval of their material, and providing access to subscribers and on occasion the general public (e.g., BBC Archives, the Guardian Archive).

Distance education cannot escape the uncertainties created by the so-called disruptive technologies given its longstanding and fundamental reliance on technologies. Earliest distance education relied on the writing and print technologies, and mechanized transport for distribution. While higher education, generally, eschewed the mass communication technologies of radio, television and cinema, elements of distance education engaged them. (Although schools, especially since the 1950s, had used educational radio and (later) television broadcasting to enhance their provision.) For example, both China and Japan instituted 'radio and television' universities. However, perhaps the most iconic incorporation of radio and television in distance education occurred within the origins of the UK's Open University and its relationship with the BBC. Initially much of the programming was supplementary to the printed course material. Television was described as 'chalk and talk on the screen' and radio as a 'read lecture.' Although not without its tensions, the influence of the BBC saw a steady improvement in the production values of the radio and television programmes (Perry, 1972, 1976). This audiovisual material grew to become a key component, especially of the mass-enrollment foundation courses. These skills were transferred and further developed as digitalization provided opportunities to include email, the Web, CDs, DVDs, teleconferencing and videoconferencing. Contemporaneously from the late 1980s, education in general began to engage with digital technologies to a level and in a manner not previously seen with any other technology since the advent of print. Classrooms were equipped with digital displays, and higher education in particular engaged with digital content management systems, used digital technologies to distribute, store and manipulate data, and increasingly added audiovisual content to classroom teaching.

In March 2008 the Australian Communications and Media Authority identified six 'top trends' for the next ten years:

1. An accelerating pace of change driven by overlapping developments in technology, and connections between people, databases and objects.
2. Diversity in the development of physical infrastructure including broadband, digital broadcasting, smart radio systems, sensor networks, mesh networks, efficiency techniques in multimedia transmission, location sensing and context-aware technologies, intelligent transport systems and satellite services.
3. Continuing spread of distributed connectivity through the integration of information processing beyond the desktop into everyday objects and activities.
4. Enhanced content and network management capabilities driven by developments in deep packet inspection and content filtering technologies, coupled with the need to improve e-security, identity management, intellectual property protection and energy efficiency.
5. The emerging social Web acting as both a platform and a database, enabling innovation and creativity by users and service providers.
6. Continuing scientific and technological innovations which, in combination, are driving advances in computing power, display technologies, artificial intelligence and nanotechnology.

(ACMA, 2008, p. 1)

Effectively distance education, and higher education generally, are entangled in a double helix of spiraling technological change linked with perpetual obsolescence as 'continuing scientific and technological innovations' (point 6, above) create discontinuity, uncertainty and risk in what is becoming an increasingly technologically dependent sector. These

202 TERRY EVANS & BRIAN PAULING

circumstances create potentially profound implications—both positive and negative—for teaching and learning. These also affect the management of educational organizations, not just in higher education, but in all educational and training circumstances.

Web 2.0 has seen the burgeoning of social networks (point 5), and some educators argue that virtual worlds such as Second Life "substantially enhanced the quality and experiences of student learning" (Jarmon, Traphagan, & Mayrath, 2008, p. 157). Teachers are using virtual worlds to "develop educational activities across many disciplines" (Wankel & Kingsley, in press). However, others wrestle simultaneously with issues of whether education should occupy such 'disintermediated' worlds (Aldrich, 2007). But the developing 'Internet of Things' (points 1 and 3) which enables the Internet to extend into the physical world using short-range wireless communications, real-time localization and sensor networks (point 2) foreshadows an even more complex world (ITU, 2005). Here the virtual and the 'real' interact using 3-D vision, animation and holographs to provide the platform that eventually becomes the hyper-reality that Tiffin and Terashima (2001) saw as revolutionizing both classroom and distance teaching of such complex curricula as science, engineering and medicine. Sophisticated blends of digital technology, biotechnology and nanotechnology (point 6) will produce environments for informing, entertaining and learning that could be reminiscent of current science fiction.

Examples of recent or nascent technologies include:

- The Grapefruit Cam, a geodesic streaming video dome camera the size of a grapefruit with eleven lenses that films 360 degrees and permits the viewer to use the "mouse to move where the spinal column can't" (Wsj.com., 2008), thereby providing enhanced content (point 4). It not only re-maps the world (see Google Street View) but provides new ways of viewing and exploring in geography, oceanography and most disciplines that rely on visuals to communicate (point 6).
- Ultra high-speed Internet (point 5), as demonstrated by the latest Internet technologies linking 100,000 desktop computers to the CERN Large Hadron Collider. This provides download and

upload data speeds 1000 times faster than publicly available in 2008, but is predicted to "revolutionise the speed at which information is downloaded to all personal computers" (Ahmed, 2008).

- Flexible and mobile screen technologies (point 6) that permit high-definition 3-D reception and projection, and enable sophisticated interactive responses to bring the teacher and the classroom ever closer for the distance education student (Troy, 2008).
- Three-dimensional imaging and holographic technologies used in the classroom with the potential to "save millions in unnecessary costs" and provide students with real-time access to "top professors" using !virtual and augmented reality" (Winslow, 2007).

How these technologies will be used can only be speculation at this stage. However, education, and especially distance education, increasingly relies on visual communication, email and the Internet to deliver teaching and learning. Therefore, it is not difficult to imagine ways in which these and other technologies may affect educational processes.

An important technological platform of significant importance to distance education is mobile telephony, especially when this is linked with multimedia devices, such as iPhones. As mobile telephony becomes more ubiquitous, services other than phone and text are migrating to mobile platforms. Mobile TV and video services have been available for a few years. This permits two of the largest digital industries—mobile connectivity and entertainment—to merge to create a new audience. By early 2008 it was claimed that in the U.S. three out of ten adults watched some media content on their mobile phones (Accenture cited in Troy, 2008). The evidence suggests that mobile devices are increasingly being used in a laptop computer manner as a source for all media activity, such as Flickr, YouTube, Google and Amazon. GPS compatibility, integration with voice recognition technology and movement-sensitive screens are available. One key element will be the ability of the mobile device to 'sense' or understand the world around it and respond to it, providing seamless access to a range of devices, networks and services and possessing an 'intelligence' that understands and anticipates what the user wants it to do (point 3) (ITU, 2005). Mobile devices and their corresponding media technologies are playing increasingly significant roles in the everyday lives of millions of people.

Mobile technology is being adapted for educational purposes in several developed (for example, Canada) and developing (for example, Egypt) nations. Mobile learning (m-learning) takes advantage of opportunities offered by mobile technologies to deliver 'across locations,' thus reducing the barriers of place and reliance upon fixed services by creating a mobile 'always on, always available, anywhere' service. For example, educators are using m-learning to 'connect' young people who are 'disconnected' from school, and examination results are 'messaged' to mobile phones by some universities and examination authorities.

It should be noted that the adoption rate of mobile phone technologies is the fastest of any new technology to date. Its impact is demonstrated by the phenomenal uptake (90 percent penetration in some markets) and the thousands of applications that have been created for mobile devices, turning what was once just a mobile phone into an object equipped with many services which have prospective educational uses. While these uses are highly appropriate for many contemporary learners—especially for those who are 'addicted' to their iPhones and 'Crackberries'—there are limitations, as with any technology. The best uses are probably those that complement other forms of education, as the following discussion shows.

One indication of the ascendancy of m-learning was the decision of the UK's Open University to cease BBC television broadcasts and replace them with DVDs and podcasting. Brabazon (2007, p. 20) uses this shift as evidence that universities have 'tropes' and that these have moved from the 'empowerment' of the 1970s, 'student-centered learning' in the 1980s, to 'flexibility' in the 1990s and now 'mobility' in the 2000s. Previously the educational value of mobile technologies was thought to be the 'delivery of content' to mobile devices. De Freitas and Levene (2003) argue that m-learning can be used in three ways: for the delivery of lectures over mobile devices, for the augmentation of the physical campus with a virtual and mobile component, and for the use of mobile devices in field studies. However, the emphasis appears to be changing. Its focus now is on the capabilities that enable users to create and share their own learning, thus moving students from being 'consumers' of content to 'creators' of content. This captures the skills of the 'digital natives' and their ubiquitous mobile appliances to offer an "immense potential for teaching and learning" (IADIS, 2009). "Mobile phones, PDAs, Pocket PCs and the Internet can be blended to engage and motivate learners, any time and anywhere" (M-learning. org, 2008). Not only does this create on-the-move learning opportunities, but, perhaps further, it incorporates Brabazon's aforementioned 'tropes,' thereby providing a learning environment that is not just mobile but student-focused, empowering and flexible.

Some have argued that there is a progression of learning technologies (Conde, Muñoz, & García, 2008). E-learning is generally defined as the use of Internet technologies for the purposes of teaching. Conde et al. (p. 61) argue that e-learning has reached "maturity as a learning method" and that any further developments will "evolve alongside the technology that made it possible." M-learning arises out of the universal acceptance of mobile devices which provide the opportunity for an 'evolution of e-learning,' with students able to make use of their devices to support their learning, especially through Web-based uses and the 'always-on' nature of the technology. The ultimate development of technology-based learning, according to Ramón (cited in Conde et al., 2008, p. 61), is "u-learning (ubiquitous learning)—a set of formative activities, supported by technology, that are readily accessible in any place." Of course, to the distance educator, ubiquity was afforded from the earliest days of correspondence, assuming that everyone was within reach of a postal service. However, subsequent technologies, such as radio and television, or audio and video cassettes, always challenged distance educators about the ubiquity of access—especially in large, geographically dispersed nations, such as Australia and Canada, or in developing nations, such as Nigeria and Papua New Guinea, where broadcast reception and even electricity could not be assumed as ubiquitous. Given the development of photovoltaic (and other independent) power generation and battery storage, and satellite and microwave transmission, *technically* even the most remote inhabited parts of the globe have access to learning. Although one could argue this was almost the case for postal-based distance education, the difference is that u-learning not only covers the distances, but does so simultaneously.

Jorma Ollila, Chairman of the Nokia Corporation (cited in Rossiter, 2003), envisions a form of u-learning in his discussion of the three "technology pillars" that are reshaping society—digital convergence, Internet protocol and mobility— which form "a networked and mobile information society." Hence, as Slaughter (2007, p. 113) suggests, "the future of education is a network, and not a place." Arguably, this is not new for distance education which has often 'networked' its students and tutors through face-to-face, telephone, contact lists or online study groups. For 'traditional' classroom education it represents a much greater disruptive force, as both its physical infrastructure and organizational culture—not to mention its business model—are threatened.

> *One of the features of the 'digital native' generation is their interactive engagement with the screen, whether it is the screen on the remote-controlled digital television, the mobile phone, the computing or the gaming console.*

## Students

One of the features of the 'digital native' generation is their interactive engagement with the screen, whether it is the screen on the remote-controlled digital television, the mobile phone, the computer or the gaming console. Rushkoff (1996) calls them "screenagers." They are very comfortable with multimedia, sharing vast quantities of material with each other, linking images and sound, designing graphics. It is common to find teenage users of the more sophisticated mobile phones creating their own small multimedia productions and sharing them. They are engaging with digital media to unprecedented degrees. In the United States 87 percent of teenagers use the Internet, 81 percent play games online and 76 percent receive news online (Pew, 2005a). Half of US teenagers use mobile (cell) phones daily and in Europe 88 percent of early teenagers (12-14) own a mobile phone (Woods, 2005). In New Zealand a staggering 99 percent of young teenagers own a mobile phone (Hendery, 2008). Between 2000 and 2005, British 16–19-year-olds' weekly television viewing declined from 22 hours to less than 16 hours (Highfield, 2005). According to the Pew survey, 16–19-year-olds are engaging weekly in SMS or IMS messaging for 6 hours, in digital gaming for 15 hours, and in Internet use for 9 hours (Pew, 2005b). This correlates with Brown and Dubber's (2007) findings, which show that interactive participation rates using the newer technologies is

> What was once 'the audience' now combines traditional activities, such as searching, reading, watching and listening, with producing, commenting, sharing, and classifying its own content.

highest among 12–30-year-olds in New Zealand, with 37 percent of 18–21-year-olds creating their own material for the Web.

What was once the 'audience' now combines traditional activities, such as searching, reading, watching and listening, with producing, commenting, sharing and classifying its own content: activities that many educators from schools to universities have encouraged within broadly constructivist approaches. New genres of filmmaking and photography, where the message gains ground over the form, are developing. The proliferation of user-generated content (UGC) is fueled by the wide availability of at-hand technology, such as mobile telephones, and the wider broadcasting outlets. While these are mainly Web-based at present, increasingly UGC, such as videos of breaking news stories and amateur footage of sports events, features on traditional broadcasting channels. Some argue that the concept of 'self-production' leads to learners finding "the process of learning more compelling," and that education becomes "more like a conversation and learning content is something you perform, some kind of operation on rather than 'just' reading it" (Anderson, 2007, pp. 32–33). The rise of Web 2.0 applications facilitates the development of UGC and provides opportunities to meet and collaborate. Arguably, these offer immense potential for teaching and learning, especially in forms of distance education.

Perhaps the most significant change in young people's behavior as a result of digital technologies is gaming. A vast new industry has been created to cater for the demands of the gaming market. Strategy Analytics (2007) predicted that the online games market would triple from $3.8 billion between 2006 and 2011. Even more significant is the role that will be played in the gaming market by the next generation of mobile phone enabled devices, such as the iPhone.

Online games are becoming an increasing part of cultural experience in the West and they are starting to be explored for educational purposes, too. This is most clearly demonstrated by the increased use of simulation programs, a form of gaming, in many applied learning

environments such as pilot training, surgery and other medical procedures, use of heavy industrial equipment and electronic role-playing.
The online segment of the population is continuing to grow and the
demographic is broadening. Once the major preoccupation of young
males, from 2005 the gender balance was nearly equal, with 49 percent
women and 51 percent men (Nielsen, 2005). Nielsen (2005) states that
what was once "considered the domain of teen boys has evolved into a
medium that is now capable of reaching expanding demographics of
gamers, including females . . . and older players, . . . it's quite possible
playing video games will assume a significant role as a common cultural
experience, in the way that movies and television do today." According
to another source, among teens in 2005, 71.5 percent of all males and
47.7 percent of all females played video games weekly either on
consoles or online, with males spending an average of 114 minutes
daily and females an average of 36 minutes daily (Myers, 2005). These
characteristics suggest that there is rich potential for distance educators
to use these sorts of approaches in their educational design. Gaming
has potentially strong connections for developing problem-based
learning and other simulation-based learning activities online, both for
individual students to use and for use in networked learning.

Online social networking is a fundamental part of many people's
lives, as is amply demonstrated by Carter-Ross when citing the
comment of a Baylor University student: "First thing in the morning,
I check my email, Facebook and MySpace;
before brushing my teeth.' While spending
less than three hours watching television this
student claimed she and her friends spend all
day on the social networking site[s]" (Carter-
Ross, 2008). The immersive and interactive
virtual world of Second Life has 15 million
inhabitants (www.secondlife.com /whatis/economy_stats.php), and
users are able to "interact and immerse themselves in situations above
and beyond what is achievable by words alone" (IBM, 2007). As of
2008 there are 30 million active users on Facebook. With more than
40 billion page views every month, Facebook is the sixth most popular
site in the United States, and the top photo-sharing site. MySpace is
even larger, with 120 million active users worldwide.

> "First thing in the
> morning, I check my
> email, Facebook and
> MySpace; before
> brushing my teeth."

Saffo (2005) argues it is possible "to select from a vast cyber-sea of media and utterly saturate [our] information space." By the time they reach university, these young people will have been exposed to thousands of hours of television, a medium that in their lifetime has moved from being a few regulated and relatively conservative channels to an unregulated, aggressively commercial, multi-channel environment. The rising generation of students who have been "empowered by new media . . . [will] demand media on their own terms and will continue to do so in the future" (Greenslade, 2007, p. 6). This is a far cry from the Reithian broadcasting tradition of educate, inform and entertain! Distance educators and especially traditional higher education practitioners face challenges, not just from the technology but from other media sources in gaining and keeping the new "learning audience." Other media organizations with deep pockets and vast skills in making compelling content in the genres and platforms mentioned above will challenge distance education, and higher education in particular, for the eyes and hands of the digital natives.

### Educational Institutions

Distance education is not only challenged by technological change and changes in the nature of the student; it is also enmeshed in a range of changes affecting higher education institutions. These include not just the obvious effects of globalization but the political, economic and cultural changes facing Western society and individuals within society. It may be argued that the status of the modern educational institution—particularly in the post-secondary sector—is under threat or at the very least faces changes to the way it functions, perhaps in order to survive. Bradwell, Hannon, & Tims (2008, p. 3) make the point that:

> "As young people experiment with taking on powerful roles as reporters, distributors, commentators and artists, they are increasingly plotting their 'route around' existing political and cultural institutions. This poses profound challenges for [educators] but it also creates opportunities."

As young people experiment with taking on powerful roles as reporters, distributors, commentators and artists, they are increasingly plotting their 'route around' existing political and cultural institutions. This poses profound challenges for [educators] but it also creates opportunities.

Although this comment is about young people, as we have argued above, the influences extend to older generations too. Indeed, as Esmond (2001) and others have argued in the context of Australian 'baby boomers' retiring, people in their mid-50s to mid-60s are not only relatively asset rich but are conspicuously well educated and often 'tech savvy' in comparison with older generations. As distance educators in the 'developed' world have experienced for several decades, retirees often look to further their education once they throw off the shackles of work. Therefore, institutions in the 'developed' world have to move with the technological times for all generations up to and including the 'baby boomers.'

The generational, technological and cultural pressures on higher education today are complex and, sometimes, ambiguous. Outside are the social, political, economic and cultural pressures that are leading to change, considered by some as positive or benign (Bhagwati, 2004; Wolf, 2004), while others see them as negative, antidemocratic and even dangerous (Giroux, 2006; Kuttner, 1996; Morris & Janiewski, 2005; Saul, 2005). Internally there are shifting intellectual values and new ways of viewing the constructions of knowledge. Again, these are welcomed by some (Clark, 1998; Daniel, 1997; Newman, Couturier, & Scurry, 2004; Noll, 1997; Shattock, 2003), more cautiously received by others (Bok, 2003; Deem & Johnson, 2001; Williams, 2005), and strongly criticized by still others (Aronowitz, 2000; Readings, 1996; Shumar, 1997).

One analyst (Ankrum, 1999) asserts that the business of higher education is governed by just three essential elements, all financial. They are: the number of enrollments, the cost of gaining students, and student retention. Ruch (2001, p. 67) agrees: "If an institution can lower the cost of acquiring its customers while maintaining enrollment and improving retention, it will generate increased revenue, favorable cash flow, and improved financial returns."

Such commercial imperatives may jar with many educators; however, few would disagree that the management of their institutions is increasingly imbued with the discourses of business and that they shape institutional behavior. Kumar (1997) suggests that higher education institutions, in their attempts to remain relevant, mimic the behavior of commercial organizations. An ineluctable conclusion to this, claims Giroux (in Mourad, 1997, p. xi), is that the university and other higher education institutions have lost their major hold on "pedagogical practices," with other institutions within the mass media, popular culture and other public and private spheres providing learning over "multiple sites" and in direct competition. These "new media" institutions have the potential to displace distance education organizations, or at least to reduce their services to areas that the new media do not find attractive and/or profitable.

The development of the corporate classroom, where great importance is now being placed on the advanced training needs of knowledge-based companies, and large research and development units in both industry and government also provide competition. It has been suggested (Gibbons et al., 1994; Smith & Webster, 1997) that these organizations offer more effective managerial models because they are not constrained by collegial government, the need for consensus, or the scepticism that often accompanies tradition. Thus, they can respond with greater speed and flexibility and carry less 'baggage.' They "seem to belong to a forward-looking enterprise culture, sceptical of the traditional demarcations, taxonomies, hierarchies that clutter the old academic culture" (Gibbons et al., 1994, p. 82). Kenny-Wallace (2000, p. 61) argues that "[t]raditional universities are no longer the dominant players in the creation and communication of knowledge." Recognized brands such as BBC Television, Thomson Learning and Internet sites like Plato.com, Google Scholar.com and Interclass.com are claiming authenticity and authority beside traditional institutions of higher education. Smith & Webster (1997) argued over a decade ago that the fragmentation of knowledge sources is inevitable in the cyberspace age.

The 20th century saw universities' primary 'production functions'—teaching, learning

*The 20th century saw universities' primary 'production functions'— teaching, learning and assessment, the authorship of knowledge, scholarly discourse and debate—largely located in academe. By 2005 there were many businesses and institutions outside of the universities offering these services.*

and assessment, the authorship of knowledge, scholarly discourse and debate—largely located in academe. By 2005 there were many businesses and institutions outside of the universities offering these services. As well as a range of integrated platforms (Click2Learn, Docent, KnowledgePlanet, GeoLearning) emanating from private providers, there are a host of competing platforms for the other learning functions, exemplified by, among others:

- Author (authoring tools): DigitalThink, Harvard ManageMentor, Mindleaders, SkillSoft, Thomson, ThinQ.
- Deliver (course management tools): Blackboard/WebCT, Moodle, eCollege, Emind, Unext/Cardean, BlueU.
- Discuss (IP/satellite communication tools): Arel, Centra, HorizonLive, Polycom, Microsoft/PlaceWare.
- Assess (assessment and testing tools): ACT, Brainbench, Thomson Prometric, QuestionMark, SkillView.

Davis & Botkin (1994, p. 16) conclude that "the private sector will eclipse the public sector and become the major institution responsible for learning." The use of new media and technologies—rather than having to invest in classrooms, labs and libraries—seduces this privatization of education to occur predominantly in the 'virtual worlds' of learning. The 'user-pays' culture of neo-capitalism suggests that course credits will be paid for with the 'credit' card!

In future, higher education 'bricks and mortar' institutions may form only parts of the knowledge-producing center. No university has the resources to match the large transnational media conglomerates that are staking claims to knowledge creation (Warner-AOL, Disney, Viacom). The total revenue of the very rich Harvard University in 2005 was US$2.9 billion (https://post.harvard.edu/mhr/financial review). That year Time-Warner earned US$43.6 billion (http://en/ wikipedia.org/wiki/Time_Warner). Which of these two institutions, then, is best able to cope with technological obsolescence and other legacy issues, has the best understanding of the screen technologies that consume young people's time and the resources to spend on the production of 'compelling' content to attract and keep the young audience and the savvy marketing and promotions skills to maintain share in a competitive environment? Where would the typical, more modestly funded universities find their futures? Do distance education institutions stand a better chance?

Understandably, the university struggles to find its 'rightful' place in all of this, as do the distance teaching universities. It seems as if the post-industrial (post-Fordist) society, in particular in the postmodern period, coupled with the primacy of market theory, has undermined the formally privileged position of higher education by creating new centers of knowledge generation, training and research. These are challenges to educational institutions on their own territories as they come to grips with the fact that a range of new specialist organizations can offer at least as good a service to government, business and the community as they can.

### Future Issues

Anticipating the future, it seems that the following scenarios are possibilities that distance educators need to consider:

- An open educational market: many institutions, as many as the market will support, will operate locally, nationally and internationally. Students will enroll at their institution of choice after considering a range of criteria that will include not just the traditional ones of subject, institutional status, and faculty quality but ease of access, speed of delivery, levels of technology, such as asynchronicity, the quality of the 'bots' and perceived 'value' of the 'product' in the marketplace.
- Immense diversity: subjects and courses will be of a diversity limited only by human creativity. Courses will be flexible and designed for or tailored to the individual student. The technologies of cyberspace will enable large storage devices to hold thousands of courses that will be delivered over high-capacity telecommunications infrastructures, seamlessly organized to individualized menus.
- The 'educational supermarket': much learning will become commodified and the pedagogical processes reduced to distributive logistics. Courses will compete against each other for purchase by the student. Much energy will go into 'positioning' the courses to ensure attention and long 'shelf life.'

- Navigators: students become the controllers of their own learning environment. Teachers will be 'called up' at the student's behest. They will employ intelligent navigational agents to search out, access, enroll and deliver the courses that best suit the student's needs at the time. A student may enroll at multiple institutions, seeking approval for an award that is unique to their own situation. They will be much influenced by the 'front window' of the possible competing institutions' 'displays.'

- Asynchronicity: students will learn what they want to learn when they want to learn it and where they want to learn it. The educational institution of the future will be 'open' on-line continuously, the notion of a term or semester will be reformed into more flexible learning periods with both economic and logistical implications for the institution as 'just-in-time' learning increasingly makes sense to the lifelong learner. (The long summer break will evaporate like summer rain!) Face-to-face tuition will be a fee-for-service 'add-on' as required by the 'consumer.'

- Customized learning: students will design their own learning environment. The economic costs of learning will be balanced against such concepts as just-in-time learning, lifelong learning and the needs of the workplace. Students want "the kind of relationship with a college that they had with their bank, their supermarket, their gas company" (Levine, cited in Malcolm & Tarling, 2007, p. 45).

- The virtual university: the virtual university provides ubiquitous access regardless of location. With the development of asynchronous learning networks a global learning infrastructure that is student-centric, virtual and provides a seamless web of educational services is envisaged.

- "The global learning infrastructure will encompass a flourishing marketplace of educational services where millions of students interact with a vast array of individual and institutional suppliers. It will be delivered through multiple technologies, including the Internet, mobile telephony, broadband cable and satellite. It is being developed in phases, but will ultimately cross all institutional, state and national boundaries" (Jensen, 1998, p. 16).

Conclusion

This chapter addresses some of the challenges facing distance education's future. It argues that the continuously changing 'faces' of the three key elements—technology, the student and the institution—will shape this future, but there are choices to be made and actions to be taken by distance educators to create their particular institutional and professional

*The synergy between digital media and digitally mediated learning is such that the creators of digital learning media need to appreciate and compete with the production values of commercially orientated mass media.*

futures. The synergy between digital media and digitally mediated learning is such that the creators of digital learning media need to appreciate and compete with the production values of commercially oriented mass media. There is a danger of the teacher being displaced by the creator of products, unless procedures are adopted to provide teaching facilitation and support, for example. Distance educators will need to use the constantly changing technology platforms to produce compelling and useful courses. Sophisticated interactivity, elements of simulation and gaming, and opportunities for the creation of user-generated learning are essential considerations for the future of distance education. Distance education institutions need to engage with the student in their own 'space,' and 'capture' the 'audience' in an attractive and engaging manner. The synergy between digital media and digitally mediated learning could be marshaled for the benefit of both distance education and students.

Earlier we asked if distance education institutions stand a better chance than the traditional universities of forging a future for themselves. In many respects they do, in that their infrastructure, culture and values are geared to mediated learning and, therefore, the shift to new media is not revolutionary in itself. Enduringly, distance education institutions have often been student-focused in their courses and services, and keen to evaluate these to ensure 'customer satisfaction' (see, for example, Evans, 1994; Morgan, 1993). They have also grappled with matters of 'access' and 'equity' to ensure that their educational provision was inclusive and, particularly, not exclusive in terms of excluding needy students. However, distance education

So, does distance education stand a chance? Yes, if it recognizes and adapts creatively to the changing technology, and the diversity and capacities of digital learners. If not, it will be off to the scrap yard, although we hope many of its useful parts will be recycled!

## TERMS AND DEFINITIONS

**Convergence:** A mathematical term with many connotations but it is commonly used in digital technology to refer to a trend where a range of technologies having distinct functionalities evolve to technologies that overlap or merge. For example, television came over the airwaves whereas telephones used a wire. Now, using digital technology, both sound and vision can be transmitted on the same platform. Also multiple products can come together to form one product, with all the advantages of each of the initial components. For example, a mobile phone can also be a camera, a radio receiver a television receiver and a Web browser.

**Corporate classroom:** A term that describes the trend for businesses to provide education and training, in house, for staff and clients. For example, the Motorola University offers programs for different levels of management at what it terms its 'academies,' and they range from basic skills training through to high-level leadership training and education.

**Digital natives:** A term coined by Marc Prensky to distinguish a person for whom digital technologies existed at the time they were born, and hence has grown up with digital technologies like computers, the Internet and mobile phones, from *digital immigrants*, people who lived before the advent of digital technologies and had to learn and adapt.

**Disruptive technology:** A term used to describe a new technology that unexpectedly displaces an established technology. Whereas *sustaining technologies* rely on incremental improvements to an established technology, *disruptive technologies* either improves a product or service or replaces it in ways that the market does not expect. Alexander Graham Bell's telephone was a disruptive technology at the time; the mobile telephone is an example of one today.

**Hyper-reality:** *Virtual-reality* is created by computer-generated programs as an alternative to physical reality. *Hyper-reality* includes virtual reality, but it is more than that. Hyper-reality merges virtual with physical reality, providing a 'hyper-world' that blurs the line between what is 'real' and what is 'virtual' and makes the virtual appear 'natural.'

**M-learning:** The use of mobile communications devices (mobile phones, personal digital assistants, mini-computers) to provide teaching and learning services.

**Nanotechnology:** The study of matter at the level of atoms and molecules. It involves manufacturing products by building or altering atoms. *Nanotechnology* makes use of minuscule objects— whose width can be 10,000 times narrower than a human hair— known as nano-particles. The properties of these products depend on how those atoms are arranged. For example, it is possible to rearrange the atoms in coal to make a diamond, or rearrange the atoms in sand (and add a few other trace elements) to make computer chips.

**Screenagers:** A term coined by Douglas Rushkoff to describe 'teen-agers who are online' and 'always looking at the screen.'

**Techno-capitalism:** An emerging form of market capitalism that is based on new technological invention and innovation. It is a new term used to describe the changes to traditional capitalism brought about by the developments of digital technology. Intangibles are at the core of techno-capitalism. Creativity and knowledge are to techno-capitalism what tangible raw materials, factory labor and capital were to industrial capitalism. It is also used to describe the corporate environment and the complex and sophisticated venture capital relationships within a hi-tech economy.

**Teleconferencing:** The process of linking people and places by telephone to interact with each other in real time.

**Videoconferencing:** The process of linking people and places by television to interact with each other in real time.

## QUESTIONS FOR REVIEW AND REFLECTION

1. This chapter identifies a number of 'recent or nascent technologies' that will impact on distance education. Can you think of any other emerging technologies that may also affect the delivery of distance learning?

2. Identify and explain some of the behaviors of what are identified as 'digital natives' that may change the ways in which students engage with distance education.

3. In what ways do you think that developments in mobile technologies may be used by institutions and students to assist in distance learning?

4. This chapter suggests a number of ways in which distance learning universities, and universities in general, may be affected by digital technologies. Identify them and rank them in terms of their likely impact.

5. This chapter identifies a number of 'future issues' that may influence the behaviors of both universities and students. Choose the ones that you believe could be significant and explain the reasons for your choices. (You might also be able to identify other issues not mentioned in the chapter that you see as having significant impact.)

6. The chapter identifies digital interactive gaming and social networking as possible tools in distance learning. Using your experience of either gaming or social networks, explain how you believe these platforms may or may not have value in distance education.

7. There are six relevant technological trends identified by the Australian Communications Authority and quoted in this chapter. Choose two of these and explain how you feel they may impact on you as a student and learner in the 21st century.

8. Slaughter (2007, p. 113) suggests that "the future of education is a network, not a place." Use the information in this chapter to describe in your own words what you believe this statement means.

**Significant Contributor**

**Ron Oliver** is Pro-Vice-Chancellor (Teaching and Learning) at Edith Cowan University in Perth, Western Australia. Previously he was Associate Dean of Learning and Teaching in the Faculty of Education and Arts at ECU and Professor of Interactive Multimedia. He is Chair of the Academic Board at ECU, a member of the ECU Council, Chair of the University Curriculum Teaching and Learning Committee, a member of the University Research and Higher Degrees Committee and the Vice-Chancellor's Planning and Management Group. He is also active on many sub-committees and working parties. He is also a member of various editorial boards including *The British Journal of Educational Technology, The Journal of Educational Media and Hypermedia, Distance Education, The Journal of Interactive Learning Research, The Australian Journal of Educational Technology, Australian Educational Computing and ALT-J*. He is an Associate Fellow of the Carrick Institute for Learning and Teaching in Higher Education, and a Fellow of the Association for Advancement of Computers in Education.

**References**

ACMA (2008). *Top six trends in communications and media technologies, applications and services—Possible implications*. Canberra: Australian Communications and Media Authority.

Ahmed, M. (2008). New era dawns at home of the Internet. *The Times*, September 29, 3.

Aldrich, C. (2007). Second Life is not a teaching tool. Retrieved October 29, 2008 from: http://learningcircuits.blogspot.com/2006/11/second-life-is-not-teaching-tool.html.

Anderson, P. (2007). *What is Web 2.0? Ideas, technologies and implications for education.* London: JISC.

Ankrum, M. (1999). Roundtable forum on the education industry. *Wall Street Transcript: Special Focus, the Education Industry,* April 26, 13.

Aronowitz, S. (2000). *The knowledge factory: Dismantling the corporate university and creating true higher learning.* Boston, MA: Beacon Press.

Bates, A.W. (1995). *Technology, open learning and distance education.* London: Routledge.

Bauman, Z. (1997). Universities: Old, new and different. In A. Smith & F. Webster (Eds.), *The postmodern university? Contested visions of higher education in society.* Bristol: Open University Press.

Beck, U. (2000). *What is globalization?* Malden, MA: Polity Press.

Bhagwati, J. (2004). *In defense of globalization.* New York: Oxford University Press.

Bok, D. (2003). *Universities in the marketplace.* Princeton, NJ: Princeton University Press.

Bonnett, T.W. (1999). *Governance in the digital age: The impact of the global economy, information technology and economic deregulation on state and local government.* Washington, DC: National League of Cities.

Brabazon, T. (2007). Mobile learning: The iPodification of universities. *Nebula,* 4(1), 19–30.

Bradwell, P., Hannon, C., & Tims, C. (2008). *Video republic.* London: Demos.

Brown, R. & Dubber, A. (2007). *We're all in this together—Public broadcasting in the Digital Age.* Wellington: New Zealand On Air.

Carter-Ross, T. (2008). Social media success demands listening. *NAB Show Daily News,* April 15.

Clark, B. (1998). *Creating entrepreneurial universities* (2001 edn). New York: Pergamon.

Conde, M.A., Muñoz, C., & García, F.J. (2008). mLearning, the first step in the learning process revolution. *International Journal of Interactive Mobile Technologies,* 2(4), 61–63.

Daniel, J. (1997). *Mega universities and knowledge media: Technology strategies for higher education.* London: Kogan Page.

Davis, S. & Botkin, J. (1994). *The monster under the bed.* New York: Simon & Schuster.

de Freitas, S. & Levene, M. (2003). Wearable technology: Evaluating wearable devices, PDAs & other mobile devices in FE & HE institutions. Retrieved September 30, 2008, from: http://www.jisc.ac.uk/whatwedo/services/techwatch/reports/horizonscanning/hs0305.aspx.

Deem, R. & Johnson, R. (2001). Managerialism and university managers: Building new academic communities or disrupting old ones. In I. McNay

(Ed.), *Community: Higher education and its communities*. Buckingham: Open University Press.

Esmond, J. (2001). Boomnet: Capturing the baby boomer volunteers: A 2001 research project into baby boomers and volunteering. Victoria Park, Western Australia: MTD and Team Consultants.

Evans, T.D. (1994). *Understanding learners in open & distance education*. London: Kogan Page.

Evans, T.D. & Nation, D.E. (1993). Educational technologies: Reforming open and distance education. In T.D. Evans & D.E. Nation (Eds.), *Reforming open and distance education*. London: Kogan Page.

Evans, T.D. & Nation, D.E. (2007). Globalisation and emerging technologies. In M.G. Moore (Ed.), *The handbook of distance education* (2nd edn). Mahwah, NJ: Lawrence Erlbaum and Associates.

Friedman, T.L. (2005). *The world is flat: A brief history of the twenty-first century*. New York: Farrar, Straus & Giroux.

Garrison, D.R. (1985). Three generations of technological innovation in distance education. *Distance Education*, 6(2), 235–241.

Gibbons, M., Limoges, C., Nowotny, H., Schwartzman, S., Scott, P., & Trow, M.A. (1994). *The new production of knowledge: The dynamics of science and research in contemporary societies*. London: Sage.

Giroux, H.A. (2006). *America on the edge*. New York: Palgrave Macmillan.

Greenslade, R. (2007). Changing media summit: Onward to an unknown and challenging future. *Guardian*, March 22. Retrieved October 7, 2009 from: http://www.guardian.co.uk/media/greenslade/2007/mar/22/changing mediasummitonward.

Hawkridge, D. (1976). Next year Jerusalem! The rise of educational technology. *British Journal of Educational Technology*, 12(1), 7–30.

Hawkridge, D. (1995). The Big Bang theory in distance education. In F.G. Lockwood (Ed.), *Open and distance learning today*. London: Routledge.

Hendery, S. (2008). Broadband stealing TV viewers. *New Zealand Herald*, May 21. Retrieved October 7, 2009 from: http://www.nzherald.co.nz/broad band-stealing-tv-viewers/search/results.cfm?kw1=Broadband%20Stealing %20TV%20Viewers&kw2=&op=all&searchorder=2&display=10&start= 0&thepage=1&st=gsa&mediatype=Any&dates=Any.

Highfield, A. (2005). BBC Online: Digital and the BBC. Paper presented at the Ministry of Culture and Heritage, Wellington, November 23.

Hughes, B.B. & Hillebrand, E.E. (2006). *Exploring and shaping international futures*. Boulder, CO: Paradigm.

IADIS (2009). Call for papers. Paper presented at the Mobile Learning International Conference, Barcelona, February 26–28.

IBM (2007). *Second Life: What is Second Life?* Dunedin: Otago Museum.

ITU (2005). *ITU reports 2005: The Internet of Things*. Geneva: International Telecommunications Union.

Jarmon, L., Traphagan, T., & Mayrath, M. (2008). Understanding project-based learning in Second Life with a pedagogy, training, and assessment trio. *Educational Media International*, 45(3), 157–176.

Jensen, R.E. (1998). Emerging techologies in education. Paper presented at the Seminar on Technology and Learning, University of Canterbury, October 16.

Kenny-Wallace, G. (2000). Plato.com: The role and impact of corporate universities in the third millennium. In P. Scott (Ed.), *Higher education reformed*. London: Falmer.

Kristof, T. (2006). Is it possible to make scientific forecasts in social sciences? *Futures*, 38(5), 561–574.

Kumar, K. (1997). The need for place. In A.W.F. Smith (Ed.), *The postmodern university*. Buckingham: Open University Press.

Kuttner, R. (1996). *Everything for sale: The virtues and limits of the markets*. Chicago: University of Chicago Press

M-learning.org (2008). Take hold of your learning. Retrieved October 3, 2008 from: http://www.m-learning.org/index.htm.

Malcolm, W. & Tarling, N. (2007). *Crisis of identity*. Wellington: Dunmore.

Morgan, A.R. (1993). *Improving your students' learning*. London: Kogan Page.

Morris, P. & Janiewski, D. (2005). *New rights New Zealand*. Auckland: Auckland University Press.

Mourad, R.P. (1997). *Postmodern philosophical critique and the pursuit of knowledge in higher education*. Westport, CT: Bergin & Garvey.

Myers, J. (2005). Gaming medium growing in pervasiveness, not fully tapped. Retrieved February 21, 2006 from: <http://www.adrants.com/2005/11/gaming-medium-growing-in-pervasiveness.php>.

Newman, F., Couturier, L., & Scurry, J. (2004). *The future of higher education: Rhetoric, reality, and the risks of the market*. San Francisco: Jossey-Bass.

Nielsen (2005). Benchmarking the active gamer. Retrieved December 1, 2005 from: <http://biz.gamedaily.com/features.asp?article_id=11161&section=feature&email>=.

Noll, J.W. (1997). *Taking sides: Clashing views on controversial educational issues*. Guilford, CT: Dushkin/McGraw-Hill.

Pearson, I. (2000). Beyond digital (how technology will change our lives). *New Statesman*, 129, 23.

Perry, W. (1972). *The early development of the Open University*. Bletchley: Open University Press.

Perry, W. (1976). *Open University: A personal account by the first vice-chancellor*. Milton Keynes: Open University Press

Pew (2005a). Teens forge forward with the Internet and other new technologies. Retrieved April 20, 2008 from: http://www.pewinternet.org/PPF/r/109/press_release.asp.

Pew (2005b). *Teens and technology, youth are leading the transition to a fully wired and mobile nation*. Washington, DC: Pew Institute.

Readings, B. (1996). *The university in ruins*. Cambridge, MA: Harvard University Press.

Rossiter, K. (2003). Address to the New Zealand Broadcasting School. Christchurch, July 16.

Ruch, R.S. (2001). *Higher Ed, Inc. The rise of the for-profit university*. Baltimore, MD: Johns Hopkins University Press.

Rushkoff, D. (1996). *Children of chaos: Surviving the end of the world as we know it*. London: HarperCollins.

Saffo, P. (2005). Farewell information, it's a media age. Retrieved April 16, 2006 from: http://www.saffo.com/essays/essay_farewellinfo.pdf.

Saul, J.A. (2005). *The collapse of globalism*. Toronto: Viking Canada.

Shattock, M. (2003). *Managing successful universities*. Buckingham: Open University Press.

Shumar, W. (1997). *College for sale: A critique of the commodification of higher education*. New York: Taylor & Francis.

Slaughter, R.A. (2007). *New thinking for a new millennium: The knowledge base of futures studies*. London: Routledge.

Smith, A. & Webster, F. (1997). *The postmodern university? Contested visions of higher education in society*. Philadelphia, PA: Open University Press.

Strategy Analytics (2007) Online games: Global market forecast. Retrieved October 7, 2009 from: http://www.marketingcharts.com/interactive/online-games-to-generate-one-third-of-game-revenue-by-2011-1736/.

Tiffin, J. & Terashima, N. (2001). *Hyper reality: Paradigm for the third millennium*. London: Routledge.

Troy (2008). The networks take charge, sort of. Paper presented at the National Association of Broadcasters, Las Vegas, April 17.

Walker, R. (1993). Open learning and the media. In T.D. Evans & D.E. Nation (Eds.), *Reforming open and distance education*. London: Kogan Page.

Wankel, C. & Kingsley, J. (in press). *Higher education in Second Life*. Charlotte, NC: Information Age.

Williams, B. (2005). *Making and breaking universities*. Sydney: Macleay Press.

Winslow, L. (2007). Holographic projection technologies of the future. Retrieved October 1, 2008 from: http://www.worldthinktank.net/pdfs/holographictechnologies.pdf.

Wolf, M. (2004). *Why globalization works*. New Haven, CT: Yale University Press.

Woods, A. (2005). Kids supplement—total engagement. Retrieved December 6, 2005: from http://www.mediaweek.co.uk/features/index.cfm?fuseaction=detail.

Wsj.com (2008). Tech diary: The grapefruit cam. Retrieved September 29, 2008 from: http://online.wsj.com/video/tech-diary-the-grapefruit-cam/5DEE3C6F-69F7-4FD2-94DF-FD0A87B3960E.html.

# PART IV
## SUMMARY AND CONCLUSION

# 11

# LEADERSHIP IN A NEW ERA OF HIGHER DISTANCE EDUCATION

## DR. M.F. CLEVELAND-INNES
Associate Professor and Program Director
Athabasca University

## DR. ALBERT SANGRÀ
Professor and Director
Open University of Catalonia

> Tomorrow's leaders need to be capable of handling dynamic agendas of possibilities and see the future as discoverable rather than predictable.
>
> (Latchem & Hanna, 2001, p. 60)

## Introduction

Today we stand at the beginning of many changes that are shifting the social, economic, political and cultural conditions of our society. According to Castells (1997), we may say that we live in a new society because it has transformed in many ways. We are experiencing:

- Economic globalization.
- Education and training as the foundation to manage change.
- The democratization of the access to information and knowledge.
- The delocalization of knowledge and the approaching of distances.
- The growth of accumulated knowledge.
- New operators in the training market.
- An ever more competitive labor market.
- The advent of a media culture.

This complex system of emergent, dynamic and opposing stagnant forces has created a kaleidoscopic social context within which higher education now must create, present and maintain itself. Changes in technology, economics, global connections and social awareness are imposing on all societal institutions, including higher education. The requirement for systematic, strategic effort to deconstruct and reconstruct higher education has never been more important.

Traditional methods of operating in higher education date back to the monastic schools of the 7th century AD and early European schools of the 13th century. The time lapse alone provides an impetus to assess and revitalize systems of higher education still employing these methods. Education philosopher John Dewey (1933) suggested that the so-called 'transmission method' of education, where content is shared in ways that allow it to be absorbed as presented, is not an appropriate education model in democratic and open societies. However, the academy's resistance to change is well documented; nothing less than systematic development processes under intense pressure to transform will do (McGuinness, 2005). "Critics of higher education lament that technology has changed, the economy has changed, families have changed, religious values have changed, race relations have changed ... [yet] colleges and universities have remained relatively unchanged" (Keller, 2008, p. 4). Existing organizational realities must give way to new structures and new pedagogical models as current socioeconomic trends, technology, and new roles for faculty and students become part of higher education.

Specific processes must be implemented in the deconstruction and restructuring of an organization wishing to realize all types of change. First, challenges in the current situation that make current ways of operating difficult or impossible must be illuminated. These challenges point to social and economic pressures imposing upon higher education, and can point the way to new directions or organizational redesign to meet these challenges. Second, leadership must be in keeping with the culture of the organization, as it currently exists, but requires action to create structures, procedures and technology to overcome challenges and move institutions in new directions. This

*"Neither the purpose, the methods, nor the population for whom education is intended today bear any resemblance to those on which formal education is historically based" (Pond, 2002, p. 1).*

view of 'leadership in context' must consider leadership during change and innovation, leadership in collaborative partnerships, leadership in networked environments, and leadership for a new era of teaching and learning. Third, this leadership practice must support continuous strategic planning. This chapter outlines the challenges in the current situation in higher education, the leadership issues and requirements for a new era in higher education, and the strategic planning that will support this process of transformation.

### Current Situation Assessment

Every time change happens, or is close to happening, we are invaded with insecurity due to the uncertainty it generates. But often change also brings about new opportunities—opportunities for progress, for a general improvement in society and particularly in the everyday life of the citizens. Changes in the society affect approaches to innovation and leadership in organizations and among individuals.

The convergence of the latest scientific discoveries in telecommunications and technology allows for important changes in information production, storage and access. This has initiated what has been called the third revolution, the post-industrial revolution or the information society.

The transformation process produced by the changes outlined above has had an enormous influence on several dimensions of society itself. Political institutions, such as ministries of education, that represent the will of the people, now demand that higher education institutions (HEIs) play an active role in the construction and consolidation of the information society. These institutions are being forced to undergo a process of restructuring that will enable them to face new challenges and, possibly, offer a new service with new perspectives. Previously, HEIs have been slow to respond to societal changes. As a result, institutional leadership has generally not met the transformational challenge required in a knowledge society (Keller, 2008).

Hanna (2000), Bates (2000), Neave (2001) and Bricall (2000) offer evidence that the HEIs need to transform in order to improve services and lead to innovation. These authors agree on the following factors:

• The limited public funding.

- The increasing costs of higher education.
- The growing demand of educational services for an increasingly diverse type of student.
- The increasing role of the information and communication technologies (ICTs).
- The emerging view of teaching and learning as an investment for the future.
- All leading to the need for new organizational models.

These factors coalesce into the broader challenges related to economic issues, changing demographics, emerging technology, and new models of teaching and learning.

*Economic Issues*

*Global Economic Change, and the Current Recession, Means Scarce Resources for Higher Education*
The global economy is a corporate structure without representation from either the general public or countries with little power or economic infrastructure. Those least educated are the most vulnerable in turbulent economic times. In addition, the education system itself can fall victim. Government deficits, competition for public funding, limited corporate funds and diminishing philanthropic activity combine to paint a picture of flat, if not diminishing, budgets for higher education (McGuinness, 2005). Institutions of higher education have two choices: to look for innovative ways to self-fund or to create corporate models that bring in investment dollars.

*Funding for Higher Education Has Been in Decline since the Postwar Era*
The National Center for Public Policy and Higher Education in the U.S.A. recently issued a press release regarding the tuition crisis and a significant loss of college opportunities. Education institutions are forced to spend valuable teaching and research time resolving these challenges. Without adequate and continuously increasing numbers of student enrollments, institutions cannot sustain themselves. This creates a market-driven environment for education institutions that should be immune from market forces and focused the development of knowledge and the citizenry.

*Changing Demographics*

*Existing Higher Education Systems Will Not Satisfy the Growing*
*Demand for Enrollment*
A combination of changing student characteristics and rising enrollments will change the culture and climate of higher education in the
next decade. Add to this the need for programs for seniors and lifelong
learners, and governments are recognizing that more students will seek
higher education than current facilities can accommodate (Oblinger,
Barone, & Hawkins, 2001; Hanna, 2007). Accommodating the ram-
pant individualism in 21st-century culture will be required (Keller,
2008). This social fact, in combination with increasing participation of
older adults in higher education, requires greater attention to individual
needs. This means creating course and program schedules that are
flexible, convenient and accessible. The development of learner-
centered curriculum and instruction is now imperative (Cleveland-
Innes & Emes, 2005).

*Globalization and Intercultural Relations*

Geographic mobility, immigration and education technology mean
intercultural experiences are part of daily student life. Institutions face
the requirement to create a culture and climate that offers respect and
support in all aspects of learning for every student, regardless of
language background, nationality, race, gender or culture.

   Learner-centered curricula must take into account this changing
student body and, in particular, the globalization of society and
learning environments. Globalization refers to operating in reference
to, or ensuring application to, the whole—in this case, the whole world.

*Emerging Technology*

*Technological Opportunities for Higher Education Are Becoming More Diverse*
*and Ubiquitous*
Information and communication technology is transforming human
activity and social organizational structures broadly; higher education
is part of this transformation. "New technology will transform higher
education as we know it today" (Oblinger et al., 2001, p. 2). This is

so for managing the infrastructure of the institution and is so for one of higher education's central mandates—teaching and learning. Infrastructure has increased in size and efficiency as the technology increases in speed and decreases in cost. High-speed networks offer expanding connections. In the past two decades, if higher education has not embraced new technology, it has reached out to utilize the Internet and other forms of technologically mediated learning. This has transformed interaction opportunities among students and between student and teacher, affecting both program management and the teaching–learning experience.

*There Is Huge Growth in Internet Use*

Internet technology is not only ubiquitous; more people from more nationalities, age groups and lifestyles use it competently. The number of Internet users was approximately 500 million worldwide in 2003 and had doubled by 2005. The opportunity to network and access information is a significant change in the way people approach, use and share information. Higher education, in the business of vetting, creating and disseminating information in the form of knowledge, has to engage and analyze Internet practices and progress.

*Technological Fluency Is a Graduation Requirement*

Technology literacy and fluency is both a requirement to succeed in education and a graduation requirement; individuals will need such skills to function in a global, networked world (Oblinger, 2000). "Universities are beginning to list the fluent use of technology as an outcome skill, encourage students to take online courses, and even requiring students to take at least one online course before they graduate" (Howell, Williams, & Lindsay, 2003).

*Teaching and Learning*

*Information and Knowledge Are Growing Exponentially*

The proliferation of new information makes the job of teaching more dynamic and constructive than ever before. Those involved in teaching will put in more hours to stay at the cutting edge of knowledge in the field. They will be continually constructing new ways of understanding content as new ideas are integrated with previous knowledge. This knowledge proliferation increases demands on everyone to keep content current, eating up resources already in short supply.

*Instruction Must Become More Learner-Centered and Self-Directed*
Pedagogy, or the art and science of teaching, has been ostensibly absent from delivery models in higher education. The best we can say is that since the inception of HEIs, information has been transmitted to students. This transmission model is evaluated harshly in light of constructivist and meta-cognitive models of teaching and learning. Applying learner-centeredness to teaching and learning models will allow students to participate more fully in the arrangement of their own learning experiences. Curriculum objectives will expand to learning about learning processes, strategies and methods, i.e., 'metalearning.' Individual education plans will emerge, plans created by the student in consultation with the teacher, rather than by the teacher in consultation with the student (Cleveland-Innes & Emes, 2005).This requires a level of self-direction that must be allowed, encouraged and developed.

*The Role of Faculty as Teacher and Student as Learner Must Change*
In the transition to a learner-centered curriculum, roles for faculty and students will be agreed-upon and explicit, embedding role clarity into a new curriculum structure. For the students, required behaviors, attitudes and values as a participant in higher education must translate into the role of self-directed, continuous, active learner. For the faculty, the current role of teacher is highly variable across institutions, disciplines and faculty members. An adjustment to behaviors, attitudes and values more considerate of students is required. Faculty will include teaching strategies that foster deep rather than surface learning. In addition, faculty will support increased responsibility for students.

*Changing Faculty Roles Increases the Need for Faculty Development and Support*
Currently, faculty members serve as content experts, selecting disciplinary content that aligns with universal requirements. Unfortunately, most faculty members do so with limited knowledge of pedagogy, learning technology or learning evaluation. This means that teaching and assessment strategies used by instructors vary widely. Teaching is

based on personal preferences and disciplinary traditions. Without direction from the institution, teaching quality is not systematic but sporadic. "The absence of a common basis for understanding and evaluating teaching makes it more difficult for members of the academy to agree on what good teaching is" (Zemsky, Wegner, & Massy, 2005, p. 125).

## Leadership in Context

Over the past few years, higher education institutions have started to develop a more strategic approach in their leadership, based on the awareness that they need to undergo a transformation process to maintain their role in the current society. Institutions must change in response to the challenges outlined above, and in reference to the way the society in which they reside has changed. To do so it will be necessary to make careful decisions about new structures and directions, based on a thorough analysis of the context in which they operate. This requires leadership that is appropriate for the times.

Research and scholarship regarding higher education leadership takes a back seat to discussions of school leadership. In addition, traditional theories of leadership have largely focused on hierarchical relationships in which there is a clearly delineated power structure with a small minority of individuals in leadership roles and a great number of individuals in the follower role. Highly trained academics exist in an environment of self-governance and expect shared leadership models. In this arena, leadership must go beyond central administration to include the rank and file. Relationships between and among administrators and faculty must be collaborative and communicative if the challenges outlined above are going to be addressed (Cleveland-Innes, Emes, & Ellard, 2001).

Adjustment in the way of doing business and producing newly identified outcomes in higher education will not proceed smoothly without new types of leadership; that is, leadership is a key ingredient in the successful addressing of significant challenges and transformation to a new higher education. For the purposes of this discussion, leadership is defined as a set of characteristics and behaviors that together enable organizations, and the individuals in them, to create optimal organizational conditions for realizing organizational goals (Beaudoin, 2007).

The higher education leader of the 21st century will exhibit strong character, well-developed personal skills and the ability to create and communicate vision (Garrison & Vaughan, 2008). In addition to these personal traits, this new leader will be willing and able to: manage change and innovation; listen to and assist stakeholders, maintaining and enhancing relationships between the institution and relevant partners; embrace the realities of network environments; and ensure transformation to a new model of teaching and learning.

*Change and Innovation*

Virtual universities can stand as an example of intensive ICT-driven innovation. This requires a very particular model of organization in order to take the maximum advantage of learning in a network, as they become 'network organizations' themselves. The integration of new technology in support of learning leads to the integration of new technology in the institution. This leads to a dynamic of change that has to be managed by involving the affected parties with a clear, shared and well-communicated vision.

In recent research (Sangrà, 2008) findings indicate the need for a strong leadership in HEIs in order to overcome resistance and realize success in education innovation. Innovation in open and distance education and e-learning in an HEI are elements of a process of change and have to be considered as such. High levels of resistance to change among the university staff can be explained in several ways.

First, the level of knowledge among the teachers tends to be very low. This causes resistance to the unknown, and the uncertainty and insecurity it implies. Second, there are ideological aspects that influence acceptance. One of them is the conservative attitude of teachers in most universities. These teachers are against any change of their own teaching models and consider that any innovation jeopardizes the final outcome of traditional knowledge transmission.

On the other hand, there is a third variable that causes a situation where a teacher does not receive any information about the possibility of improving his or her teaching results with the use of ICT because there is no evaluation process in place. This lack of evaluation means a lack of evidence regarding the effects of new teaching and learning models, thus leaving benefits, if any, of the transition in the realm of the unknown.

### Collaborative Partnerships

HEIs now face the difficulty of being competitive in a global educational world. Some years ago, collaboration was easier if you took into account the fact that universities from different continents were not competitors, but potential partners; now they are competing for the same students.

ICT development and, particularly, the extensive use and presence of the Internet in education have reduced distances. Even the smallest and farthest university in the world can become a competitor if it offers a similar program online. ICT and the Internet have given distance education credibility as an innovative, legitimate and modern way to learn.

In this new scenario, collaboration is the counterpart of competition. A partner may become a competitor and, simultaneously, an ally. Thus, new competences should be developed by those who lead a university and want to establish strong and fruitful partnerships with other institutions. The following criteria should be taken into consideration when starting a process for a partnership:

- *Flexibility:* any agreement cannot be based on an immovable position. We should also understand the interests of our partner and will be available to move from one position to another in a range of possibilities. To prepare different scenarios in which we can feel comfortable can be a good strategy for this. We should always pursue a win/win relationship.
- *Freedom:* by agreeing to a partnership, neither we nor our partner should feel that significant freedom has been lost. It is not necessary to impose our solutions as the only ones, but respect the way in which other institutions manage their organization. Only when feeling free can we feel involved in important challenges.

- *Commitment:* we are not just developing the project at hand. We should show our willingness to engage in a committed relationship with the other partner. And we can ask them for a similar commitment.
- *Excellence:* this should be our target. A collaborative partnership should be based on the fact that together we can reach a higher, even the highest, level of excellence. No level of accomplishment less than excellent is acceptable.
- *Segmentation:* sometimes, HEIs try to carry out very general and institutional agreements that do not take into consideration particular needs and possibilities of smaller units of departments within them. It is recommended that objectives be segmented, narrow and appropriate to the units involved. Only from this perspective can we then be flexible and work with different solutions.
- *Academic collaboration and acknowledgment:* we should start from the basis of the acknowledgment of the other partner. We are all academic institutions, and it is from the respect of the other and from a frank collaboration that we will build a strong, competitive partnership.
- *Feasibility:* finally, our agreement should be considered on the basis of its feasibility. Even if our main aim is academic, our purpose should be sustainable to avoid failure.

It is also important to consider some issues regarding the characteristics of our partners. First of all, it is important to share a common educational background. Unproductive discussions on different educational approaches may be avoided. Second, find partners that can become complementary. If your partner is doing the same as you, it may be quite difficult to agree on what you will do and what will be done by the other. Also find an experienced partner, which adds value to your proposal. And finally, try to find a balanced partner, in the sense that the partnership provides as much benefit for your institution as you provide to it, and that the cost of the partnership is in balance with the gain received.

*Leadership in Networked Environments*

The 'networked' university is already a reality. ICTs and the knowledge economy are the roads on which the future of the university is being built. Distance education has to take advantage of, and manage, the technological change (Bates, 2000). Improved leadership and management are key enablers for it (Leitch, 2006, quoted in Bolden, Petrov, & Gosling, 2009).

Leadership is "a set of attitudes and behaviours that create conditions for innovative change" (Beaudoin, 2003, p. 519). Thus, distance education leaders should carry the flag to foster this change based on innovation. Challenges in the transition from traditional distance education to online learning are similar to those found when traditional face-to-face classrooms seek to integrate information and communication technologies into teaching and learning activities. Never has the agenda of distance education governance been so similar to that of the conventional universities.

The following issues emerged as a result of poor or limited leadership in the face of transition to a networked environment:

- The lack of a defined strategy to disseminate and implement the project. People do not know anything about it, or what they know is only based on rumors, which leads to a situation where the perception of a strategy is very limited and the possibilities of involvement shrink considerably or even turn into potential opposition or reluctance.
- The lack of a general and overall strategy or a very defensive position of the university's governing board alongside the lack of coordination between strategic actions and operative decisions. This usually leads to a certain chaos in the organization and results in not having a clear view of what the message is and how everybody is supposed to react.
- Occasionally, this could be accompanied by too frequent organizational changes that increase the feeling of living in a provisional moment or a phase of uncertain leadership. It is important not to confuse necessary restructuring in a moment of change with the constant modifications in structure and responsibilities. Such continuous changes can even lead to problems in keeping a con-

stant rhythm of innovation. Also we have to see the lack of evaluation of the initiatives that are carried out. What is not evaluated is labeled as being not very important.

Any change like ICT integration in a university requires a process of strategic thinking in order to redefine the roles of the different agents, to create new functions and departments and develop a new concept for the educational model. It also leads to the reorganization of routines and administrative processes and to the restructuring of production and educational design processes.

The ICT integration process is easier to understand in a context of reconfiguration of an institution's organizational and pedagogical characteristics in harmony with the new opportunities and limitations that technology brings about. Therefore, we see technology, organization and pedagogy (TOP) as a triangle of factors that are closely related to each other in a symbiotic way (Sangrà, Guàrdia, & Fernández-Michels, 2009)

Analysis of factors and mechanisms promoted in the studied cases enabled us to observe how the universities' visions and strategies— the ICT integration models—condition the configuration of the TOP triangle under which we can arrange the identified actions and activities.

Technology, organization and pedagogy are three elements that become the main factors for the development of a successful initiative if they are adequately combined. They are very often taken into consideration but looked at independently. The proposed TOP triangle presents the three elements in a situation of mutual influence and correspondence. Therefore, the initiatives for ICT integration or for e-learning development in universities have to be based on a strong link between all three vertexes and have to create the appropriate context for the development of an ICT-integrated environment that leads us to efficiency and sustainability through a strategy of institutional dimensions.

In relation to the three vertexes of the TOP triangle, it is important to reflect upon the profiles of the university leaders and the process managers. They should have a strong capacity for implementation of a very concrete strategic plan in which they have to manage the organizational and economical aspects, adding a high level of understanding

for the technological aspects in the context of a well-defined pedagogical approach.

Distance education institutions that shift toward ICT-based course
delivery have a shorter distance to go than traditional universities that
usually have to try to integrate a wholly new teaching and learning
concept into their existing administrative, organizational and pedagogical frameworks. This means having to overcome old conceptions
and the reluctance of teaching staff who see change as a threat.

Distributed leadership takes on a new and useful meaning when we
see it in reference to developing virtual communities. In fact, from the
Megatrends project (Paulsen, 2007), a number of skills for leadership
in successful e-learning institutions should be considered. They are the
ability to:

- build high competence and tradition in online education
- promote continuing research and evaluation related to online
  education
- develop high competence in ICT
- develop effective administrative systems
- make sure to give support to the bottom-up initiatives
- attract enthusiastic employees who believe in online education
- develop strategies that support online education and make sure
  that the employees are loyal to the strategy
- focus on quality
- consider collaboration with other educational institutions
- utilize the pressure on the necessity to change as a means to be
  flexible, to stay in business and to adapt to the changing market
- define precisely the institutional model you will adopt
- plan carefully to manage both educational and business activities
- avoid consortia of institutions that compete with each other and
  the consortium.

## Strategic Planning

The definition of 'strategy' offered by Mintzberg, Quinn, & Voyer
(1997, p. 7) is: "the pattern or plan that integrates the main aims and
policies of an organization and at the same time . . . establishes the
coherent sequence in which action has to be carried out."

The concept of strategic planning comes from the corporate context, where changes happen quicker, more frequently and in a more radical manner. Strategic planning is now a corollary to strategic leadership processes within companies and institutions. It is an attempt to gain market advantage, obtain better results, be more efficient and effective, and conquer a market, all in a determined period of time.

In order to carry out strategic planning it is important to initiate a process called 'strategic thinking' (Boar, 2001) or 'strategic formulation' (Andrews, 1971). In this sense, HEIs must start a process of strategic reflection that allows evaluation of the strong and weak points that could be brought about by change, particularly by the incorporation of ICT. This reflection should also help in determining which strategic decisions would be necessary in order to generate maximum benefits for the institution. All this can be called the development of a strategic plan for the integration of ICT in the HEI.

Indeed, the development of an ICT implementation strategy seeks to generate knowledge about how to use technology in order to create information and adequate systems with the aim of developing competitive advantages within an organization (Porter, 2000). The university has to determine in each case which competitive advantage it is looking for. Previous research (Sangrà, 2005) was conducted to identify how universities were integrating ICTs from a defined and planned strategic viewpoint. This study produced the following conclusions:

- ICTs represent a transversal axis of institutional change.
- Strategic planning is increasing but it still has a low impact on academic activities.
- There are fields of priority strategic action: access and infrastructure, administration processes, communication, research, and teaching and learning.
- The chosen strategies are not the same in every university.

As a consequence there is a lack of balance in the ICT integration process; this does not lead to integral solutions. Findings from this study demonstrated that ICT-driven innovation can become the driver of organizational and cultural changes within the institutions themselves. Such objectives are not always openly expressed and can lead to confusion. Unclear or unstated objectives can lead to a lack of implementation with negative results regarding the desired outcomes.

## Conclusion

New leadership for a new and distributed higher education will proceed with identification of challenges in the existing situation that make current ways of operating counterproductive. Next, addressing challenges will involve leading through change toward innovation. Advancement is only innovation until it becomes the new normal; leading is required until the new normal has been reached.

We suggest that this new normal will involve collaborative partnerships, networked environments, new models of teaching and learning and continuous strategic planning. Leadership will manage and evaluate the emerging new structures, driven in large measure by networking technology (Beaudoin, 2003). It is the technology integration that will be central to many changes. Beaudoin states that some institutional leaders "would not acknowledge that technological innovation is perhaps the single most compelling factor driving them towards new organizational structures and new pedagogical models" (p. 521). Technology integration in higher education, whether traditional face-to-face or distance delivery, is one of the most demanding challenges; we have the opportunity to put it in the very center of the discussion, not as a second-class education method, but as a driver for innovation and change.

Leaders in higher and distance education must rise to the challenge of the knowledge society and the transformational impact of ICTs. This calls for courageous and collaborative leaders willing to address important but difficult problems. Technology integration, into both the institutional infrastructure and the teaching and learning system, is one these challenges. Distributed leadership offers a persuasive discourse that embeds concepts of both collegiality and managerialism (Bolden, Petrov, & Gosling, 2009). It is time to utilize this leadership model in response to the needs of higher education, as distributed learning did some time ago. The need for strategic planning, clear vision and direction from the leaders of higher education institutions is a must for the future.

## TERMS AND DEFINITIONS

**Culture:** In reference to organizations, culture is a system of common and shared beliefs, values and perspectives about the work the organization does, and the context in which the organization operates. This influence affects patterns of interaction, patterns of common duties and activities and choices made by leaders. These patterns then allow actors (people) in the organization to create and recreate the patterns of action and functional systems that sustain and/or change the organization.

**Faculty development:** Refers to maintenance and/or improvement of competence for an academic employed in the position of faculty member. This is a term borrowed from the human resource vernacular that describes professional or staff development. For faculty, development may fall into multiple categories: development related to improved scholarship, development related to course design and teaching or other kinds of training/career enhancement.

**Leadership:** Definitions of leadership vary with the theory used and the field in which leadership is being proffered. Leadership in post-industrial, post-Fordist society must embrace the collaborative, recursive nature of the context. This means a focus on the leader is no longer adequate. Leadership must be defined as the collaborative activities that the leader and followers do together to carry out organizational imperatives. According to Beaudoin (2007), leadership is a set of characteristics and behaviors that together enable organizations, and the individuals in them, to create optimal organizational conditions for realizing organizational goals.

**Organizational climate:** This ambiguous concept is often compared to the concept of personality in individuals. Climate refers to the enduring characteristics of organizational life. This is noted by individuals operating in coordination with the organization. Climate can be seen as 'positive' or 'negative,' depending upon the ability of the characteristics of organizational life to realize its public functions effectively. Positive or negative climate can also refer to the perceived comfort of individuals working in the organization, and one's sense of fit with organizational characteristics.

**Role:** A sociological construct describing a collection of behavioral requirements associated with a certain social position in a group, organization or society (Kendall, Murray, & Linden, 2000).

**Strategic planning:** Strategic planning in the 21st century requires iterative activity of discussion and consensus-building to clarify shared direction and build commitment to future direction and priorities; attention to continuous change and the dynamic environment is what makes this planning *strategic* (Rogers, Finley, & Galloway, 2001).

## QUESTIONS FOR REVIEW AND REFLECTION

1. What are the central challenges faced by higher education in the current social and economic climate?
2. How can leadership actions remedy these situations?
3. What makes higher education institutions unique in relation to leadership strategies?
4. What are the central requirements of a strategic plan? How must these be shaped in reference to higher education?
5. What will the higher education institution of the future look like?

### Significant Contributor

**Donald E. Hanna** received his Ph.D. in Adult and Continuing Education from Michigan State University in 1978. His experience in online education began in 1987, when he was the coordinator of an online conference as part of the Kellogg National Leadership Program. He is the author of numerous articles and book chapters. Most recently he authored and edited *Higher Education in an Era of Digital Competition: Choices and Challenges* (Atwood, 2000). He is also the co-author and editor (with Colin Latchem) of *Leadership in Open and Flexible Learning* (Kogan Page, 2001) and *Bridging the Gap: Leadership, Technology, and Organizational Change* (Atwood, 2003). Dr. Hanna served as Chancellor of the University of Wisconsin-Extension (1993–1997) and was previously Associate Vice-Provost for Extended University Services at Washington State University. He was a visiting scholar on a Fulbright specialist grant to Vietnam and Thailand in 2005–2006.

## References

Andrews, K. (1971) *The concept of corporate strategy.* Homewood, IL: R. Irwin.

Bates, A.W. (2000) *Managing technological change. Strategies for college and university leaders.* San Francisco: Jossey-Bass.

Beaudoin, M.F. (2003) Distance education leadership: An appraisal of research and practice. In M.G. Moore & W.G. Anderson (Eds.), *Handbook of distance education.* Mahwah, NJ: Lawrence Erlbaum Associates.

Beaudoin, M.F. (2007). Institutional leadership. In Moore, M.G. (Ed.), *Handbook of distance education*, 2nd edition. New Jersey: Lawrence Erlbaum Associates.

Boar, B. (2001) *The art of strategic planning for information technology.* New York: John Wiley and Sons.

Bolden, R., Petrov, G., & Gosling, J. (2009) Distributed leadership in higher education: Rhetoric and reality. *Educational Management Administration & Leadership*, 37, 257–277.

Bricall, J.M. (2000) *Universidad 2mil.* Madrid: Consejo de Rectores de las Universidades Españolas (CRUE).

Castells, M. (1997) *La era de la información: Economía, sociedad y cultura. Vol. I: La sociedad red.* Madrid: Alianza.

Cleveland-Innes, M.F. & Emes, C. (2005). Principles of a learner centered curriculum: Responding to the call for change in higher education. *Canadian Journal of Higher Education*, 35(4), 85–110.

Cleveland-Innes, M.F., Emes, C. & Ellard, J. (2001). On being a social change agent in a reluctant collegial environment. *Planning in Higher Education*, 29, 25–33.

Dewey, J. (1933). *How we think* (rev. edn). Boston: D.C. Heath

Finley, D.S., Rogers, G., & Galloway, J.R. (2001). Beyond the mission statement: Alternative futures for today's universities. *Journal of Marketing for Higher Education*, 10(4), 63–82.

Garrison, D.R. & Vaughan, N.D. (2008). *Blended learning in higher education XE "higher education" : Framework, principles and guidelines.* San Francisco: Jossey-Bass.

Gairín, J. (2006) Las comunidades virtuales de aprendizaje. *EDUCAR*, 37, 41–64.

Hanna, D.E. (Ed.) (2000). *Higher education in an era of digital competition: Choices and challenges.* Madison, WI: Atwood.

Hanna, D.E. (2007). Organizational change in higher distance education. In Moore, M.G. (Ed.), *Handbook of distance education*, 2nd edition. New Jersey: Lawrence Erlbaum Associates.

Howell, S.L., Williams, P.B., & Lindsay, N.K. (2003). Thirty-two trends affecting distance education: An informed foundation for strategic planning. *Online Journal of Distance Education*, 6(3). Retrieved September 24, 2008 from: http://www.westga.edu/~distance/ojdla/fall63/fall63.htm.

Keller, G. (2008). *Higher education and the new society.* Baltimore, MA: Johns Hopkins University Press.

Kendall, D., Murray, J., & Linden, R. (2000). *Sociology in our times*, 2nd edition. Ontario: Nelson Thompson Learning.

Latchem, C. & Hanna, D.E. (2001). Leadership in open and flexible learning. In Latchem, C. and Hanna, D.E. (Eds.), *Leadership XE "Leadership" for 21st century learning: Global perspectives from educational perspectives.* Sterling, VA: Stylus.

McGuinness, A.C. (2005). The states and higher education. In Altbach, P.G., Berdahl, R.O., & Gumport, P.J. (Eds.), *American higher education in the 21st century*. Baltimore, MA: Johns Hopkins University Press.

Mintzberg, H., Quinn, J.B., & Voyer, J. (1997) *El Proceso estratégico: Conceptos, contextos y casos.* Mexico: Prentice-Hall Hispanoamericana.

Neave, G. (2001) *Educación superior: Historia y política. Estudios comparativos sobre la universidad contemporánea.* Barcelona: Gedisa Editorial.

Oblinger, D.G. (2000). *The nature and purpose of distance education.* Technology Source. Retrieved June 2009 from: http://www.technologysource.org/article/nature_and_purpose_of_distance_education/.

Oblinger, D., Barone, C.A., & Hawkins, B.L. (2001) *Distributed education and its challenges: An overview.* American Council on Education (ACE). Retrieved January, 2009 from: http://www.acenet.edu/bookstore/pdf/distributed-learning/distributed-learning-01.pdf.

Paulsen, M.F. (Ed.) (2007). *Megaproviders of e-learning in Europe.* Bekkastua: Megatrends Project. Retrieved January 30, 2009 from: http://nettskolen.nki.no/in_english/megatrends/.

Pond, W.K. (2002). Distributed education in the 21st Century: Implications for quality assurance. *Online Journal of Distance Learning Administration*, 5(2). Retrieved August 12, 2006 from: http://www.westga.edu/%7Edistance/ojdla/summer52/pond52.html.

Porter, M.E. (2000) *Estrategia competitiva: Técnicas para el análisis de los sectores industriales y de la competencia.* Mexico: Continental.

Rogers, G., Finley, D., & Galloway, J. (2001). *Strategic planning in social service organizations: A practical guide.* Toronto: Canadian Scholars' Press.

Sangrà, A. (2005). Introducing ICT in higher education: A strategic planning approach. *Journal of e-Learning and Knowledge Society*, 1(3), 331–340.

Sangrà, A. (2008). ICT integration at the university: Models, problems and challenges. Unpublished Ph.D. dissertation, Universitat Rovira I Virgili, Tarragona.

Sangrà, A., Guàrdia, L., & Fernández-Michels, P. (2009). Matching technology, organisation and pedagogy in e-learning: Looking for the appropriate balance leading to sustainability and effectiveness. In M. Santasfield &

T. Connolly (Eds.), *Institutional transformation through best practices in virtual campus development: Advancing e-learning policies.* Hershey, PA: Information Science Reference.

Zemsky, R., Wegner, G., & Massy, W. (2005). *Remaking the American university: Market-smart and mission-centered.* Piscataway, NJ: Rutgers University Press.

# 12

## CONCLUSION

### DR. D.R. GARRISON
Professor and Director
University of Calgary

### DR. M.F. CLEVELAND-INNES
Associate Professor and Program Director
Athabasca University

It has become more than evident that approaches to teaching and learning in higher education are being transformed in response to information and communications technology. What is not so clear is the impact of teaching and technological developments in

*Through the varied perspectives of the contributors we have gained insight into the issues and state of distance education as well as the challenges for the study and practice of distance education as we move forward.*

distance education institutions. The guiding question is: what impact will these developments have on the evolution of distance education institutions? The sine qua non of distance education has been independent study through prepared course materials that would guide the individual learner. Teaching was embedded in the instructional materials provided to the student. The exclusive goal of this approach was to provide access at a minimal cost. Serious pedagogical compromises were necessary to reach this goal of greatly expanded access. What has radically changed as a result of these developments is a focus on the nature and quality of the educational transaction. Interaction and independence are no longer a zero-sum game. Access is no longer tied to low-cost independent study approaches.

The purpose of this chapter is to extract the key themes embedded in each of the chapters and use them to explore likely developments in the theory and practice of distance education.

Themes

We began this book with a number of probing questions. Through the varied perspectives of the contributors we have gained insight into the issues and state of distance education as well as the challenges for the study and practice of distance education as we move forward. An overview of the themes found in these perspectives is described next.

In the second chapter, the editors review significant events of central influence on distance education. In so doing, foundational principles and practices of distance education are identified, in past and current forms. In describing the industrial era of distance education, we outline how the emergence of a new era of distance education – the post-industrial era – is evolving. This occurred, in part, through changes in technology, and, in part, with the demonstrated uses of that technology. In industrial models of distance education, geographical constraints necessitate use of available technologies to neutralize distance and increase access. The current focus on transactional issues and ubiquitous communications technologies is illuminated as a logical extension of post-industrial characteristics. The remainder of the book is organized to consider how new and emerging communications technology and the Internet impact distance education

In Chapter 3, Gary Miller provides an exploration of organizational changes in distance education. He starts us on this quest of understanding changes in distance education by describing the social, technological and institutional changes through the various developmental stages, beginning with correspondence study, progressing to the industrial period, and setting the stage for online learning. He notes how distance education overcame or replaced earlier forms to move increasingly into the mainstream of higher education. However, there is some way to go, as reflected by Gary's pedagogical challenge to determine "how to create a common sense of community among students of very diverse backgrounds and interests." This theme of community is prevalent throughout this book. A more challenging question for distance education is: how do you create community in a context of continuous enrollment and self-pacing?

In Chapter 4, Margaret Haughey provides a unique historical perspective of teaching and learning in distance education. This perspective is crucial if we are to understand the current state of distance

250    D.R. GARRISON & M.F. CLEVELAND-INNES

education and begin to understand its evolution during the current communications revolution. She provides a detailed context for the provision of distance education that helps us appreciate the growth of traditional distance education and the challenges that it faces in a digital age. Similar to the other authors, she notes the importance of support and student–instructor dialogue and identifies the intellectual leaders who attempted to address these issues in the Industrial Era. Finally, she notes the theme of flexibility for the learner but with the choice of seeking help. Her concluding challenge for distance educators is to maintain this flexibility (i.e., independence) in a digital age. From this perspective, it would seem that it is very difficult for distance educators to let go of this independence.

In Chapter 5, Heather Kanuka and Charmaine Brooks increase our depth of understanding of the development of distance education through a critical analysis of post-Fordism characterized by the replacement of industrial approaches such as the division of labor with flexible, mass-produced learning materials and experiences using Net-based communication tools. The first two goals are flexible but cost-effective educational outcomes. As well, integral to the post-Fordist movement has been constructivist approaches to learning. In this, the authors move on to their third goal (in addition to flexible access and cost-effectiveness) to achieve a quality learning experience. The culminating argument is that it is not possible to provide a quality learning experience with flexible access (large enrollment classes) in a cost-effective manner. Establishing collaborative relationships and personal interaction and support requires "an investment in human capital." As such, post-Fordism provides only the appearance of providing flexible access and quality learning in a cost-effective manner. The challenge for distance education to provide "accessible and flexible learning opportunities, while continuing to offer a quality commodity that is also cost effective for a mass market" continues to this day.

Before we leave this chapter, let us pick up on the theme of quality of an educational experience that very much relates to the theme of learning communities. To this

[W]hy has campus-based enrollment thrived in the midst of ubiquitous interactive and collaborative technologies?

point much of our discussion has indirectly been focused on distance education moving toward that of online and higher education. There is the alternative explanation that needs to be acknowledged: that is, will higher education evolve and merge with distance education practices? That is a distinct possibility if we see online learning as a distance education practice. However, online learning is very much more aligned with higher education. In this context of predictions that conventional higher education will morph toward distance education (Annand, 2007), Kanuka and Brooks ask an important question: why has campus-based enrollment thrived in the midst of ubiquitous interactive and collaborative technologies? Perhaps the strongest explanation is the sense of community and common purpose created in a collaborative face-to-face environment. When we better understand the qualities of a community of learners to create and sustain discourse and quality learning outcomes, it may be the full potential of online learning that will reveal how we can achieve flexible access, quality learning and cost-effectiveness, and shape the direction for the future of distance education.

The challenges of post-Fordist distance education are explored from a slightly different perspective by Doug Shale in Chapter 6. He begins with the premise that the development of distance education has been about the organizational "ways and means to bridge the separation of teacher and student." Doug provides an interesting perspective on the organizational dynamics of early correspondence study in higher education institutions as well as the dedicated distance teaching universities. The challenge for distance education and its Achilles heel, according to Doug, is "weak and inefficient interaction with students." Doug states that the industrialized approach, with its economies of scale, presents education as "a commodity that can be packaged up by an educational institution (not a professor—an institution) and transmitted to students." He goes on to state that the "notion that a course package (however constituted) is sufficient to induce learning has been the source of much misconception" and may be the source of the marginalization of distance education. The point is that distance educators can no longer make a virtue out of idealizing independence and excessive self-direction. Cost-effective communications technologies and new approaches challenge these views and again raise the theme of community and a quality educational experience for our times. Finally, Doug notes that we see conventional higher education and traditional distance education both adopting Web-based technologies. As a result, consideration of the convergence between distance and traditional education is an important issue.

In Chapter 7, Karen Swan makes the point that online learning is in essence post-industrial distance education. More importantly, she goes on to say that what distinguishes online learning are the pedagogical approaches grounded in social constructivist learning theory that focuses on collaboration. The digital technologies of post-industrial distance education that enable online learning is an important cultural influence. This development combines with a second cultural influence, social constructivism, "that resonates with age-old academic ideals." Karen explores the technical and constructivist cultural influences and the confluence that has created the conditions for computer-mediated communication (i.e., computer conferencing) to emerge in the form of online learning. This leads directly to the theme of a quality distance education experience associated with collaborative learning communities. In this context Karen explores the Community of Inquiry framework as a model for online learning.

In Chapter 8, Phil Ice does a remarkable job of exploring and assessing the myriad new and emerging learning technologies with the potential to support connectivity and collaboration in an educational environment. He has done a masterful job of making sense of the complex array of Web 2.0 tools and providing us with a vision of future applications. Phil wisely notes the virtually impossible task of trying to predict future applications of technologies in an educational context even a few years hence. He does, however, build his exploration around the premise that the role of technology will be focused on providing increased connectivity and collaboration for education purposes.

In Chapter 9 Norm Vaughan explores a fast-emerging use of information and communications technology that combines online learning and face-to-face learning experiences. Blended learning approaches build on the capabilities of the technology to create and sustain communities of learners. As such, blended learning creates opportunities and challenges to both distance and higher education institutions. The power to fuse the strengths of online and face-to-face educational environments and create collaborative constructivist learning experiences in a cost-effective manner is transforming higher education (Garrison & Kanuka, 2004). The core theme again is the nature and quality of the learning experience founded in collaborative approaches to learning. The experience with blended learning speaks to its enormous potential to impact distance education and transform higher education.

In Chapter 10, Terry Evans and Brian Pauling provide a provocative perspective with regard to educational institutions and distance education. Their point is that technology and the fluidity of educational practices will have an enormous impact on distance education. To emphasize this point, Terry and Brian state, "it is possible that 'distance education'—the term and its history—will be towed to the scrap yard," with many of its useful parts recycled. This speaks directly to the essence of this book, which is about the transformational future of distance education. The authors argue that this transformation will not be confined to distance education. Practices such as blended learning suggest that higher education institutions will lose their control of pedagogical practices. The implied challenge is whether distance education is to be reformed or scrapped. This is the stark reality that faces distance education and the focus of this book.

The reform of distance education from the perspective of organizational change and leadership is the focus of Chapter 11. Martha Cleveland-Innes and Albert Sangrà examine the current situation of higher education, how distance education can and has informed higher education broadly, and how leadership and strategic planning can enable transformation. There is opportunity in the move to post-industrial states to change education in ways that will improve access, and improve communication and collaboration such that the teaching and learning transaction is enhanced. In the end, it is this enhancement and realignment of education structures and process for a new era, such that education access and teaching and learning quality improves, that should be at the center of any education-related change.

## Post-Industrial Distance Education

Online learning may be the best representation of post-industrial distance education. Post-industrial distance education practice has been shaped most strongly by ubiquitous communications technology and collaborative constructivist approaches to teaching and learning. These two factors have set the stage for the creation of online educational communities. That is, communities that can sustain discourse and knowledge construction over time and space. However, distance education institutions have not been influenced evenly by these developments. Online learning has raised serious questions as to the assumptions and practices of industrial distance education.

Developments in online learning have provided a unique perspective on the theory and practice of distance education. Online learning emerged largely from the work on computer-assisted learning and computer conferencing. This represents a distinct line of research that has considerable overlap with distance education but is driven by very different principles and practices. Online learning represents a new era of distance education that capitalizes on the new communications technology but, more importantly, represents a shift in pedagogical practices. The connective ability of online learning is distinguished by its ability to create and sustain communities of inquiry, the hallmark of higher education. Online learning does not limit access nor appreciably increase cost; yet it can provide unconstrained membership in collaborative communities of learners.

Online learning is brought to life in communities of inquiry that offer possibilities inconceivable in industrial distance education. Collaborative approaches to learning online are not congruent with the characteristics of continuous enrollment and self-paced learning synonymous with industrial distance education. Moreover, in industrial approaches teaching presence remains a passive and often virtual experience. The difference in teaching presence is that between tutor support and continuous facilitation and direction. Industrial distance education practices are greatly resisted by conventional higher education institutions. This is not the case, however, for online learning as its adoption in conventional higher education institutions has increased significantly (Allen & Seaman, 2007).

Distance Education Theory

There is a conceptual divide between traditional distance education and online learning as reflected in commitments to independence versus collaboration. Moreover, theoretical development in distance education (entrenched in the industrial paradigm) has largely stalled compared to the research associated with online collaborative communities of learners (Garrison, 2009). If the relevance and terminology of distance education are to be preserved, then coherent theory must be developed that can accommodate independence and collaboration concurrently. Online learning has shown this to be possible and not a contradiction in terms. Distance education theory must begin to accommodate technological and pedagogical developments that are currently being manifested under the theory and practice of online learning.

As we have seen in previous chapters, the Internet and communications technology have been powerful catalysts to rethink how we approach teaching and learning in education generally. While distance educators are trying to provide increased access and flexibility through the adoption of information and communications technology, "this has challenged not only the theories but also the practice of distance education worldwide . . . [T]he 'distance' between teacher and learner was likely to disappear in distance education" (Wei, 2008, p. 370). Wei asks if "distance in distance education goes, what will happen to distance education then?" (p. 340). The great risk for distance education is increased marginalization if we keep to the outdated ideals of independent study and continuous enrollment that essentially block the creation of collaborative learning communities.

The theoretical challenge for distance education theorists is to incorporate sustained two-way communication in the form of critical discourse and collaborative learning activities. Distance education theorists have attempted to address the issue of conversation and dialogue (Holmberg, 1989; Moore, 1990, 2007), but they did not fundamentally challenge the premise of independence and self-pacing. As such, there has been little theoretical progress in transforming industrial constructs associated with distance education institutions. Theory developed in distance education has largely stalled (Garrison, 2009). The core assumptions of distance education (i.e., access, independence, economies of scale) need to be re-examined in the context of online learning theory and practice (i.e., collaboration, community, quality assurance). A concerted effort is required if we are to achieve a comprehensive theory that encompasses distance and online learning. Much greater emphasis must be focused on transactional and collaboration theories of learning mediated by information and communications technology. Consideration must also be given to the possibility of combining online and face-to-face learning experiences that have become so prevalent in higher education (Garrison & Vaughan, 2008).

At this time, the dilemma for distance education is whether distance education theorists should be grappling with the challenge to fuse theoretical developments in online learning with accepted distance education theory based on industrial assumptions; or should they wait and create theory based on emerging practice and the inevitable evolution of traditional distance education institutions? The latter was largely the case with Peters' industrial model of distance education. While theory may be shaped by practice, theory can also help us shape practice. It would seem to us that the latter is where we find ourselves. The theory of online learning could and should have a strong influence in shaping the direction and identifying the possibilities for distance education. The challenge for distance educators is to maintain access and efficiencies of the industrial approach while increasing interaction and collaboration.

## Conclusion

Will the traditional approach to distance education begin to dissolve at some point in the near future? Will the distinguishing phrase, 'distance education,' become an anachronism? Have the traditional assumptions around independence and industrial production shifted in any appreciable degree? Have the collaborative possibilities of online learning changed the essence of the distance education process and experience? Will we see a convergence of distance and higher education through the mutual adoption of online learning theory and practice? The question is whether distance education will join the mainstream of higher education or be scrapped theoretically and practically.

Guri-Rosenblit (2009) argues that it is a misconception to think that e-learning (i.e., online learning) is a new generation of distance education. The reality is essentially that there is a disconnect between distance education and online learning. Distance education institutions do not use online learning approaches to an appreciable degree. Guri-Rosenblit (2009, p. 107) states that "distance education and e-learning constitute two distinct phenomena," which is not surprising considering their distinctly different origins. The goal of distance education remains access, while online learning is about the enhancement of teaching and learning. The question is whether and how these two goals and approaches can merge.

To what extent will there be a shift theoretically and practically in distance education? Are the issues of access and economies of scale reasons to hold to the ideals of independence and self-directedness? Are these approaches necessary and sufficient to prepare students for an increasingly connected and knowledge-based society? Has the focus shifted from access to content, to access to communities of learners and people with common interests who wish to explore deeply and collaboratively construct meaning and knowledge? Engaging in collaborative learning is being accepted as a richer and more relevant educational experience. Will this ideal inevitably shape distance education in the future?

We need to view distance education from multiple perspectives and with a questioning attitude. What we hope we have accomplished here is to provide a range of perspectives and challenging questions with regard to the future of distance education. What we must not do is blindly accept the dogma of past practice. Change has been too great for this to be a comfortable or lasting position. Distance educators must critically analyze new developments, particularly in online learning, and begin to position themselves for the inevitable transformation of how we approach learning in distance education. It is time that distance educators think through the changes and possibilities of both flexible access and collaborative learning experiences. Are these to remain disjointed realities and ideals? The quality of the teaching and learning transaction must always remain the prime mover in any educational experience, including distance education. This is the future of distance education as online theory and practice permeates traditional distance education institutions and practices.

Significant Contributor

**Andrew Feenberg** is Canada Research Chair in Philosophy of Technology in the School of Communication, Simon Fraser University, where he directs the Applied Communication and Technology Lab. He has also taught for many years in the Philosophy Department at San Diego State University, and at Duke University, the State University of New York at Buffalo, the Universities of California, San Diego and Irvine, the Sorbonne, the University of Paris-Dauphine, the Ecole des Hautes Etudes en Sciences Sociales, and the University of Tokyo. He is the author of *Lukacs, Marx and the Sources of Critical Theory* (Rowman and Littlefield, 1981; Oxford University Press, 1986), *Critical Theory of Technology* (Oxford University Press, 1991; 2nd edn titled *Transforming Technology*, 2002), *Alternative Modernity* (University of California Press, 1995), *Questioning Technology* (Routledge, 1999), and *Heidegger and Marcuse: The Catastrophe and Redemption of History* (Routledge, 2005). Translations of several of these books are available. Dr. Feenberg is also Co-editor of *Marcuse: Critical Theory and the Promise of Utopia* (Bergin and Garvey Press, 1988), *Technology and the Politics of Knowledge* (Indiana University Press, 1995), *Modernity and Technology* (MIT Press, 2003), and *Community in the Digital Age* (Rowman and Littlefield, 2004). His co-authored book on the French Events of May 1968 is *When Poetry Ruled the Streets* (SUNY Press, 2001). With William Leiss, Dr. Feenberg has edited a collection entitled *The Essential Marcuse* (Beacon Press, 2007). A book on Dr. Feenberg's philosophy of technology entitled *Democratizing Technology* appeared in 2006. In addition to his work on critical theory and the philosophy of technology, Dr. Feenberg has published on the Japanese philosopher Nishida Kitaro. He is also recognized as an early innovator in the field of online education, a field he helped to create in 1982. He led the TextWeaver Project on improving software for online discussion forums under a grant from the Fund for the Improvement of Post-Secondary Education of the U.S. Department of Education. For the latest Web-based version of this software, see http://www.geof.net/code/annotation/. Dr. Feenberg is currently studying online education on a grant from the Social Science and Humanities Research Council (SSHRC).

## References

Allen, I.E. & Seaman, J. (2007). *Online nation: Five years of growth in online learning.* Needham, MA: Babson Survey Research Group (Sloan Consortium).

Annand, D. (2007). Re-organizing universities for the information age. *The International Review of Research in Open and Distance Learning*, 8(3). Retrieved December 11, 2007 from: http://www.irrodl.org/index.php/irrodl/article/viewArticle/372/952.

Garrison, D.R. (2009). Implications of online learning for the conceptual development and practice of distance education. *Journal of Distance Education*, 23(2), 93–104.

Garrison, D.R. & Kanuka, H. (2004). Blended learning: Uncovering its transformative potential in higher education. *The Internet and Higher Education*, 7(2), 95–105.

Garrison, D.R. & Vaughan, N. (2008). *Blended learning in higher education.* San Francisco: Jossey-Bass.

Guri-Rosenblit, S. (2009). Distance education in the digital age: Common misconceptions and challenging tasks. *Journal of Distance Education*, 23(2), 105–122.

Holmberg, B. (1989). *Theory and practice of distance education.* London: Routledge.

Moore, M. (1990). Recent contributions to the theory of distance education. *Open Learning*, 5(3), 10–15.

Moore, M.G. (2007). Theory of transactional distance. In M.G. Graham (Ed.), *Handbook of distance education* (2nd edn). Mahwah, NJ: Lawrence Erlbaum.

Peters, O. (1994). Distance education and industrial production: A comparative interpretation in outline (1973). In D. Keegan (Ed.), *Otto Peters on distance education: The industrialization of teaching and learning.* London: Routledge.

Wei, R. (2008). *China's radio and TV universities and the British Open University: A comparative study.* Nanjing: Yilin Press.

# Contributors

**Charmaine Brooks** was the Coordinator, Curriculum and Resources Implementation with Alberta Education (K-12). In this role, she worked closely with the Provincial Curriculum Coordinators throughout the province to support the development of implementation plans and activities for the new and revised curriculum. Prior to this position, she served as a Learning and Technology Consultant for Alberta Education. In this role, her work focused on supporting K-12 stakeholders with the integration information and communication technologies across the curricula. Charmaine received her B.Ed. and M.Ed. from the University of Lethbridge.

**Dr. M.F. Cleveland-Innes** is a faculty member and Program Director in the Center for Distance Education at Athabasca University in Alberta, Canada. She teaches Research Methods and Leadership in the graduate programs of this department. Martha has received awards for her work on the student experience in online environments and held a major research grant through the Canadian Social Sciences and Humanities Research Council. She received the best paper award in 2005 from the

Canadian Association of Distance Education. In 2009 she received the President's Award for Research and Scholarly Excellence from Athabasca University. Her work is well published in academic journals in North America and Europe and she sits on the editorial boards of *The Canadian Journal of Distance Education* and *Revista de Universidad y Sociedad del Conocimiento* in Spain. Current research interests are in the area of leadership in open and distance higher education, teaching across the disciplines in online higher education and emotion and learning.

**Dr. Terry Evans** is a Professor in the School of Education at Deakin University, Geelong, Australia and was Associate Dean of Education (Research) for 13 years until 2008. He is Chief Investigator on two Australian Research Council projects— *Research capacity-building: The development of the Australian Ph.D. programs in national and emerging global contexts* (with M. Pearson & P. Macauley) and *Australian doctoral graduates' publication, professional and community outcomes* (with P. Macauley)—and an AusAID Australian Development Research Grant entitled *Identifying strategies to sustain professional learning communities for teachers in remote primary schools in Papua New Guinea* (with E. Honan, S. Muspratt, A. Kukari, & P. Paraide). Terry has published widely on distance education and doctoral education. He has edited (with D. Nation) *Changing University Teaching: Reflections on Creating New Educational Technologies*, *Opening Education: Policies and Practices from Open and Distance Education*, and (with C. Denholm) *Doctorates Downunder: Keys to Successful Doctoral Study in Australia and New Zealand*, *Supervising Doctorates Downunder: Keys to Effective Supervision in Australia and New Zealand* and *Beyond Doctorates Downunder: Maximising the Impact of Your Australian or New Zealand Doctorate*.

**Dr. D.R. Garrison** is currently the Director of the Teaching & Learning Center and a full professor in the Faculty of Education at the University of Calgary. Dr. Garrison has co-authored a book titled *E-Learning in the 21st Century*, where he provides a framework and core elements for online learning. He has most recently co-authored a book titled *Blended Learning in Higher Education* that uses the Community of Inquiry framework to organize the book. This book received the University Continuing Education Association (USA) Frandson Book Award in 2008. Dr. Garrison won the 2004 Canadian Society for Studies in Higher Education Award for distinguished contribution to research in higher education and the 2005 Canadian Association for Distance Education Excellence in Research Award. Since 2001, he has been overseeing the long-term direction and development of programs at the TLC. He is committed to enhancing teaching and learning on campus and works with senior administration, faculties, departments and university committees to meet this goal. He is inspired by the challenge of facilitating transformative change in teaching and learning.

**Dr. Margaret Haughey**, Vice-President Academic, Athabasca University, has a background in education administration and policy, and an active research and publication file on distance education and online learning. Over the years, she has been an instructor, instructional designer, course producer, administrator and researcher in various aspects of distance education, using a variety of media from print and live satellite broadcasts to online learning and from audioconferencing to learning objects. Margaret is a regular conference presenter and invited speaker, and has published a number of books on aspects of distance education, most recently *The International Handbook of Distance Education*, with co-editors Terry Evans and David Murphy. Her roles as President of the Canadian Association for Distance Education and Editor of its *Journal of Distance Education* (1998–2006) have given her close ties with the network of practitioners and researchers in the world-wide distance education community, and with provincial and federal government agencies.

**Dr. Phil Ice** holds an Education Doctorate in Curriculum and Instruction with minor concentrations in Instructional Technology and Science Education. Currently Dr. Ice is the Director of Course Design, Research and Development at the American Public University System. His research is focused on the impact of new and emerging technologies on cognition in online learning environments. Work in this area has brought Dr. Ice international recognition in the form of two Sloan-C effective practices, a Sloan-C Effective Practice of the Year Award—2007, application of his work at over 50 institutions of higher education in 5 countries, membership in Adobe's Higher Education Leader's Advisory Committee and multiple invited presentations, workshops and book chapters related to the integration of emerging technologies in online courses. Examples of his research include the use of embedded asynchronous audio feedback mechanisms, using Web 2.0 tools for collaborative construction of knowledge through integration of RIAs and remote observation of student teaching experiences using asynchronous, Flash-based environments. Phil is also involved with seven other researchers in the United States and Canada in numerous other research initiatives related to the Community of Inquiry framework, including the development of a validated instrument that captures the intersection of teaching, social and cognitive presence in online environments.

**Dr. Heather Kanuka** is Academic Director of University Teacher Services and Associate Professor of Educational Policy Studies at the University of Alberta, Canada. Prior to her recent appointment to the University of Alberta, Heather was a Canada Research Chair in e-Learning at Athabasca University. Her research has tended to revolve around academic development, e-learning and philosophies of educational technology.

**Dr. Gary E. Miller** is Executive Director Emeritus of the World Campus at Pennsylvania State University. He previously served as Associate Vice President for Outreach and Executive Director of Penn State Continuing and Distance Education. He was the founding Executive Director of Penn State World Campus, the University's online distance education program. From 1987 to 1993, Dr. Miller served as Associate Vice President for Program Development and Executive Director of the International University Consortium at the University of Maryland University College. In 2004, he was inducted into the International Adult and Continuing Education Hall of Fame. He received the 2004 Weidemeyer Award from the University of Wisconsin and *The American Journal of Distance Education*, the 2007 Irving Award from the American Distance Education

Association for his contributions to distance education, the 2008 Disting-uished Service Award from the National Telecommunications Network, and the 2008 Award for Most Outstanding Achievement in Online Teaching and Learning by an Individual from the Sloan Consortium. Dr. Miller earned a Doctor of Education in Higher Education from Pennsylvania State University. He is the author of *The Meaning of General Education: The Emergence of a Curricular Paradigm*, and numerous articles and book chapters on distance education.

**Dr. Brian Pauling** began the broadcasting program at Christchurch Polytechnic Institute of Technology in 1983 and was the first head of the New Zealand Broadcasting School. He has a background in broadcasting, publishing and adult education. He has a particular interest in the educational theories of capability learning, cooperative education, immersion learning and independent learning, all of which inform the BBc degree and the teaching practices of the school. His current research includes the impact of converging technologies (television, telecommuni-cations and computers) on the delivery of teaching and learning, digital broadcasting, public broadcasting, access and community broadcasting. He is a media consultant for a number of regional and national organizations. Recent publications include: *The Digital Future and Public Broadcasting*, Engaging the Digital Natives, Climbing Everest May be Easier, in T. Evans (Ed.), *The International Handbook of Distance Education*, and *The Changing Technologies of Learning: Reshaping the Boundaries of the University*.

**Dr. Albert Sangrà** is Full Professor at the Universitat Oberta de Catalunya (UOC), where he has been Director for Methodology and Educational Innova-tion (1995–2004), in charge of the educational model of the university. He is currently Academic Director of the Accredited Master's Degree in Education and ICT (e-learning). His main research interests are the organizational issues regarding the use of ICT in education and training and quality in e-learning. He has played the role of consultant in several virtual training projects in Europe, America and Asia, and has served as a consultant for the World Bank Institute. He is currently a member of the

Executive Committee of the European Distance and E-learning Network (EDEN) and a member of the Advisory Board of Portugal's Universidade Aberta. He earned his Ph.D. in Education at the Universitat Rovira i Virgili, a Degree in Education at the Universitat de Barcelona, a Postgraduate Degree in Applications of Information Technology in ODE at the Open University of the UK, and a Diploma on Strategic Use of IT in Education at Harvard University. He also serves or has served on the editorial and advisory boards of several academic journals, including *The International Review for Research in Open and Distance Learning* (*IRRODL*, Canada), *The European Journal for Open, Distance and E-learning* (*EURODL*), *The American Journal of Distance Education* (USA), *The Journal of e-Learning and Knowledge Society* (Italy), *Distance & Savoirs* (France) and *Pixel-Bit* (Spain).

**Dr. Doug Shale** was Director of the Office of Institutional Analysis at the University of Calgary. He is now retired. He has written a number of articles and book chapters over the years and his particular interest in distance education has been the pedagogy of distance education. He also has an interest in the organization and administration of higher education, especially higher distance education.

**Dr. Karen Swan** is the James J. Stukel Distinguished Professor of Educational Leadership at the University of Illinois Springfield, and the very proud grandmother of Case Shazaam and Zack Flash Rosenfeld. Karen's research is in the general area of electronic media and learning. She has authored over 70 journal articles and book chapters, produced several hyper-media programs, and co-edited two books—*Ubiquitous Computing in Education* and *Social Learning from Broadcast Television*—on educational technology topics. Her current research focuses on data literacy, online learning and ubiquitous computing in education. Karen has directed projects funded by the National Science Foundation, the U.S. Department of Education, the New York City Board of Education and several foundations. She is the Special Issues Editor for the *Journal of Educational Computing Research*, Chair of the 2009 Sloan-C International

Conference on Online Learning, and serves on the review boards and/or steering committees for many educational technology journals and conferences. Karen was the 2006 winner of the Sloan-C award for Most Outstanding Achievement in Online Learning by an Individual.

**Dr. Norman Vaughan** is an educator and researcher with interests in blended learning, faculty development and primary to high school education. He is an Assistant Professor in the Department of Education, Faculty of Teaching and Learning at Mount Royal University in Calgary, Alberta. Norman's teaching background includes graduate and undergraduate courses in educational technology, school education in northern Canada, technical training in the petroleum industry, and English as a Second Language in Japan. In addition, he has been involved in several consulting projects with book publishers and higher education institutions to develop online courses and resources. He recently co-authored the book *Blended Learning in Higher Education* and has published a series of articles on blended learning and faculty development. Norman is currently the Research Director for the Canadian Network for Innovation in Education, the Associate Editor of *The International Journal of Mobile and Blended Learning* and is on the editorial boards of *The Canadian Journal of Learning and Technology* and *The Journal on Centres for Teaching & Learning*.

# Index

Note: Page numbers in **bold** indicate figures. Page numbers in *italic* indicate tables

challenges: blended learning
169–70, 172–3, 176–8, 191, 252;
of interaction/separation 15,
18–19, 70, 91, 251, 255;
organizational 41, 50, 60, 100,
115, 191–2, 209–10, 213,
228–30, 234–5; pedagogical 41,
111, 118, 183, 249–50;
technological 129, 155, 189, 205,
209, 238, 253; theoretical 50, 61,
255–6
Chang, V. D.-T. 126
change *see also* continual change
culture; resistance to change:
economic 1–3, 230; and
leadership 235–6; organizational
177; social 1–3, 26–7, 49, 198,
209, 227; student/teacher roles
233
Chataqua movement 91
Chickering, A. W. 82
Chinese Central Television
University 52
Chinese Radio and Television
University 96
Cho, K. 176
Christian, W. 183
Christie, B. 121–2
Clark, B. 210
Clark, D. 165
Clark, R. E. 99
Cleveland-Innes, Martha 7, 124,
231, 233–4, 260–1
Click2Learn 212
Cloud Computing 142–4, 146,
156–7, 159
CNED, France 49
Cochrane, C. 79
Cocking, R. R. 114–15, 117,
119–20
cognitive presence 125–7
cognitive psychology 109
collaboration 16, 18–19, 109, 145,
148, 188, 236–7, 250–4, 256–7;
definition 22; inter-institutional

29, 32–5; and organizational
structure 177–8; and SaaS 142–3;
and technologically mediated
environments 111–13; and
Web 2.0 technologies 141–2
collegial processes 54, 61
Collins, A. 76, 113
commercial elements 210–13, 215
commodification 101, 213
Common Library 151
Commonwealth of Learning 101
communities of learners 18, 114,
249–52, 254, 257
community colleges 30, 32–3
Community of Inquiry (CoI)
framework 19–20, 104, 109,
122–7, **123**, 140, 155, 165, 178,
**179**, 193, 252, 254
community-centered learning
environments 120–1
competition 101, 103, 236
Conde, M. A. 205
confluence 109, 126, 252
connectivity issues 144–6, 252, 254
constraints 126–7
constructivism 20, 76–80, 84, 109,
112–17, 119–20, 127, 137, 140,
252–3
consumerism 74, 79, 101
Contact North/Contact Nord 38–9
continual change culture 157–8,
201, 238
Continuing Education units 29
continuity of counselling 58
convergence 20–2, 146, 216, 229,
252; of traditional/distance
education 18, 21, 36, 100–2, 174,
238, 256–7
conversational model 15, 60
Cooperative Extension Service 29,
38
coordinated delivery 40
corporate classroom 211, 216
correspondence study 14, 27, 29, 43,
46, 48–9, 59, 91–4, 97, 251;